Reuben Snake

Reuben Snake
Your Humble Serpent

Indian Visionary and Activist

As told to
JAY C. FIKES

Introduction by **Jay C. Fikes**
Foreword by **James Botsford**
Epilogue by **Jay C. Fikes**
Afterword by **Walter Echo-Hawk**

Clear Light Publishers
Santa Fe, New Mexico

Copyright © 1996 Jay C. Fikes

Clear Light Publishers, 823 Don Diego, Santa Fe, N.M. 87501

Library of Congress Cataloging-in-Publication Data

Fikes, Jay C. (Courtney), 1951–
    Reuben Snake, your humble serpent / by Jay C. Fikes ; foreword by James Botsford ; afterword by Walter B. Echo-Hawk.
        p.   cm.
    Includes bibliographical references and index.
    ISBN: 0-940666-60-X : $24.95
    1. Snake, Reuben. 2. Winnebago Indians—Biography. 3. Native American Church of North America. I. Title.
    E99.W7S634   1995
    299'.7'092—dc20   94–43554
    [B]   CIP

First Edition
10 9 8 7 6 5 4 3 2 1

Contents

Foreword
by James Botsford

*"If we don't change our direction,
we're going to wind up where we're heading."*

With those words of what he liked to call "Winnebago Wisdom," Reuben Snake gently nudged the hearts and minds and spirits of all who had ears to hear him . . . and there were many.

Some few people seem to have the ability to see the whole world at once, to see across all the chasms and through all the obstacles that occupy so much of our daily lives. Few indeed have the ability to see through time, to live knowingly as the embodiment of all that has gone before and simultaneously as the compassionate giant who selflessly prepares a high road for the journeys of future generations.

You are about to read the story of such a man. It is a humble story because he tells it himself. In this book, you will not find a litany of his accomplishments because that was neither his purpose nor his style. Besides, if someone were to begin today to recite the many good things Reuben Snake did in this world, the time it would take could be counted in seasons.

Jay Fikes has very thoughtfully used the trust Reuben placed in him to illuminate the astonishing transformations Reuben made in his lifetime. Reuben's spiritual journey exemplifies hope, demonstrating how he overcame the prejudice and abuse which were directed toward most Indians of his generation. But this book provides more than mere testimonial about individual redemption. Reuben Snake emerged from an archetypal passage. Having learned the lessons taught by suffering and injustice, he rose up to become a champion of his people.

Reuben said that his grandfather told him there are three things that make the enjoyment of human life possible—three things that people should try to exhibit in their everyday lives. Respect. Compassion. Honor.

Here is what Reuben Snake said about them a few years back:

Respect: "Each one of us is endowed by the Creator with his spirit. The spirit that makes you stand up and walk and talk and see and hear and think is the same spirit that exists in me—there's no difference. So when you look at me, you're looking at yourself—and I'm seeing me in you."

Compassion: "When you look at all the other parts of creation, all the other living creatures—the Creator endowed them with gifts that are far better than ours. Compared to the strength of the grizzly bear, the sharp sightedness of the eagle, the fleetness of the deer, and the acute hearing of the otter, we're pitiful human beings. We don't have any of those physical attributes that the Creator put into everything else. For that reason, we have to be compassionate with one another and help one another—to hold each other up."

Honor: "It's easy to point fingers at one another for our shortcomings, but to show somebody the feelings of pride that you have in them for what they do that's beneficial to their fellow man—that takes effort. But if you go to that kind of effort, then you're going to have that good feeling that we have to have one for another. And that's what makes life enjoyable."

These are the kinds of teachings, the depth of understanding that wise men and women have spoken of for thousands of years from all the great spiritual traditions of the world. Reuben was right up there with all those great sages, patiently waiting for the rest of us. Each and every being is brought into Creation by the great mysterious power we in some languages call God; each being embodies the sacred gift of life, yet each and every one is unique. So many times I saw how Reuben respected all the beings in Creation, how he honored them, how he showed compassion with his skillful and humorous patience for the problems of daily life that so many brought to his door.

He was such a huge man. His mind was in the spirit world of the Creator, his feet compassionately on Mother Earth, his heart flowing freely in between. Some few people throughout time have had the ability to talk of the important things of life from a place of understanding. Reuben was one of the precious few of those who not only spoke that way, but lived it. Whether conversing with an astrophysicist, or listening to the tongue of God speak to him through a holy fire in a tepee prayer meeting, or sitting at the kitchen table with a neighbor or stranger and a cup of coffee made by his wife, Kathy, Reuben was one of the precious few who walked his talk. Of whom among us will such a thing be said? May the Great Spirit bless you, brother Reuben. May your spirit soar with eagles and find a home with God.

Through his story, Reuben gently nudges us to realize that if we are true to our spiritual bearings, if we live our lives with respect, compassion, and honor, and if we are thereby guided to do things in this world, we can and do change the course of the future we leave for our children. You've heard about the stereotype . . . herein you can listen to the archetype.

Lest the reader feel that I am exaggerating the man, consider this: How many of us are able to accomplish transforming our vision of the world we want to live in into the policy and law of the United States? In his Afterword to this book, Walter Echo-Hawk succinctly describes the history of legal and political oppression perpetrated against Indian people—particularly in the area of religious expression, and most pointedly against Reuben's beloved Native American Church.

The horrendous injustice committed by the U.S. Supreme Court in permitting the practice of this venerable spiritual tradition to be criminalized in American law stirred Reuben to his last courageous fight. I will never forget the day after that

9

dreaded decision in the *Smith* case in April of 1990 when Reuben asked me to help him "overturn the ruling of the Supreme Court."

When I reminded him that neither he nor the Native American Church had any of the money or resources necessary for such a daunting task, he smiled broadly and said, "We'll find good friends along the way." When I reminded him of his poor health, his expression grew stern and he said it was something that simply must be done. He looked at me and said, "I'll give the rest of my life to this if I have to."

Reuben was right. There were good, strong, committed friends along the way . . . enough to accomplish the task. And he was also right on the other count. He quit his job and committed himself to his final battle. With prayers by night and work by day he poured his energy into this seemingly impossible task. In the end, he gave it more energy than he actually had and died along the way, but not before he had singularly and clearly set the wheels in motion that resulted in a strong new federal law that ended literally hundreds of years of persecution against the peyote religion. His essential and catalytic efforts helped restore this ancient way of worship to the dignified place it deserves among the profound spiritual traditions of the world.

Even though he was a prayerful man, Reuben believed in rolling up your sleeves and getting things done in a responsible way. He often illustrated the point by telling the story of the family whose home was about to be flooded by a swollen river. First a truck came down the road urging the people to get in and be taken to higher ground. The family declined, saying they believed in God and that he would take care of them and see to their needs. The water rose up to the ground floor of their home and a boat came by calling for the family to get in and ride to safety. Again, they declined and climbed to their roof. A helicopter came overhead to lower a rope to them, but the family said again that they were putting their faith in God who would take care of them. Finally the waters rose over the roof and the family was swept away.

When they got to Heaven, they cried out, "Dear God, we put all our faith in you and yet were swept to our deaths! How could you do this to us?" To which God replied, "Hey! I sent you a truck and a boat and a helicopter. You have to do something, too!" Reuben Snake did something, too.

What an honor it was not only to know Reuben, but to go out and fight the good fight with him for the last ten years of his life as his lawyer, his friend, and his adopted brother. Because of his vision and his wisdom, he chose the fights worth fighting, and because of the respect he engendered, he found friends in both likely and unlikely places, and he prevailed. His people prevailed. Righteousness prevailed.

Whether it was in accomplishing the thousands of little things few will ever remember, or whether it was undertaking the huge battles that I sometimes thought were too big, it was an unspeakable honor to have walked beside him—one step behind. Reuben showed us all how to overcome evil and ignorance with dignity and compassion. Such are the ways of a Warrior Sage.

Reuben Snake had the good fortune to be born into a culture that is rooted in the perennial values, the old ways. He had the intellectual capacity and the presence of being to understand the spiritual truths within those ways. I watched those understandings wash right through him, as if he were passing them from the past to the future—and indeed, he was. This Sweet Earth has never had a better friend.

Acknowledgments

I am deeply indebted to Kathy Snake. She graciously welcomed me into her home while her husband was living, and supported this project without hesitation. I feel certain that Reuben would have dedicated his autobiography to her had he lived to see it published.

Reuben's eldest son, Darren Snake, has been enthusiastic and cooperative from the moment he learned that I was intent on completing his father's autobiography. He and his wife, Lena, kindly hosted my wife and me in their home so we could attend the day of tribute paid to Reuben Snake on January 12, 1994. Darren also shared his memories of his father's last months on earth and explained numerous details of Winnebago culture to me. His trust, support, and guidance were indispensable in completing the Epilogue to this book.

James Botsford provided numerous clear and effective suggestions for correcting defects he identified in earlier drafts of the manuscript. He generously gave me legal counsel and sent me various biographical notes and tributes published about Reuben Snake. The profound admiration each of us had for Reuben Snake, our adopted brother, became the cornerstone of our relationship and enhanced enormously the quality of this book.

Ginger Miles helped ignite my initial interest in doing this autobiography. Reading excerpts from her interviews with Reuben Snake and helping her conduct interviews with Reuben and other members of the Native American Church (of the Omaha, Winnebago, and Yankton Sioux tribes) in November of 1992 did much to awaken my curiosity about

Reuben's life. Ginger's ability to communicate effectively with radio audiences, as exemplified by her National Public Radio program "Hymns of Praise: the Native American Church," inspired me to write this book in a more popular style than I might otherwise have chosen.

I am grateful to many of Reuben's relatives for welcoming me during my visits to Winnebago. I am most obliged to Michael Snake, Elaine Snake, Dawn Snake, Serena Snake, Roger Snake, Norman Snake, William Hensley, John Earth, and Janet Bass. Special thanks are also due to several other Native American friends, including Shawna Robbins, Johnny White-Cloud, Harley GoodBear, Colleen GoodBear, Irene Herder, Frank and Virginia Dayish, and Yvette Joseph.

My parents, JC and Virginia Fikes, were especially pleased that Reuben and I decided to write this book. Their steadfast support quickened completion of this project.

The constant encouragement of my wife and daughter, from my tape-recording of Reuben Snake in May of 1993 to the final editing of this book, has been invaluable. Each of them contributed significantly, both directly and indirectly, to making this book a reality.

Peter Canby, author of *The Heart of the Sky,* was at Winnebago during my interviews with Reuben Snake in late May of 1993. We discussed many details of Reuben's life and the liturgy of the Native American Church both before and after Mr. Canby attended a peyote meeting among the Yankton Sioux. He kindly consented to permit publication of Reuben's responses to his questions.

The first transcription of my tape-recorded interviews with Reuben Snake was done by Chuck Freidel. He is to be commended for the accuracy and speed of his work.

David Christie enthusiastically supported the writing of this book and is involved in marketing the audiotape "Hymns of Praise."

I am much obliged to Professor Kathleen Danker for several suggestions which significantly improved certain aspects of the introduction, notes, and bibliography. Aided by her

Winnebago consultant, Felix White, Sr., she graciously provided an ethnographic dictionary of Winnebago words.

Several anonymous reviewers of an earlier draft of the manuscript deserve praise for their insightful criticism. The comments from the University Press of America reviewer were particularly constructive.

Photographs for this book were graciously provided by Darren and Kathy Snake, Gary Rhine, Phil Cousineau, and Elizabeth Sackler. My heartfelt thanks go to Marcia Keegan, Sara Held, and Sunny Elliott of Clear Light Publishers for improving vastly the visual quality of this book.

Walter Echo-Hawk's eloquent Afterword concisely portrays the circumstances in which Reuben Snake grew up and rose up to struggle for justice. I am sure Reuben would be pleased by Walter Echo-Hawk's appreciation of his achievements, both political and spiritual. Walter's brave heart, humility, and commitment to serving native people remind me of what I like best about Reuben Snake.

Jay C. Fikes

Introduction
by Jay C. Fikes

I am one of hundreds of people whose life has been enriched by the words and deeds of Reuben Snake, one of the preeminent political and spiritual leaders among American Indians of his generation. During the three years I knew him, Reuben gently but accurately pointed out some of my shortcomings in private while praising lavishly my accomplishments on all ceremonial and public occasions. I trusted him because he treated me with respect, honor, and compassion. Because I trusted him, I considered seriously whatever constructive criticism he offered me. Whenever I observed Reuben I noticed others also responding to his love. This extraordinary educator, activist, and spiritual leader showed me, without preaching, that if people are to take greater responsibility for the relationships in which they are involved, their freedom must be fully respected.

During what was to be the final month of Reuben's life we tape-recorded almost two weeks of conversations describing all the events worth remembering about his life. As I edited our discussions and reflected upon the numerous insights they contain, the significance his life held for me became clear. His words and deeds demonstrated that great leaders are able to inspire others to do the right thing, for the right reasons, because they have honored and served their followers. Reuben Snake led by being a humble serpent.

Two severe heart attacks and extensive damage to his kidneys from diabetes had left Reuben physically weak when we taped our conversations. His memory was excellent and it was obvious that he had given much thought to our task of recording his life story. As we began recording, he advised me that he "wanted to put this autobiography in a proper context." To provide the "proper context" Reuben wanted readers to have about his life as a member of the Winnebago tribe, I offer some historical background in this introduction and the notes at the end of the book.

From the first moment of contact between the two peoples, European immigrants tried to implement various and sundry schemes to force American Indians to abandon their aboriginal cultures. Few immigrants questioned the wisdom of their attempts to assimilate Native Americans into the Euro-American culture they were creating on this continent. Euro-American efforts to conquer and convert the Ho Chunk people, commonly known by the name Winnebago,[1] were particularly devastating. The Winnebago were physically relocated five times, exposed to various versions of Christianity presented by impetuous missionaries, and robbed of most of their homeland, first by coerced treaties and force, and later by act of Congress—the Dawes or General Allotment Act of 1887.[2]

Reuben Snake was well aware of how such tragic events had affected his people. I vividly remember the profound emotion he displayed one morning while reminding members of the Yankton Sioux tribe of how an influential Winnebago named John Rave had first taught the Yankton how to conduct prayer meetings in which peyote (a small, spineless cactus whose scientific name is *Lophophora williamsii)* is reverently consumed as a divine medicine and sacrament. Rave shared his knowledge of this ancient ceremony with the Yanktons out of gratitude for the generosity and hospitality the Yanktons had extended to a group of destitute Winnebago during the winter of 1863–1864. Reuben recalled that these Winnebago had been forced to flee for their lives to escape starvation while imprisoned on barren land in South Dakota following the American offensive ignited by the Santee Sioux uprising which began August 18, 1862, in southern Minnesota. The Winnebago who fled were neither allies nor accomplices of the Santee Sioux.[3] The Santee revolt provided the American government with justification for deporting all Winnebagos from southern Minnesota, even though the Winnebago were clearly innocent bystanders. Reuben mentioned that most of the homeless Winnebagos who survived that winter among the Yankton Sioux later found refuge among the Omaha Indian tribe. In 1865 the Winnebago gained title to land in northeastern Nebraska (Jackson 1964; Lurie 1978: 700).

Reuben Snake was born on January 12, 1937, and grew up in the deep woodlands along the bluffs of the Missouri River in Nebraska. His earliest years were spent in poverty. Like many other Winnebago children his age, Reuben attended a private boarding school run by German-speaking missionaries of Swiss ancestry at Neillsville, Wisconsin. This kind of educational institution has frequently been condemned by Native Americans because it did so much to assimilate them into the mainstream of American culture. Reuben knew from personal experience how diligently such schools tried to suppress Winnebago language and culture, yet he confessed that the discipline they instilled had helped prepare him for serving as a Green Beret in the United States Army.

Reuben was stationed in Berlin in the mid-1950s, giving him an opportunity to learn about German culture. After receiving his honorable discharge from the Green Berets and leaving Germany, he encountered numerous obstacles to entering the mainstream of American society. Like many other American Indians, Reuben learned that being Indian meant being subjected to discrimination by non-Indian employers and by representatives of Christian religious denominations. His personal encounters with prejudice, and his experience of being homeless and dependent on alcohol, made him more patient with human frailties and more compassionate toward homeless people, and moved him to dedicate his life to achieving justice for American Indians.

During Reuben's childhood his older relatives had allowed, while complaining privately, Winnebago students at boarding schools to be penalized for retaining their language and culture. When Reuben's daughters asked him why their public school teacher claimed that "Indians have weird beliefs,"

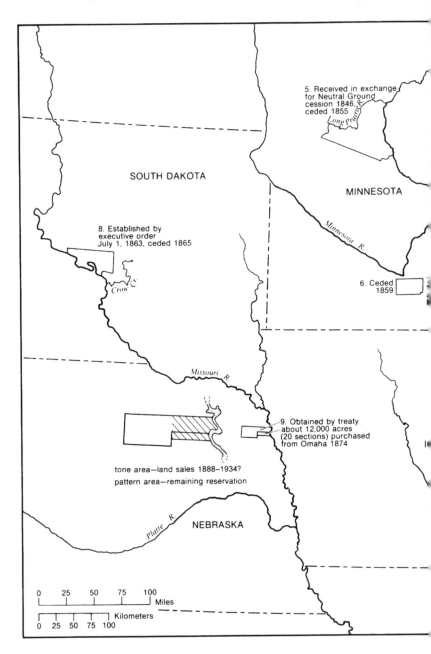

Territory, land cessions, and removals 1829–1934. Detail of Nebraska lands shows most recent sales and modern Winnebago Reservation. Source: *Handbook of North American Indians*, vol. 15 (Washington, D.C.: Smithsonian Institution, 1978), page 691.

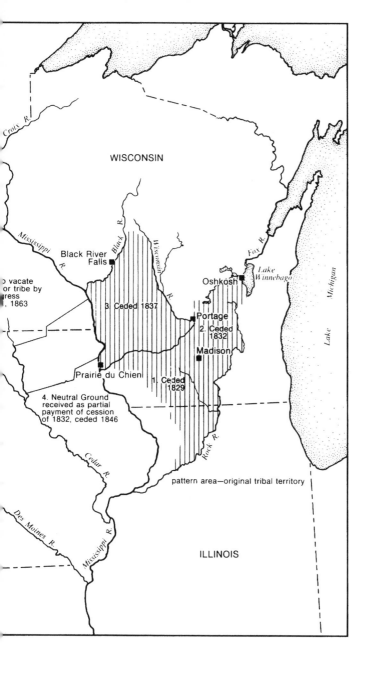

WISCONSIN

Croix R.

Mississippi R.

Black R.

Black River
Falls ■

Wisconsin R.

Fox R.

Oshkosh ■

Lake Winnebago

Lake Michigan

3 Ceded 1837

Portage
2. Ceded
1832

Madison ■

o vacate
or tribe by
ress
, 1863

Prairie du Chien ■

1. Ceded
1829

4. Neutral Ground
received as partial
payment of cession
of 1832, ceded 1846

Cedar R.

Rock R.

pattern area—original tribal territory

Des Moines R.

Mississippi R.

ILLINOIS

he got ready to return to the Winnebago Reservation. Seeing his children suffering from the same insensitivity he had endured, he decided some changes were needed.

Reuben's rejection of absolute assimilation into American society epitomized and contributed to a tremendous turnaround taking place among American Indians. Late in 1968, when Reuben became president of the All Nations Club, the organization dedicated to preserving Winnebago culture, he was making a commitment to reclaim his Winnebago heritage. Inspired in part by the success of the civil rights movement, Reuben organized the boycott of Walthill, Nebraska, in 1969. This successful economic boycott defended Indian civil rights and revived Indian self-respect. It marked the beginning of Reuben's political activism and ended his drift toward assimilation. He was now clearly heading down a path toward restoring respect for Winnebago culture and making his people self-sufficient economically.

Reuben's activist orientation was given a firm spiritual foundation shortly after he rejected the Mormon church's de facto segregation of Native American and immigrant American worshipers in South Dakota. When Reuben was ordained as a Roadman (spiritual leader) in the Native American Church (NAC) on October 26, 1974, he was already well along on the road to retaining only the best of both worlds, the Euro-American and the Native American. By late 1977, when he was installed as the Winnebago Tribal Chairman, he was committed to implementing programs which would bring only the best for future generations of Winnebago people. He was dedicated to being their humble serpent.

To appreciate Reuben's accomplishments, the magnitude of the obstacles he confronted must be fully understood. The era when Winnebagos fled to Nebraska in the wake of the Santee Sioux uprising was one in which government programs promoted unconditional assimilation and many immigrant Americans were convinced that "the only good Indian was a dead Indian." Reuben grew up during a time when schemes supporting assimilation of American Indians into the "mainstream" of Euro-American society continued, despite the promise of the "Indian New Deal" heralded in 1934 with the Indian Reorganization Act. To pass this act, Congress diluted and altered the innovative policies for American Indian tribes proposed by a particularly progressive commissioner of the Bureau of Indian Affairs (BIA) named John Collier (Collier 1947: 154–158). Nevertheless, the Indian Reorganization Act represented an immense improvement in federal Indian policy over the preceding period in United States history (Deloria and Lytle 1984).

Collier's policies encouraged Indians to inaugurate modern tribal governments and to begin regaining control over their land and lives. Some forty-three years later, Reuben Snake's bold and innovative leadership of the modern tribal government established among the Winnebago of Nebraska moved his people toward self-sufficiency. Reuben's efforts as Winnebago Tribal Chairman supplemented and extended the reform movement launched a few years before his birth by BIA Commissioner John Collier.

In 1970 Reuben successfully confronted the U.S. Army Corps of Engineers, whose project would have condemned precious Missouri River front land located in Iowa, on the eastern boundary of Winnebago territory. Although Reuben jokingly referred to himself as the "Rear Admiral of the Winnebago Navy," he "commanded" only a tiny rowboat in helping to defend Winnebago interests against the U.S.-backed invasion. To enforce its title to that riverfront land, land recognized by the 1865 treaty, the Winnebago tribe had to win two federal lawsuits against the U.S. Army Corps of Engineers. Reuben's actions as "Rear Admiral" and the court battles the Winnebago tribe subsequently won prevented the forced appropriation of more than 600 acres of land, now the site of the Winnebago tribal casino (near Sloan, Iowa).

A few years later, Nebraska Public Power District also tried to condemn Winnebago land. Their unsuccessful confrontation with the Winnebago was settled out of court. Chairman Reuben used the money this settlement provided to help put Winnebago tribal economic development on a firm foundation.

Reuben was also a great advocate of tribally controlled economic development and education. In his lifetime, tribally controlled community colleges (including the Nebraska Indian Community College he helped establish) and tribally controlled schools began replacing schools dominated by the BIA or by Christian evangelist/teachers. Near the end of his tenure as Winnebago Tribal Chairman, tribal gaming operations were launched on the land he successfully defended against invasion by the Army Corps of Engineers. The revenue gained from gambling bolstered his hope that the poverty Winnebagos and other Native Americans have endured in the wake of Euro-American conquest and colonialism will eventually be overcome.

Reuben's political leadership took many forms but always exemplified how to resolve the foremost challenge facing Native American leaders of his generation: how to retain valuable and viable aspects of aboriginal culture while selecting and incorporating the most desirable features of immigrant American culture. He was among the foremost Indian political leaders of his generation, serving as Chairman of the Winnebago Tribe of Nebraska, as National Co-Chairman of the Trail of Broken Treaties, National Chairman of the American Indian Movement, and President of the National Congress of American Indians.

Reuben was a master at settling differences and building consensus among divergent factions of Native Americans. His passage into the spirit world on June 28, 1993, was mourned deeply by virtually all Native Americans. By that time his unique blend of spirituality and political activism had attracted the attention and earned him the respect of non-Indian leaders and statesmen such as Senator Daniel Inouye, Senator Robert Kerrey, Vice President Al Gore, Representative Doug Bereuter, Governor E. Benjamin Nelson, and the Reverend Jesse Jackson. But Reuben was more than a prominent politician. He was respectful of the teachings of Winnebago and other tribal elders and committed to preserving traditional Indian religious customs and institutions.

Reuben was christened and baptized in the Native American Church on Easter Sunday morning in 1937. During his twenty years of service as an ordained Roadman in the Native American Church, he conducted hundreds of all-night prayer meetings. The combination of aboriginal American symbolism, reverence for peyote, and faith in Christ which characterized the Native American Church meetings Reuben conducted has never been well understood by non-believers. Reuben recognized that Jesus Christ's spirit and teachings were distinct from the dogma disseminated by most Christian/European churches. Yet he did not allow the inconsistency between Christ's message and the (mis)conduct of people professing to be Christians to diminish his personal commitment to serve the Creator, as Christ had done. Reuben believed deeply in the message of Jesus Christ and the priority Jesus placed on obeying the two greatest commandments: "The first was to love the Lord thy God with all thy might, with all thy strength and with all thy soul. The second commandment was like unto the first, to love thy neighbor as thyself." Reuben was disinclined to call himself a Christian because he knew that "literally hundreds of millions of people have died at the hands of Christians through the Crusades and all the various 'holy wars' that have gone on." Moreover, Reuben was convinced that the Winnebago people had appreciated the value of teachings comparable to those of Christ long before immigrant Americans brought their Bibles to preach to them. For Reuben, the core of Jesus Christ's teachings and the essence of traditional American Indian spirituality were compatible. His skill in selecting the best from both worlds, native and immigrant American, continues to inspire younger American Indians to do likewise.

While tape-recording Reuben's life story, I recognized how his political activism embodied overlapping meanings conveyed by his Winnebago name, *Kikawa Unga*. The original meaning of his name, "to rise up," indicates the manner in which a snake elevates its head in self-defense. This ancient image of a coiled serpent was appropriate for Reuben Snake, who belonged to the Snake Clan, one of twelve patrilineal clans of the Winnebago tribe (Radin 1970). Moreover, as Reuben explained, his Winnebago name, "to rise up," had been bestowed at a Native American Church meeting on Easter Sunday in 1937. Accordingly, it had acquired Christian connotations, signifying to struggle for justice, and to be resurrected. After Reuben became a Roadman in the Native American Church his life began speaking eloquently. Prayers uttered by his ancestors were being brought to fruition by his choices and conduct.

Reuben's greatest personal challenge was learning how to balance his concern for family life with the demands of political activism. When his wife Kathy left him in January of 1974, he prayed to the Creator to guide him in making amends and restoring their marriage. In resolving their problem he relied upon the power of prayer and the divine medicine, peyote. When his wife returned and their life together improved, Reuben remained dedicated to fulfilling the pledge he made to serve the Creator. From that moment on, his devotion to Kathy and his commitment to serve others rested upon his promise to put God first in his life.

Kikawa Unga worked at aligning his actions with words of enduring value because he had faith in the power of the Creator's Word. He believed "this universe was created through a word of prayer from the Creator-of-all-things," that in the beginning, the Creator "spoke the words that brought this universe into reality." His commitment to live according to this spiritual vision of life gave him the strength and courage required to work for justice. It was his unpretentious but profound spirituality that kept his pursuit of justice and Winnebago self-determination free from malice and resentment toward Indian and non-Indian detractors alike. He prayed for those few individuals who treated him as if he were their enemy.

Reuben's quest for a better life for the Winnebago and all

Native Americans took a tremendous toll on his health and family life. He suffered his first heart attack in October of 1986, during his tenure as President of the National Congress of American Indians. Although he never recovered his physical health again, his mind remained clear and he continued working to build a better world.

Everyone who knew Reuben appreciated his keen sense of humor. One day he telephoned me at work in Washington, D.C., identifying himself as Luke Warm Water. Mr. Warm Water talked quite earnestly about his participation in a rally I was organizing to promote protection of the Native American Church's religious freedom. This rally, in which Reuben was to be the keynote speaker, was to be a solemn event at the site of the future National Museum of the American Indian on the Mall. I laughed when one of Mr. Warm Water's ludicrous statements made me realize it was Reuben Snake playing a joke on me.

I had to swallow another dose of Reuben's comic relief tonic one day after he had finished reading my book, *Carlos Castaneda, Academic Opportunism and the Psychedelic Sixties*, which criticizes the ways certain anthropologists had badly misunderstood, if not actually mocked, some of the most sacred elements in Huichol Indian religion.[4] Reuben understood I was indignant about several sacrilegious statements anthropologists had made about sacramental peyote use. He knew that Huichol Indians are obliged to eat their supreme sacrament, peyote, raw to honor the precedent set by their ancestors. Sensing my annoyance with the preposterous claim that Huichols give peyote enemas, he informed me with a mock-serious tone that everything in the whole world could be made right again if only peyote enemas were given to everyone in need.

He often ended his letters with the phrase, "Your humble serpent." This jocular play on the word *servant* nicely conveyed his membership in the Winnebago tribe's Snake Clan and his heartfelt desire to remain humble while serving his people. It also allowed him subtly to tease people who automatically condemn snakes, which Reuben viewed as healers and humble creatures who rarely elevate themselves far from the earth. His joy at being a humble serpent of his people was made possible because he had reconciled his reverence for Winnebago customs with his commitment to live up to Christ's message.

Observing Reuben's constant practice of humility helped me gain greater insight into the value of a cardinal rule of conduct to which he had dedicated himself as a Roadman: to treat all people with respect, compassion, and honor. He adhered to a single standard of conduct, regardless of a person's social status, economic standing, or station in life. Reuben Snake was dedicated to acting in precisely this caring way with everyone he knew. That benevolent quality is what made him the greatest humble man I have ever known. Reuben's life demonstrated that sincere efforts to keep that benevolent quality central in our conduct will make this world a better place.

Minutes after learning that the Supreme Court, in *Oregon Employment Division v. Smith,* had refused to extend First Amendment protection to members of the Native American Church who revere peyote in their religious rituals, I received a telephone call from Shawna Robbins, a Navajo woman who was then employed by LaDonna Harris, President of Americans for Indian Opportunity. Shawna urged me to get in touch with Reuben Snake to determine what I could do to help preserve the religious freedom of the Native American Church. I immediately called Reuben and explained the scope of my work as the lobbyist on Native American issues for the Friends Committee on National Legislation. I also informed him of my admiration for Huichol Indian singers, whose singular reverence for peyote, the spineless cactus they have venerated for centuries as the heart of the Creator, had become evident during my research among them (Fikes 1985, 1993a). I told Reuben that my observations of Huichol peyote rituals and my reading about the prayer meetings of the Native

American Church (NAC) convinced me that the Supreme Court's decision was unjustified. I remember promising him I would do whatever I could to help secure legal protection for the NAC, whose sacramental use of peyote in bona fide religious rituals had just been imperiled by the Supreme Court's landmark decision.

The commitment I made in that conversation on April 17, 1990 became the cornerstone of my friendship with Reuben Snake. My appreciation for Reuben increased gradually during what were to be his last three years of life. I knew him primarily as a spiritual leader, a Roadman in the NAC. As I participated in meetings to devise and enact national legislation to protect sacramental peyote use and to secure religious freedom for American Indians, I became aware of Reuben's standing as an exceptionally talented Native American political leader. I was impressed with his ability to reconcile and combine Christ's message with Native American spirituality and ethics. His conviction that peyote is a divine medicine and teacher, and his remarkable experiences as a Roadman, are well represented in his book.

Reuben believed that for me to be an effective advocate for the NAC I needed to attend several of their all-night prayer meetings. He invited me to Winnebago, Nebraska, to attend my first such meeting in July of 1990. After participating in a conference he organized to help officers of the NAC devise a strategy for introducing and passing national legislation to protect their religious freedom, I found myself seated inside a tepee next to his eldest son, Darren Snake. I managed to remain awake all night and until noon the next day. During the feast which concludes the prayer meeting, I was delighted by a young Winnebago boy who innocently asked me if I was the President of the United States. My observations of numerous other NAC meetings strengthened my efforts to obtain full legal protection for what I regard as a remarkable and wonderful way of worship.

Reuben was the Roadman at one NAC prayer meeting in New Mexico in June of 1992. He honored me by inviting me to speak during the pre-dawn hour set aside for the sermon. The next day he presented me with the bolo tie he had been wearing. It was adorned with a silver rattlesnake, the same species of snake I had spoken about with great reverence at the prayer meeting. As he took it off his neck and handed it to me he informed my grandmother and parents that sometime in the near future he planned to sponsor a ceremony to formally acknowledge me as his brother. We had already been calling each other "brother," but I felt especially pleased by his promise to confirm our relationship in a ceremonial way. Reuben did not live long enough to perform that adoption ceremony. A few weeks before he passed on, he told his sons he considered me his brother and asked them to treat me accordingly.

Reuben Snake will always be my spiritual brother. I recognize him as a humble serpent who rose up to struggle for justice and religious freedom for American Indians. Our prayers and hard work helped reverse the shocking 1990 Supreme Court ruling which first led me to call him. In October of 1994 the enactment of Public Law 103–344 brought to a successful conclusion our crusade to gain full legal protection for members of the Native American Church who rely on peyote as a teacher, Holy Medicine, and supreme sacrament.

Listening to Reuben explain the premium he and other Native Americans place on extended-family living and spirituality has inspired me to work to overcome the impatience entailed by my pursuit of individual achievement. What he taught me about the traditional Winnebago concept of the four hills of life has enhanced immensely my sense that the life of an individual human being must be seen within a spiritual and multi-generational spectrum. As Reuben suggested, each of us comes into this world from the spirit world and our lives seem to be devoted to getting back into it. There are four hills of life and each of us is walking uphill all the time. The first hill of life is a time for individual exploration and personal growth. The second hill begins with our commitment to marriage and family life. The third hill is about raising our grandchildren. The fourth hill is reached when we become great-grandparents. From this elevated position in life we have a unique perspective on life's significance. We may eventually be blessed with white hair before the Creator-of-all-things calls us back to the spirit world from which we originally came. Reuben emphasized that each of us is following in the footsteps of our ancestors. We are renewing their trail so that our children, and eventually their children, will be able to follow in our footsteps. The way we actually walk up this road of life will have far more influence than whatever we may say to our children. Reuben's Winnebago philosophy of life showed me that just as the prayers, words, and deeds of our ancestors have paved the way and made life possible for us, so our lives will blaze the trail, or keep it visible, for our descendants.

Reuben provided several examples illustrating his faith that human relationships extend beyond life, that ancestors present in the spirit world may aid relatives still living here on earth. He spoke from personal experience about "seeing" his "deceased" relatives inside the tepee when he prayed at sunrise at the first NAC meeting he attended upon returning home from the Green Berets. He spoke of having heard and felt the presence of the deceased relatives of a young woman who had been scheduled to have a hysterectomy coming to heal her as he prayed and prepared to doctor her. He spoke about a dream he had on the night a funeral service for his aunt was held. In this dream Reuben saw his long-dead cousin riding toward his mother (who was Reuben's aunt). Reuben's cousin picked his mother up, put her on his horse, and then "they rode on up the hill and disappeared from my sight." Reuben's dream symbolized what the spirit world is all about. Reuben's experiences of love enduring beyond life were profoundly comforting, and much more vivid than descriptions of heaven conveyed by orthodox Christians.

Such experiences convinced Reuben that our earthly existence is part of an unending cycle of life. As he sometimes declared during the NAC Half-Moon meetings he conducted, the half-circle composed of sand symbolizes the half-moon[5] and reminds worshipers that their journey through the portion of the life-cycle which is visible to us here and now is only a fraction of what is contained in life's circle.

I consider it providential that Reuben Snake selected me to write his autobiography. I had given much thought to helping him complete his autobiography before a dream stimulated me to ask if he would be willing to tell his life story. I briefly disclosed what my dream meant to me and stated that I anticipated that publishing his autobiography would prove beneficial to the younger generation of Native Americans. When he modestly accepted the challenge of tape-recording his life story I was pleased and declared again that I felt he represented an indispensable role model for younger Native Americans.

I am convinced that the saga of Reuben's struggles with injustice, prejudice, alcohol, and the appeal of unconditional assimilation does indeed provide an example that can help younger American Indians persevere and overcome adversity. His life story should encourage them to take only the best from both worlds, native and immigrant American. Reuben Snake's reverence for the Creator and his testimony about spirituality and the extended family may help all readers of this autobiography walk the four hills of their lives with greater humility and compassion.

Thunder at Big Bear Hollow

I was born on January 12, 1937, at the Winnebago, Nebraska, Indian Hospital, as it was called in those days. My father was Reuben Harold Snake. My mother was Virginia Greyhair Snake. I was their fourth child. I had two older brothers and an older sister. When I was born, our community was still struggling through the Depression. A lot of things were being done to try to generate employment and improve people's lives on the reservation. There were Works Project Administration (WPA) and other governmental programs. The government had provided funding for materials to build houses and the government employed the local Indian men to build the houses. Little houses popped up on different parts of the reservation. There was a place down along the bluffs of the Missouri River where one of these projects had built a forest ranger station, with a lodge and a fire tower. There was housing available in that area.

It was into one of these houses, a two-roomed framed house, that my father and mother had moved. When I was born, they took me home to that house after I left the hospital. So that is how I began life with my father and my mother, my brothers, my sister, and my grandmother. My father's mother lived with us. We all lived in that two-room house along the bluffs of the Missouri River, in the deep woodlands of the reservation.

I have no recollection of my first year of life. About the time that I was three months old, my grandmother had an especially compassionate feeling for me. She wanted me to have a good life, a healthy life. So she went to see her uncle, an old man by the name of John Painter Senior. He was a

BEING INDIAN IS. . . .
Forever!

BEING INDIAN IS. . . .
Knowing the Great Spirit.

BEING INDIAN IS. . . .
*Having your teenage child come home from school
and ask about "the strange beliefs" of Indians that
his/her teacher mentioned in school today.*

BEING INDIAN IS. . . .
*Fighting with the U.S. Army to save your country
from the evils of communism and against the U.S.
Army on your reservation to keep the Corps of
Engineers from stealing all of your land.*

—From *Being Indian Is,*
by Reuben Snake

Roadman of the Native American Church and he had acquired the (ceremonial) ways of the Quapaw people. He used what they called a Quapaw fireplace.[1] My grandmother asked him to pray for my life. So they made arrangements.

When I was about three months old, on Easter Sunday morning, 1937, John Painter named me and baptized me into the Native American Church. He gave me an old Winnebago Snake Clan name, *Kikawa Unga,* which means "to rise up." But in telling of the crucifixion and resurrection of Jesus Christ, he put a Christian emphasis on my name. He said he wanted me to be like Christ, to rise up and carry on God's work. And that's how I began my life around this sacred fireplace, the Native American Church fireplace.

I vividly remember something from the second year of my life, in the spring of the year. Early one morning I woke up to a loud crash of thunder. It was lightning and then it was thundering and it scared me. I started to cry. My mother woke up and told me to not be afraid, that it was just lightning and thunder. My grandmother got up and went outside. My grandmother belonged to the Thunder Clan of our nation.[2] We have a tradition, a belief that when life is going to be renewed in the spring of the year, the grandfathers bring the life-giving rain back to us. The thunder grandfathers bring the life-giving rain. So when they hear that first thunder, the Thunder clan goes out and makes a tobacco offering. That's what my grandmother was doing. Of course I was little and didn't understand that. I was very attached to my grandmother, and when she went outside I stood in the doorway. I watched her say her prayer and make her tobacco offering to the grandfathers. I remember that very distinctly. Then she came back inside and put me back to bed and I went back to sleep.

The next morning when I woke up, my grandmother was very busy. She was outside clearing off a piece of ground. And she got my older brothers and went out into the forest. They began to cut some saplings. And when they came back she began to construct a little lodge. In our Winnebago language they call it a *chiporoke*. It is a little round house. She made the frame and covered it with canvas; then she took some bedding and arranged it in this little lodge. She built us an arbor, a sun shade, and then she built an outside fireplace in front of the wigwam. It took her all day to do this with my older brothers and my sister helping her. That evening she prepared a meal and after we sat down to eat she began talking to us children. I remember her saying that Winnebagos had a certain way of living. She could tell us about it. She could explain it to us but we wouldn't really understand it. The very best thing she could do for us was to make us live that way.

She said, "We're going to live in this little lodge this summer. We are going to sleep in here. And I'm going to cook outside here, and do everything outside under this little sun shade. And you're going to be around here and you're going to see what I do and learn something about this Winnebago way of life." She was talking to us in our native tongue and telling us these things. So that's what happened. My father and mother stayed inside the frame house. But my grandma, my brothers, my sister, and I all started living in that little wigwam.

She used to send me off to the spring for fresh water in the morning. I had two little syrup pails that I carried water in. She told me that that was going to be my responsibility, to bring the fresh water.

We used to observe her in her daily rituals, the preparation of food, washing our clothes by hand and all of these things. In the evening she would take the ashes from the fireplace, and she would walk around the lodge and spread the ashes around. She would tell us that she was doing this to keep the bad spirits away during the night. She said, "This fire is sacred. This fire is holy. We use it to sustain ourselves in this life." The ashes of the fire were used in this manner, as protection against the bad spirits that were out in the night. So we got to experience some of that old Winnebago way of life with our grandmother.

That was the way that I lived the first several years of my life down along the Missouri River. I would run in the woods and chase after my brothers. My grandmother would send my brothers out to hunt squirrels or rabbits. She'd praise them for being good hunters when they brought something back. I used to tag along after them.

I learned to have a lot of respect for the Creation through this kind of activity. Because she used to tell us, "All these things out there, all these creatures, all these trees, and all these living things were created by the Creator of all things. They all are endowed with His spirit and they all are here as our relatives. We are all connected and so we have to have respect for the Creation."

She used to wake us up early in the morning before the sun came over the horizon. She would tell us not to be laying around when the daylight came, because the Creator gave us life and we should enjoy life. So she used to stand outside this wigwam and pray in the morning and say thank you for the day. She taught us that too. These are some of the early recollections that I have of living with my grandmother in that wigwam.

The wigwam wasn't very big. It was probably ten or twelve feet in length and about eight feet wide. It was just big enough for us to have a place to sleep at night without being rained on. We were outside most of the time. That's the way Winnebago life was. We should not lie around inside our lodge during the day. We should be out in the Creation. The lodge was only canvas, all covered in canvas. There was no electricity or running water. Even that little two-room frame house we lived in didn't have electricity. We used to have lanterns, kerosene burning lamps. I remember my father used to work on the Works Project Administration project.

My grandmother washed clothes by hand in a wash tub, using a scrub board. One day my father and one of his friends brought a washing machine. It had a little gas-fueled engine on it. When we fired up the engine, the washing machine went to work. That was something wonderful in our eyes, to have a machine to wash your clothes. We couldn't believe it.

Back in those days there were very few people on the

reservation who owned cars. Most families traveled by horse and buggy. My dad had a team of horses and a wagon. Most Winnebago families had wagons. My father and mother used to cut fence posts to earn a living. They'd spend their days out in the timber cutting oak fence posts. Then they'd load up the wagon on Saturday morning, put us kids in there, and bring a wagon load of fence posts to town to sell them to the local farmers. My father was working on the WPA project as well as cutting fence posts with my mother. So we had enough money to buy our food.

There was a general store here in Winnebago where all the Indians shopped. Every Saturday all the families used to come to town in their horse-drawn buggy. They would buy their supplies at the store and then go to a little park in the downtown area. Everybody would buy a picnic lunch. They would all be out in the little park visiting and eating. Doing that on weekends was kind of a community activity. Sometimes we stayed in town, when my folks had enough money. They would give us a dime apiece. It cost a nickel to go to the show and it cost two cents for a bag of popcorn. And we could buy a handful of candy for three pennies. Our folks would leave us kids in town because we were enthralled with the weekly motion picture serials that were running—every week there was a new adventure. Our folks would go home in a wagon. We'd stay for the movie at the local theater. We enjoyed ourselves, eating popcorn and candy. When the show was over we'd have to walk home in the middle of the night, all the way back to the river.

It's nine miles from town down to the river. Walking home was a great adventure. There were many creatures of the night making noises. I used to get scared when we heard the coyotes howling, but my brothers weren't afraid. So they used to say, "Oh, don't be afraid. Everything's all right."

In those days town was primarily a place for Whites. All the government workers, all the local business men, were White. They owned the grocery store, the blacksmith shop, the gas station, and the drugstore and everything. They owned all these homes here in town. There were very few Indian families that lived in town. All the rest of us lived out in the rural part of the reservation. Down where we lived, along the Missouri River in the woodlands, there were a lot of families, particularly in the place they called Big Bear Hollow.

We developed a little cadre of guys. We called ourselves the "Big Bear Hollow Gang." We used to run through the woods playing cowboys and Indians. Life was by and large pretty enjoyable. We used to make little carts with baby-buggy wheels and some lumber. Then we'd go up on a big hill and race down the hill in these little carts.

Although we had shoes we usually went barefoot in the summer. Our families couldn't afford to be buying us shoes all the time. So they encouraged us to go barefoot. My grandmother used to make us little moccasins, too. She'd take different kinds of material and she'd make little moccasins for us. So we saved our shoes for coming to town. It's about the only time we'd wear shoes, when we came to town.

That was the way it was during the first four years of my life. It was a time that I enjoyed.

Greyhair family gathered on Winnebago, Nebraska Reservation for Thanksgiving feast, 1939. Reuben Snake, just under three years old, is standing in the front row. Some of his close relatives pictured are Josephine Greyhair, his maternal aunt *(front row, third from left)*; Pete Greyhair, Reuben's *dega*—mother's brother *(back row, far left)*; Virginia Greyhair, Reuben's mother *(fourth from left)*; next to her *(on her right)* is Reuben's maternal grandfather, Isaac Greyhair; Sarah Greyhair, Reuben's maternal aunt *(back row, second from right)*; behind Sarah is Raymond Greyhair, Reuben's *dega*—maternal uncle. Photograph courtesy of Regina Greyhair Scott.

Traces of Traditional Winnebago Ways

Then my parents broke up. My father had developed a serious problem with alcohol. So he left us. He went to Wisconsin with my grandmother. About a year later my mother remarried. My stepfather took us to Sioux City, Iowa. Moving there was a tremendous culture shock. Having grown up in the woods on the Winnebago reservation, living the carefree life, it was a shock entering the big city. Sioux City was really a boom town during the Second World War.

The war was just getting under way when we moved there. There was a large factory there that made B-24 Liberator bombers. A lot of Indian people were employed there, and many other people too. Along the southern edge of the town, next to the Missouri River, was a place called South Bottoms, where all the immigrant people lived. That's generally where the Indian people wound up living. Quite a conglomeration of people lived along the South Bottoms. A lot of European immigrants settled in South Bottoms. We used to socialize with Polish people and Norwegian people and Jewish people.

One of my most memorable experiences was the arrival of the first diesel engine in Sioux City. They had a great big celebration. We were all there, we little kids standing on the side with round eyes, looking at this great big diesel engine. We couldn't understand how it worked.

My stepfather was drafted into the army shortly after we moved to Sioux City. There was just my mother and two brothers, my sister, and I. My mother got a job working at Saint Joseph's Hospital as an assistant cook. Her salary was fifteen dollars a week. That's all she had to pay the rent and buy the groceries. She took care of our everyday needs with that fifteen dollars a week. Times got pretty hard after a while because there were five of us in the household. Fifteen dollars just went so far.

My mother decided to put my older brothers in the Catholic mission school over in Marty, South Dakota. Then she brought my sister down here to Winnebago, to Saint Augustine's Mission, and put her in that school. Then my father came from Wisconsin and took me back to Wisconsin with him.

We went to a place called Black River Falls Indian Mission, where my grandmother and my aunt were living. My father was still involved in his alcoholic activities so I didn't see too much of him. I was enjoying life with my grandmother, my aunt, and my little cousins. Then my father came after me and said: "We're going to go up north. We're going to go visit my brother."

My uncle had married into the Menominee tribe some years before. So we left Black River Falls and we went up to Neopit on the Menominee Reservation. My uncle was the Bureau of Indian Affairs' police officer. My father went about his drinking ways and left me with my uncle and his family.

I became very attached to them. They were good people. My uncle was a very forceful Baptist lay minister, what you would call a real Christian. He was raising his family that way. We used to go to church every Sunday. My uncle would do the preaching, and give us the hellfire and brimstone ceremonies that Baptists are famous for.

After a year, my grandmother sent for me. One of her relatives came over to the Menominee Reservation and picked me up and brought me back to Black River Falls to live with her. The Indian Mission, as it was called, was a settlement of probably a thousand Winnebagos. They carried on the culture of our people as best they could even though they were being proselytized by the Evangelical Reformed Church. Still, there were a lot of activities like hand games and moccasin games and things of this nature that they practiced. My grandmother had grown up this way and she would take us grandchildren around to these gatherings. Even though she had left the Medicine Lodge Society[1] to become a Native American Church member, her relatives were still active in the Medicine Lodge in that area. They used to come and talk to her when they were going to have a Medicine Lodge doing. She would help them prepare the food and we used to go along with her, me and my little cousins.

But because we had not been initiated into the Lodge, we couldn't go inside and be active participants. So we used to sit around outside listening to the music and the talk that was going on inside the long house. They were all talking in Winnebago, so I had some limited exposure to that way of life, the kind of ceremonial life that the Winnebago people used to practice. We attended Native American Church services, so we didn't have that much contact with the Medicine Lodge ways.

In those days in the Native American Church there was a certain rhythm to the drumbeat and a certain way of singing. Today we have a real fast drumbeat, and we sing real fast. The whole rhythm has changed from that time to now. The old men who conducted services back then were practicing primarily the Cross-Fire tradition. It was the tradition that had been taken back from Nebraska to Wisconsin. In their meetings there was a lot of preaching and a lot of reading of the Holy Scripture. They used to memorize the Bible, chapter and verse, and translate it into the Winnebago language. So I got to hear all that as a child. It was really done from memory. They didn't have to read the Bible. They knew it so well that they could preach without reading it. They quoted chapter and verse from the Bible in our own tongue. So what they did then made for a whole different atmosphere than the way it is today in the Native American Church. They were moderately strict in their rules. There was a certain way one had to live one's life every day, a certain way one had to conduct oneself in the Native American Church. They had some rather rigid rules of life in their ceremonial way. Like I said, today it's more relaxed. You don't have that kind of rigidity. Back in those days when you went into the church, you didn't come out just because you felt moved to come out. They used to say, "If you feel you have to do something (vomit), just eat some more medicine (peyote) and pray that you'll be all right. And don't be sitting around in here visiting with one another. If you have to be talking, talk to God. Don't talk to one another."

In our Winnebago way of life, parents didn't administer punishment directly. Whenever a child did something wrong or violated family rules, the parents would tell the uncles, the mother's brothers. They were the disciplinarians within the Winnebago family. So whenever the uncle came around, our mothers would say, "Well, your nephew here said this, or he did that, and he knows he's not supposed to." So then my uncle would grab hold of me. They never hit me or beat me but they used to let me know that I was doing something wrong. For instance, one uncle would grab me and run his knuckles along my temple. That would really sting and he'd say, "Do you feel that?"

And I would say, "Yeah, *Dega* (mother's brother), I feel that." Then he'd say, "Well if you feel that, there must be something inside there."

So I'd say, "Yeah, *Dega*, there's something inside."

"Well, if there's something inside there to tell you how to act, how come you did this dumb thing?" He chastised me by making me go out and help him. He'd be cutting firewood and he'd make me stack the wood. That's the way he used to correct me, by making me get out and work. He'd tell me, "You have to think about what you did. If you didn't do that you wouldn't have to be sweating here. But because you didn't do something right, now you have to pay for it." That's the way discipline was handled by the uncles. So within my family, I don't have any recollection of my parents or my uncles or any of my relatives beating on me or administering corporal punishment. It was just done in that way I explained, to make us think about what we did. And we knew that we should not do it again. That was a very good system they had,

Family portrait taken circa 1946 at the residence of Reuben Snake's maternal grandfather, Isaac Greyhair, in Winnebago, Nebraska. *(Left to right)* Sterling Snake (Reuben's elder brother), Laylee Likehim (Reuben's cousin), Reuben Snake, Regina Greyhair (Reuben's "little mother" or first cousin), Winnifred Snake (Reuben's sister) holding Elizabeth Greyhair (Reuben's first cousin), and Beebe Likehim (Reuben's cousin). Photograph courtesy of Regina Greyhair Scott.

very effective. And through that type of system we developed a lot of respect for our uncle. Whenever our uncle said something, we had to respond immediately. We couldn't say "no" to him if he told us to do something. Because if we said "no," we would lose face in our community. People would say, "Oh, that guy is so dumb he can't even listen to his uncle. How is he going to listen to anybody else?" It was important to respect your uncle and follow your uncle's direction. Then he would say, "Well, my nephew is a good nephew." People would respect children who knew how to behave.

So those were the teachings we learned half a century ago. A lot of that has disappeared from our life today.

Reuben Snake with Regina Greyhair, his Winnebago "little mother" (first cousin in Anglo kinship terms), circa 1949. Photograph courtesy of Regina Greyhair Scott.

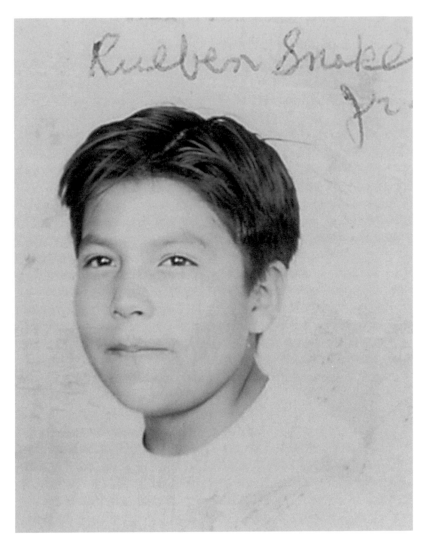

Reuben Snake, elementary school class picture, circa 1947. Photograph courtesy of Regina Greyhair Scott.

Neillsville Mission School

About 1942 my mother came to Wisconsin and took her children to a little town called Neillsville. A German-speaking immigrant named Jacob Stucki, who was a medical doctor and an ordained minister of the United Church of Christ, had started an Indian mission school there. My sister, my two older brothers, and I entered the boarding school at Neillsville. Some cousins of ours from Wisconsin were also at the school. An experience that I later appreciated was getting used to a regimental lifestyle. We all had to get up at a certain hour in the morning and get cleaned up and march to breakfast. And each of us had a specific place to sit at the breakfast table. Each of us had chores to do throughout the day: washing dishes, peeling vegetables, or mopping hallways.

The founder of the school had raised his children among the Winnebago so that they would all be fluent in the Winnebago language. But the rule enforced at the school was that we couldn't speak our own native language. We had to speak English. We couldn't practice any of our cultural activities because they were condemned as pagan, superstitious ritual. When my grandmother came to visit, she and the headmaster would be laughing and carrying on a hilarious conversation in Winnebago. It used to bother me that he could do that but that when we students talked in Winnebago, we were breaking the rules. That was my first experience of hypocrisy, of the Whites preaching one thing and doing another.

Life at that school was very rigid. We had one ringleader there. He was in the eighth grade. And he was perfectly

49

Winnebago, a genuine Winnebago. He used to gather us younger guys together and he'd create some kind of drum sound, maybe by beating on a tin can. Next he'd start singing songs and get us all to dance. Then he'd talk to us in our language and tell us things. He was really impressive. But if we were caught doing this, we were punished. I remember one instance when we were caught singing and dancing and practicing our ways. The housemother tied me to a stairwell post and beat me with a razor strap. That kind of beating was standard practice at that school.

Sometimes I talked with my grandmother and relatives about the unpleasant experiences at school. They understood and they commiserated with us. But it was a White man's institution. We were there to be educated, so they said, "Well, you just have to do what they tell you to do and don't get into trouble."

Some older guys would get truly upset and frustrated with the system and would run away. And then the local law enforcement people would be informed that some Indian kids had run away from the school. They'd be out hunting them and when they brought them back they used to shave their heads. That was part of the punishment for running away, to be shaved bald-headed.

That school was far more restrictive than any public school of today could be. It had about fifty girls and fifty boys and went from first grade through eighth grade. It was a pretty well organized system. Of course, we used to find ways to react to what was happening to us. One of the housemothers was a German-American lady, so we called her "Mrs. Hitler." And then after the Japanese became enemies of America, there was this little Japanese-American lady at the school who we labeled "Mrs. Tojo." We used to bring hellfire on ourselves just for calling them that. After all, they were real proud to be Americans.

When they caught us calling them "Mrs. Hitler" or "Mrs. Tojo," we'd get punished. They'd deny us food if we got out of hand, and make us sit and read the Holy Scriptures and think about our sinful ways. Whippings and denial of food were the standard forms of discipline.

I don't want to paint too bleak a picture. Some of these people had heartfelt feelings for us. I recall certain times when the housemothers must have felt great compassion for us. They would cry when they prayed for us. It was just the system, the system that was designed to move us out of our culture into the Christian way of life. That was the most difficult part, to be denied our culture, our language, our music, and our ways. We were coerced and intimidated into adopting European, Christian values. My first years were spent as a free spirit on the reservation, living with my grandmother and my parents and enjoying life. Then I was thrust into an environment where everything was controlled. We were told when to get up, when to eat, when to go to class, when to work, and when to go to bed. It was quite a shock.

But in retrospect, I think that such early experiences helped me a whole lot later on in life. When I went into the military a lot of White guys used to complain about the rigidity of the military life, but, heck, I just accepted it because I'd grown up that way. And it was by and large a good experience to get to know all these other Winnebago people my age. There were even some Oneidas and Menominees at the school. So I developed some lifelong friendships there.

When we got out of class each afternoon, they gave us about an hour to do our chores. I was in a group that sat in the basement peeling vegetables for the next day's meal. When I finished that I was free to run about outside.

It was a beautiful setting, a great big three-story building with a lot of beautiful lawns around it. The Black River ran close by the edge of the school. It was a pretty place. We used to run around and play outside until it was time for the evening meal. We'd have to go inside and wash up. Then we'd march into the dining room and take our assigned seats. We had our prayers and vespers and Bible readings. Then we sat down to eat. After the evening meal certain people were responsible for washing the dishes and cleaning the kitchen.

Then we had to do our studying until about 9:00 p.m., when they used to put us to bed.

The boys and the girls had separate dormitories; the building was divided with the girls on one side and the boys on the other. They kept us pretty well separated, except for everyday activities. There was one big dormitory room for the older boys, the sixth, seventh, and eighth graders. There was another big dormitory room for the little boys from the first to the fifth grade.

I remember the teachers being pretty decent people. I got along better with some than with others. The first- and second-grade teacher was an extreme disciplinarian. I had a hard time with her. But when I got into the third grade, there was a real kind, gentle woman. She was truly a caring person. I got along very well with her. She was more like a mother to us than a teacher.

We were always being told to do things in preparation for some event. They organized Christmas plays. One month before Christmas, we'd all get assigned roles. I used to be one of the singing angels in a nativity scene. They would perform the whole Christmas story and it used to be a lot of fun getting ready for that play.

My relatives would come to performances. The school would send out word that we were going to have a Christmas play. Many of our relatives used to come up from Black River and fill the largest classroom, which probably held a hundred people or so.

This school was supported by a variety of people and institutions that donated a great deal of used clothing. They'd bring a truckload of used clothing in, take it upstairs, unpack it, and spread it all out. Then they'd take us up class by class, and we'd get to go through and pick out the things we wanted. Because this was during the war, we were all heavily influenced by wartime propaganda. Everybody wanted to dress and look like a combat pilot. So as soon as we reached into the second-hand clothes we'd start looking for those leather flying helmets and silk scarves. We were going to look cool if we could find one of those. We'd be running around with a leather flying helmet and a silk scarf around our neck, acting like a real war hero. That kind of thing was quite entertaining.

Getting those clothes was just part of the routine of life, part of the system we were involved in. I never felt any shame over it. I never felt deprived or anything. It was just something we did. They used to issue us work shoes called "Little Abners." The manufacturer of these shoes donated rejects to the school. So everybody wore these brown stogies with big round toes like Little Abner wore in the comics. Those were our weekday shoes. We saved our good shoes for going to church on Sunday.

I had this one buddy my age. We used to throw sand on the sidewalk and run on it real fast. Those leather-soled shoes would just skim over the top of the sand. So we could twirl around and do different kinds of pirouettes. My buddy got so good at sliding that he used to wear his shoes out in only two weeks. The leather soles would be gone. So they'd have to issue him another pair. After a while they got upset with him because he was wearing out shoes three times as fast as anybody else. They wanted to know why he wore shoes out so fast. When they saw us sliding around on the sand on the sidewalk, they realized how he was doing it. So they said, "Okay, just to teach you a lesson, we're not going to let you wear your shoes after school. That way you won't be wearing them out."

Then what they did was take his shoes away from him. So he would tie mop rags around his feet. That way he couldn't slide on the sand. But he was very creative. He found out he could slide in a hallway with the mop rags on his feet. So we took our activity indoors. He used to do all this maneuvering around on the polished floors of the hallways with mop rags tied around his feet.

Our teachers were puritanical. We could only have fun in a Christian way. For them, having a good time meant singing hymns. We had vespers every evening. At the vesper service one of the housemothers or teachers would read scripture to us and lead us in singing Christian hymns such as "The Old Rugged Cross," "Nearer My God to Thee," and "How Great Thou Art." We learned all those hymns. We had to memorize all of them and were coached on how to sing them properly.

At that time my favorite subject was reading. I developed a love for reading in that school. I'd pick up anything and read it. I enjoyed reading *Treasure Island* and all of Jack London's books about Alaska. And oh, *The Black Stallion*. That kind of storytelling was really interesting to me. I wasn't too hot in math. But English and history courses interested me. I used to contemplate about how we were taught in American History that George Washington was the father of our country. Whenever I saw a picture of George Washington I couldn't fathom how this White guy with his big nose and his powdered wig could be my father. Absolutely nothing about Native American cultures was taught. There was nothing Indian in our schooling.

The school owned a farm which was run by a White guy. He would use the schoolchildren in planting the gardens in the spring and taking care of the livestock. They had milk cows, hogs, and chickens. The older boys were responsible for tending to the livestock. And then in the fall, we would all harvest produce out of the gardens and store it in large bins in the basement of the school. We would have those vegetables available throughout the school year. There were generally vegetables like cabbages, carrots, potatoes, rutabagas, celery, and tomatoes.

All the children were sent home for the summer. I used to go back to my grandmother's. The Neillsville Indian School was around thirty miles from the Black River Falls Indian Mission, where my grandmother lived. When the school year was over she would take us back to her home. I was at my grandma's home only in the summer and during the holidays, like Christmas.

When we stayed with my grandmother during the summer we were still involved with the traditional Winnebago ways. My cousin was really a good hunter and a good trapper. So I used to tag along behind him. He was always snaring rabbits and shooting squirrels and trapping beaver and muskrat. Wild game was a fairly common part of our diet back in those days. And of course we had the standard vegetables that we bought at the store. Every evening my grandmother used to send my cousin and me down the road to an older German man who had some milk cows. We used to buy a gallon of milk from him every night. I think it cost ten cents.

The Winnebagos in Wisconsin had access to cranberries and blueberries and a variety of things that grew in the forest. We used to harvest them and my grandmother would can strawberries, blueberries, and cranberries. She knew about other kinds of natural foods like waterlily roots. She would go out in a pond where the waterlilies were growing and dig them up with her toes. She would take the long tube of the root, cut it into sections, and dry them in the sun. She cooked that in bacon fat. We ate a lot of traditional foods when we stayed with grandma, things like fried bread and baking-powder biscuits.

I never recall being hungry. It always amazes me when I reflect about it, that we didn't realize we were poor. I guess we were. But somehow or other, between my grandmother and my aunt, we always had food on the table. There never seemed to be a time when we went without.

At my grandmother's house we didn't have electricity. Everything was done by lamplight after the sun went down. We had a wood-burning stove. The house didn't have any inside plumbing. We had to haul water from a spring about 300 or 400 yards away. We never did own a car or radio.

My grandmother owned some land in Nebraska, and every month the Bureau of Indian Affairs would send her a small land lease check. So then she would get me ready, because I was the oldest of her smaller grandchildren. We would walk from the Indian mission to downtown Black River, about eight or nine miles. After a couple of miles she would carry me on her back wrapped in her shawl. I think that had a lot to do with my feelings for my grandmother. We developed deep bonds during that time. She and I would walk to town and she would cash her little check. Then she would buy a gunny sack full of staple foods like flour, oatmeal, and lard. She always saved enough to buy a little candy for all of us. Then she would hire a taxi cab to drive us back to the mission with our monthly supply of staples.

That was the type of life we had at the Indian mission. That was generally the lifestyle of all the Indian people that lived there. We had a strong communal life. There was always some kind of social function going on, a moccasin game or a hand game or something else to attend, and the Evangelical Reform Church used to have gatherings. Everybody got to know each other and got along well.

I was at Neillsville during first and second grade and halfway through third grade. Around Christmas time, my mother came. She had relocated to a small town called Hastings, about twenty-five miles south of Saint Paul, Minnesota. She had a decent source of income, so she came after us children and she took us back to Minnesota with her.

Anglo Economics
and Public Education

M oving to Hastings started another fairly exciting cycle in
my life. There were very few Indians living in the area.
I can recall only one other Indian family living in that
town of maybe ten thousand people. Our source of income
was the production of little tourist trinkets. We used to make
little drums out of old inner tubes and tin cans. We had a
working relationship with a company in Minneapolis and another in Red Wing, Minnesota. So each one of us, my brother,
my sister, my mother, and I, had a weekly goal, a weekly
quota of different sized little drums that we would make and
paint. Then, on Saturday, we'd pack them all up in big boxes
and hire a cab to take them all down to the train station.

We'd get on a train and ride to Minneapolis. We would
take the boxes over to the Bloom brothers. And they would
buy all of the drums we had produced. Then we would have
money so we could rent a hotel room and eat out and go to
a movie. We were tremendously impressed by this great big
city, by what was going on in the streets of that city. On Sunday we'd get on the train and come back to our little town.
And we'd start all over again manufacturing more souvenir
tom-toms. And the next week we'd get on a train and we'd go
to Red Wing, to the other company, and sell our drums there.

It was a good source of income for us. It kept us housed
and clothed and fed. And we got along well.

In Hastings, most people didn't know any Indians, and
they had all these misconceptions. It was primarily for economic reasons that we moved there. That town was just a
place that my mother found where she could get a house and
be located between the two places where we were going to sell

our drums. We weren't too far from Prairie Island, which is a Sioux community in Minnesota. So there were other Indians in the area.

My mother was strongly influenced by Reform Church Missionaries in her formative years. They had encouraged her to learn English. So when we children came along, even though my mother was very fluent in Winnebago, she only talked to her peers, people her own age, in our tongue. When she talked to us children, she spoke English. She told us, "That's the only way you're going to be able to get along with these people is to speak their language. So you had better learn their language."

So that's the way it was with us at home. My mother talked to my stepfather and she talked to her brothers and other people in our Winnebago tongue. We understood the conversation but we couldn't join in because we weren't schooled in the use of our tongue. So we had to use English when we talked to them. We learned simple Winnebago words like *warooj,* that's time to eat, or *menagre,* sit down, or *hoora,* come here. We all knew a few phrases but we could not carry on a conversation in our Winnebago language.

After we left the mission school in Neillsville we came back to Hastings, Minnesota. Our mother enrolled us in the local public school system. Of course, carrying the name "Snake" in a White society created a provocative situation, and we were often teased—both because we were Indians and because we had this weird name. So my sister and I were obliged to "educate" a lot of White kids. We had to give them a knuckle sandwich now and then so they would learn to respect our name. We had to go to "Duke City" every now and then to defend our identity.

We were friendly with everybody and the non-Indian kids were friendly toward us. People weren't openly racist. They just were ignorant. And once they came to know us, they realized that we weren't that much different than they were. And we'd go visit our White friends and they'd come over to our place. We had good relationships. My older brothers played on the local softball and baseball teams. They had White girlfriends. So we fit in fairly well with the non-Indian people living around us.

One of the state mental institutions was located about a mile away from the farmhouse where we lived. We used to go over and visit the people who were living there. Many of them were free to roam the grounds. They weren't confined in any way except for the ones who supposedly were dangerous. So we used to go over there and play cowboys and Indians with these mental patients.

I was about eight years old then. My brothers were just entering their teenage years. My sister was about ten years old. We had a unique kind of playground there. Maybe that's why I am the way I am today. Many of these people were very childlike in their ways, because of the different kinds of mental disorders that they had. Yet they weren't dangerous. They just talked funny.

We had many adventures with the inmates at this state mental institution. We did some naughty things. In the spring, these guys used to come out of the mental hospital to tap the maple trees. And my brothers and my sister and I and some of our friends would come creeping through the woods after they had hung their maple buckets on the trees. We would gather up all their maple sap and put it into our buckets and we'd run off with it.

This used to upset the patients. At first they didn't understand who was ripping them off. And then one day one of them spotted us coming through the woods behind them. And they said, "The Indians are coming! The Indians are coming!" Then they ran off and left their maple buckets behind. We used to build a big fire and pour all the maple sap into a tub and boil it down into syrup and hard maple-sugar candy. These were some of the fond memories I have of living in Hastings.

In 1941 or 1942 my mother and my grandmother took us up to Door County, Wisconsin. The whole peninsula of Wisconsin was covered with cherry orchards. The owners used to hire Chicanos, Jamaicans, people out of the Ozarks, and Indians to harvest the cherries every summer. So I started doing that as a very young child. I got up early in the morning to go out and start harvesting cherries all day long. That was a source of income for my family. My mother, my brothers, my sister, and I, all worked together to do this. There were a lot of other Winnebago families there as well. That became a yearly expedition for us, to travel up to cherry land, as we called it, up to Door County, Wisconsin. It was a great deal of fun, too. After a hard day's work the orchard owner would load us all in a truck and take us down to Lake Michigan, or to Green Bay. We'd jump into the water and have fun down there. After a couple of hours the owner would bring us back to our camp.

Doing migrant labor exposed me to another aspect of the dominant culture. It allowed me to interact with members from diverse groups. During the summer Door County was inhabited by a variety of people. It was very stimulating to get to know children from other cultures. I always think that associating with them in that way contributed greatly to my ability to appreciate people from different backgrounds.

The orchard owners usually built little camps with cabins on their property, so each family would have a place to stay. But we had to go to the orchard owner's home to use his pump to have access to water. The cabins had little spaces for bunks in them and a little space for a kerosene stove to cook our food. It was very primitive living. But it used to be fun. At one particular orchard there were only Winnebagos. So we got to associate every day with one another, play with each other after a hard day's work. That strengthened my ties to my Winnebago relatives.

Summer migrant work was a part of my life from the time I was four years old until I was about seventeen, when I joined the service. I worked not only in Wisconsin but in southern Minnesota, where there was a lot of truck farming. That experience motivated me to try to find something else to do with myself besides engaging in stoop labor. The work was very tiring, particularly on the truck farms. I had to crawl on my hands and knees to pull weeds all day long, from six-thirty in the morning to six o'clock in the evening.

We children used to get paid thirty-five cents an hour. I think the adults got fifty cents an hour because they didn't require as much supervision. The farmer usually hired some overseers to walk behind us to see that we were doing the job adequately.

Our mother usually collected all the money at the end of the week. Then we would go to town. She would take us out to dinner and to a movie. She would buy us the clothes that we needed. She handled all the family finances. I think my older brothers probably got an allowance from her. I didn't because I was just a young kid and didn't know how to handle money.

Summers were more fun than any other time of year because I was with my mother and my grandmother and my other relatives. I got to enjoy various aspects of our culture during the summer months. We could do those things which were denied us at the mission school during the school year.

Of course we did not speak Winnebago because it was stressed so strongly by the missionaries that we had to learn English. I spoke English all the time, even though I understood the Winnebago language. In Wisconsin there was greater retention of the language because most of the children at the mission school came from homes where Winnebago was the parent tongue. So when they went home everybody in their household spoke Winnebago. They were able to develop fluency in the language. A lot of children in my age group at the mission school were fluent in Winnebago. They probably got into more trouble than I did at the mission school because they were constantly conversing in Winnebago.

The Winnebago language and culture were suppressed at the mission school because anything Indian was considered to be inferior. For us to be "saved" we had to forfeit our Indianness. We had to adopt European values and the European life style. We could not practice our culture, speak our language, or sing our music. If we wanted to truly be children of God and followers of Christ we had to give up all of our Indian ways.

We had to have our hair cut regularly. We couldn't go to school with long hair. We weren't allowed to wear anything Indian. We had to wear White man's clothing. It was all right to wear the White man's jewelry but not Indian jewelry. These rigid standards were enforced to eliminate all the Winnebago customs from our lives and make us into little brown facsimiles of the White man. Not a trace of our culture was allowed in the school. They denied us everything.

After we left this mission boarding school and came back to Minnesota we didn't stay too long. The war came to an end, my stepfather was discharged, and he brought us back to the reservation in the late summer of 1945. But my stepfather and my mother couldn't find work on our reservation. So they put my brothers and my sister and me into the Reformed Church Mission Home, here on the Winnebago (Nebraska) Reservation. Then they went off to Minnesota to find work again.

My brothers and my sister and I spent a couple of years here at the Reformed Church Mission Home. During our time there we attended the public school every day. I think my second experience with the Reformed Church missionary people was a little more positive, although the church itself was, like all other White Christian denominations, dedicated to denying the spirituality of Indian people. They preached the Word of God, the message of Christ, very strongly. It just so happened that the housemother we had was an extremely kind and loving individual. I have real fond recollections of her. She wasn't harsh with us. She treated us kindly. She treated us like a mother. She looked after our everyday needs and counseled us and tried to express real love towards us. That was a whole different experience, being under that kind of care and keeping.

At Winnebago at the Reformed Church Mission Home

everybody had assigned duties: to mop the halls and wash the dishes and mow the lawn. We were obliged to do different chores as part of our daily routine. That was good training. It taught us responsibility and showed us that we had to do certain things in order to make our environment a nice place to live.

I wouldn't say we didn't have negative experiences here. The director of the school was a Reformed Church minister. He was very anti-Indian culture when he first came here. I remember one incident where we were doing something Indian and he lined us all up, all us boys that he had caught doing this Indian thing. He made us hold our hands out and he began to hit us with a ruler across the palms of our hands. We had been singing or doing something that he considered to be regressive behavior. We were trying to hang on to our Indianness.

Like the other missionaries, they believed very strongly that the only way we could be saved was to forgo all of our Indian cultural and spiritual ways and adopt the European value system and accept the word of Christ.

We attended church twice each Sunday. They had a morning service and an evening service. All the children in the home were obliged to be present at both services. So we got proselytized quite intensely. They used to have regular activities for us during the week. One night each week we were obliged to go down to the church and practice our singing and choir and have Bible study. Then we could be involved in some recreational activity that was provided by the church people. So there was a constant effort to brainwash us and to eliminate our native culture from our lives.

When summer came, my brothers and sisters and I went back to Minnesota and worked on a truck farm with my stepfather and my mother. That's how we spent the summers for about three years until my parents felt pretty comfortable living in southern Minnesota. Then they came after us and took us back to Minnesota to live.

Around that time, in the city of Albert Lea, in southern

Minnesota, the Winnebago population was growing. It eventually grew to about three hundred Winnebagos who were living there, in Freeborn County, Minnesota. We were part of a contingent of Winnebagos that worked on the truck farms and eventually moved into local industry. We worked at the packing house and in other industries around that area and became kind of permanent settlers there.

In 1950 I went to school at Haskell Institute, a federal boarding school in Lawrence, Kansas. I was thirteen years old when I entered Haskell as a high school freshman. Once again I had to undergo a tremendous cultural change. There were approximately five hundred Indian students at Haskell Institute. For the first time in my life I was exposed to many different tribal groups. There were Kiowas and Comanches and Creeks and Otoes and Cherokees and Navajos and Sioux and Arapahos. It was truly stimulating to get to know many of these young people who came from distinct tribal backgrounds.

Haskell Institute was where I began to get involved in athletic activities. I had always enjoyed running. It was just something I liked to do. Haskell had a good cross-country team and I got involved in that. Later on I began to play football and basketball. I was never all-star caliber but I did manage to make the varsity team. I was elected co-captain of the cross-country team because I had won a couple of races while I was a sophomore. The coach felt I had potential as a runner so he made me co-captain of the cross-country team. I used to run fifteen miles every evening just to stay in shape.

Haskell Institute has since become a junior college. But in those days it was a co-educational high school and a vocational/technical school. We lived in dormitories on the campus. There was one dormitory for freshmen and sophomores and another for junior and seniors.

We lived a regimented life. The bell would ring at a certain hour of the morning and we had to get up. And then the bell would ring when it was time for us to go to the dining hall to eat breakfast. The bell would ring when it was time to go to class. The bell would ring when it was lunch time. The bell would ring when school was over. The bell would ring when it was time to go eat our evening meal. Then the bell would ring when it was time to go to bed. We lived by a system of bells.

We were encouraged to attend church on Sundays. There were Catholic services and services conducted by some Protestant denominations. I was still somewhat active in the Native American Church. While I was growing up I had attended prayer meetings from time to time, maybe once or twice a month. So I considered that to be my religion. I never got involved in any non-Indian denomination. I was one of those people that didn't go to church on Sunday at Haskell.

There wasn't any place in Lawrence, Kansas, to attend Native American Church meetings. However, my mother's uncle was a Winnebago who had married into the Potawatomi tribe at Marquette, Kansas, about forty or fifty miles away from Lawrence. He used to pick my sister and me up and take us back to the Potawatomi Reservation, and there we would experience a Native American Church meeting.

There was a small number of Winnebagos attending Haskell. The largest part of the student body were young people from the state of Oklahoma. There weren't many representatives of the upper plains tribes. There were some Sioux students, and probably eight or nine Winnebagos.

I got along all right with those Winnebagos there who were my relatives, my cousins, but they weren't any more attuned to the culture than I was. The circumstances at the school were kind of paradoxical. They didn't want us to practice our Indian ways but they really didn't deny them. They had an Indian dance club, which served as a propaganda tool to impress the non-Indian people in the surrounding community that we were good people. Those who knew how to dance Indian and sing Indian could join this club. They had regular weekly meetings, and they gave performances around the city of Lawrence and probably in Topeka or Kansas City. It was a multi-tribal kind of activity. Students learned a little bit about this tribe and a little bit about that one. Although Haskell was an all-Indian institution, there was nothing Indian taught at the school. The Indian club was the only organization which carried on any kind of cultural tradition at all.

All Haskell teachers were in the United States Civil Service and they were predominantly non-Indian. Of course there were some good teachers and there were some bad teachers. In my second year, when I was a sophomore, I had to choose a vocation to study. I chose radio and television repair. Half my day was spent learning about radio and television sets. Our instructor in that shop was a very good, caring person who had a genuine interest in teaching us. It wasn't just a job, it was something he felt that he could do to help us. So he was very diligent in teaching us how to be good radio and television repair people.

During my freshman year I was really amazed to see that the school employed an Indian. Presley Wear was a Kiowa Indian. I don't remember what courses he taught but he was our freshman football coach. I just couldn't believe that an Indian could be a teacher and a coach. Presley Wear was the first role model I had. He helped me realize that it was possible for an Indian to accomplish something. He was a good-hearted individual, and he really encouraged us to get an education and to strive to do the very best that we could do.

I think Haskell may have employed another Indian or two in the vocational/technical section. I never really got to know them. There were other Indians on the Haskell staff, like custodians and groundskeepers. The head coach was a Potawatomi Indian, Doctor Tony Coffin. He was also a role model for me.

I was at Haskell about two and a half years. I went there in 1950 and I left in 1952. Like a lot of young people, I became involved in some things that perhaps I shouldn't have. Back in southern Minnesota, where I spent my summers with my family, some of my young relatives and friends had started to associate with non-Indian young people. I remember one particular family that owned a tavern. There were some young girls and a young boy in this family. Their children would go into the tavern's basement and take a case of beer and bring it out and share it with us.

I was thirteen years old the first time I tried alcohol. One evening they said, "Would you guys care for a cold one?" We all said, "Yeah, sure." So they went down to the basement, into the cooler, and brought a case of beer out the back door. Then we ran off to the park where we were sitting behind some bushes drinking beer.

I didn't drink every night. I drank every weekend with these young people. When their dad got busy running his bar business and the crowd showed up on Friday night, that was an ideal time to be hauling drinks out without dad noticing. So that's what we would do on Friday night and maybe even Saturday. That led us into other kinds of negative behavior. Often, after drinking so much beer, we wanted to fight somebody. So we'd go down the street and pick a fight with somebody.

We fought just about any kids we thought were in need of a "tune-up." We would be cruising the street and start bad-mouthing some people and then they'd begin bad-mouthing us back and so then we'd get out and work them over.

Nobody was ever seriously injured in the fighting. It was limited to a black eye or a fat lip. We never used any weapons, no knives or anything like that, we just duked it out. The purpose of the fighting was to prove our manhood I guess. That's what we were trying to do, to establish who was the toughest guy.

Albert Lea was a strange little town. It had been an all-White community up until the Second World War. Then they started importing migrant laborers, Mexican-Americans from Texas and thirteen families of Winnebagos from the reservation. Suddenly there was an influx of different kinds of people. The White community didn't quite know how to accept us. We were a necessary part of their life because we were out there doing all this stoop labor in their truck farms, but they didn't particularly care to see us in their eating establishments and definitely didn't care to see us in their schools.

As usual, there was always somebody trying to save us. We got proselytized by several different religious groups. A lot of people were friendly; they just accepted us. But there was a large portion of the community who, just because they didn't know any better, used to insult us. Being young and cocky, we didn't take too much of that mistreatment without fighting back. We knew that we weren't welcome and that always had us on edge.

Amateur boxing was very popular in that town and throughout the state. We developed a really outstanding boxing team composed mostly of Indians and Chicanos. We brought prestige to the city by winning a lot of championships in the amateur bouts, in the Golden Gloves tournaments and events like that. Albert Lea became known as a good fight town, a place with a lot of good Chicano and Indian boxers. In that way we earned some respect over the years that I lived there. I don't remember ever getting beat up. During those years I was in pretty good shape and had acquired a pretty good left jab and right cross. At age thirteen, I was probably the youngest guy in the crowd. Most of the kids were fifteen or sixteen years old. Those older guys all had girlfriends and we'd travel around in beat up old cars with their girlfriends. I didn't have a girlfriend at that age.

Those older guys were my cousins and relatives. We had some Winnebago girls and some White girls. The Chicanos were very jealous of their women. They liked to go out with Indian girls, but whenever an Indian guy tried to go out with a Chicana girl he got into trouble. We didn't try to pick up Chicana girls because that would have generated open warfare and we really didn't want that.

Sometimes our elders would get together and organize a traditional dance, a powwow, and occasionally we'd put on a show for some organization. But our social activities were limited largely to getting together as families and celebrating birthdays or weddings or events like that. There was no other structure to facilitate social events among our people. We younger men used to associate with the Chicanos, who were well organized. They used to rent the local armory and have big dances and invite Indian girls. The Indian guys would go along saying, "Damn, if you're going to take our women over there, we're going to go over there, too."

The only Whites interested in us were people trying to proselytize us into one denomination or another. We didn't get involved in activities organized by the White community.

Within that community of Albert Lea there were about three hundred Winnebagos. But except for the prayer meetings of the Native American Church, and an occasional pow-wow, there wasn't any active emphasis on retaining the culture. The older people that lived there, members of my mother's generation, talked Winnebago to one another and reminisced about their younger days. But they were preoccupied with just trying to earn a living.

My older relatives knew we were drinking and fighting. They would tell us that we shouldn't be doing that kind of thing. When I attended a Native American Church meeting those old men would preach at us young guys to straighten up and act right, do things the way we were supposed to, and leave the drinking alone.

I respected those elders. I really liked them. It used to give me real soul satisfaction to go to a Native American Church prayer meeting. When I was between ten and fifteen I attended prayer meetings once or twice a month. Sitting in there and listening to those old men in their sixties, seventies, and eighties was really beneficial to me. It gave me a peaceful feeling to hear them speak our language and reveal the things that were most important in life. That was all very positive for me, even though at that age I disregarded much of their advice. It was good to hear but then it was hard to practice.

From Student to Green Beret

I didn't have a girlfriend until I went to Haskell Institute. Of course, finding somebody to go out with was one of the favorite activities of everybody there. There was a nice-looking young lady, and being as young as I was, I was always tonguetied in her presence. It probably took me several months to work up enough courage just to ask her to go to a movie on Sunday afternoon at the school auditorium. When she accepted I felt like doing cartwheels. In addition to taking this young lady to shows I'd invite her to the dance. They used to have dances occasionally on a Saturday night, and even though I never was much of a dancer I'd invite her and we'd go dancing. It was a nice relationship that we enjoyed, until she found somebody better-looking and more popular than I was. I was merely the co-captain of the cross-country team. She was after the football captain or something.

By the time I left Haskell, the drinking that I had been drawn to from the age of thirteen, though only on an occasional basis, was beginning to affect my life. At Haskell I used to work on the weekends. They had a program that helped students who needed money find jobs such as cleaning people's yards, or mowing their lawns. I used to go out and do that sort of yard work perhaps two or three times during the week, in the evening after school, and all day Saturday. That way I would have enough money to do something Saturday night, to go to a dance or a movie. Some of my peers used to say, "Hey, why don't you chip in with us? Give us five dollars and we'll go down and we'll get a fifth of Jack Daniels or something."

They were always able to find somebody on the street to buy alcohol for them. They'd go downtown and maybe they'd give somebody five dollars to go in the liquor store and buy them something to drink. Then they'd bring it back to the campus and we'd find a secluded place to sit and drink. So that began to have an impact, even though I was very dedicated to athletics and I was a pretty decent student. I was doing my best to acquire the education that was available to me there. But still, due to peer pressure, I used to get involved with these kids who were drinking hard liquor. In one of those situations, my cousin and I were drinking and we got into a fight with some other guys and we beat this one guy up pretty badly. When our dorm supervisor found out what happened we were put on restriction. For thirty days we couldn't go anywhere.

After that fight my cousin said, "The hell with this noise. I don't have to stay at this place if they're going to do that to me. I'm going to go home." I said, "Well, hell, if you feel that way, I'm going home too." So I packed up all my clothes and took what money I had and bought a bus ticket back to Minnesota. I told the school people, "Hail and farewell."

At Haskell, I enjoyed my athletic endeavors and even the school work. It wasn't a bad life. But when we messed up and were put on restriction I decided to leave and go back to Minnesota. I stayed with my oldest brother a little while and then I went back to my mother's house and enrolled in school there. We lived about two miles outside of town. My mother used to get up at four-thirty in the morning and cook breakfast and wake me up and feed me. Then she would get dressed and go out on the road and start walking to work. It was cold, sometimes down to thirty, thirty-five degrees below zero. She had to walk three miles to work at a produce house, where they processed turkeys. She worked there from about six-thirty in the morning until six o'clock at night. I was going to Albert Lea High School. It bothered me that my mother had to go through all this hardship just to keep me in school. So one day I told her, "Mom, I'm going to quit school and go to work, so that you don't have to work." She said, "No, don't do that." "No, I'm going to do it," I said.

After my sixteenth birthday I quit school and I started working where she was working. I told her to stay home. I would work and she said, "No, it's all right. I'll just continue on with my job." She and my stepfather and I were all working at this produce house. She was in good health. She kept her home up, she worked every day and looked after my needs and those of my stepfather. That went on for some time. Finally one day I said, "I'm really tired of these turkeys. There's got to be something else in this world for me to do beside working with these turkeys." I decided that it was about time for me to join the service. I was seventeen years old. One day I just laid my tools down and I started walking out. Then the foreman said, "Hey you, Snake, where are you going?" I said, "I quit this job, I can't stand it anymore." So my cousin noticed me walking out, because he was working there too. He asked, "Where you going?" I said, "I'm going uptown." "Well, I'm going to go with you." He quit too.

We went uptown to the Marine Corps recruiter's office. He wasn't in, so we went to the Navy recruiter's office. He wasn't in, so we went to the Air Force recruiter's office. He wasn't in, either. Then we went into the Army recruiter's office and he was in. So we said, "We want to enlist." He was always looking for recruits so he signed us up.

We were under the legal age, and he knew it because he had signed up my two older brothers. My oldest brother had joined the Army when he was sixteen. My other brother joined the Army when he was fifteen. This man was the same one who had recruited both of them. So he said, "I know you. Being from the Snake family I know you lie about your age. So I won't believe you when you tell me you're eighteen." He paused and asked, "So, how old are you?" I said, "I'm seventeen." "Well, all right," he said. "If your mother doesn't object, I'll take you." So my cousin and I joined the Army. That was in November of 1954.

I went to Fort Leonard Wood, Missouri, for my basic training, and then to Fort Gordon, Georgia, for signal core training. In the summer of 1955 I was nearing completion of my

73

Reuben Snake prepares to join the Army, fall 1954. *(Left to right)* Raymond Greyhair, Reuben's maternal uncle; Virginia Greyhair, Reuben's mother; Reuben. Photograph courtesy of Regina Greyhair Scott.

training course in radio repair when a special forces recruiting officer came through. He announced that he was looking for men interested in becoming communications specialists. He was looking for radio repairmen and radio operators and the like. So out of a thousand men that were graduating from that particular class in signal school, one of my friends from Pennsylvania and I were the only two who volunteered for the Green Berets.

I had a couple of reasons for wanting to be a Green Beret. One day on the parade grounds, a plane flew over and all these paratroopers jumped out of the plane. Right then and there all the WACs (Women's Army Corps) went bananas. All those women exclaimed: "Oh, look over there! Look at those guys!" I thought to myself, "Hey, that's pretty cool. That is a great way to attract a woman's attention, by jumping out of airplanes."

Furthermore, the special forces recruiter told us, "If you join our organization, if you can meet our standards, you won't ever have to pull KP (kitchen patrol) and you won't be assigned to some godforsaken place. You'll be right in the middle of all that's going on." I was excited by the fact that the Green Berets were being trained in exotic places like Panama and Puerto Rico and the Rocky Mountains and Virginia. They were undergoing mountain training and underwater demolition work and jungle warfare and desert warfare. So it was much more stimulating than just being stuck in Fort Huachuca, Arizona. It was the excitement that was appealing to me, the idea that I was going to experience all these things. That is why I signed up with them.

In August of 1955 I went to Fort Bragg, North Carolina, to join the 77th Special Forces Unit. I went through jump school there, learning how to be a paratrooper, learning how to jump out of a plane and get the parachute to work. At Fort Bragg I completed all the different kinds of training required of any individual who wants to become a Special Forces Operative. We had to go through a broad range of training and we also had our own specialty. I was a communications specialist, so I was a repairman for all the various kinds of radios that we were going to use. I also went to an operator's school and I became a radio operator. We also had to go through what they called cross-training. We had to learn something about every other team member's specialty. We had to learn a little bit about what medics do, a little bit about weapons, a little bit about intelligence, so that when we finished training each of us would be a well-rounded individual capable of organizing a regimental size drill or unit. Each Special Forces Operative is supposed to have all those skills by the time he gets done with training.

In January of 1957 I was called before the board for an examination to see if I qualified to be a Special Forces Operative. I passed my exam and I was designated a Special Forces Operative. Then I was asked to take a tour of duty in Berlin, Germany. So I went to Berlin for a year, which was quite an eye-opening experience.

At that time Berlin was behind the Iron Curtain. The East Germans and Russians had the city of Berlin completely surrounded. West Berlin was occupied by the United States, Britain, and France. East Berlin was occupied by the Russians. It was, in many respects, the focal point of the Cold War.

We Special Forces Operatives were told to work with the CIA. The CIA people briefed us about the fact that there were sixty-seven different nations with intelligence units right there in West Berlin. They warned us to be aware of everything that was happening, to be alert all the time. It was an intriguing job, being stationed in Berlin at that particular time. It was exciting to practice all the assignments that we were given as A-teams. Each one of us had a specific task to do in case war ever broke out.

I drank a lot because that was part of the life style of the Special Forces. It's that way in all military units. In order to prove that you are a he-man you have to be able to drink. I smoked, but not much. I was in good physical shape. I weighed about 187 pounds and I could do a seven-mile forced march in less than fifty minutes with a forty-pound rucksack on my back. And I could box for fifteen rounds.

The Germans in Berlin were very intrigued by American Indians. In Germany right now there are probably one and a half million Indian hobbyists, people who practice how to be an Indian. They learn how to do bead work and leather work, and how to sing and dance the dances of various tribal cultures. We Indians are really popular in Germany. When Germans would find out that I was an American Indian, I always had free drinks and everybody began slapping me on the back. I know that the Germans I worked with were always impressed with the fact I was an Indian. I used to get invitations to their homes for the holidays.

This was the first time in my life when being a Native American resulted in positive experiences. I used to think about that. Here I was in a foreign country and people treated me with kindness and respect and looked up to me as a person. It was a feeling which I had never really enjoyed in my own country.

My image of the United States did not change at that time. I think I had probably been brainwashed to the point where I accepted most of the European values. My indoctrination was so complete that even though I knew I was an Indian, even though I knew I was Winnebago, and I wasn't ashamed of that fact, I didn't dwell on it either. I thought I was just a regular person, like the rest of the crowd, with brown skin, so it never bothered me too much. Of course, there were a certain number of guys in the service who didn't like Indians. They would make remarks, but that wasn't so serious a problem.

Getting into fights was a normal aspect of military life. After all, they were training us to be aggressive. So whenever we went out drinking with our buddies we usually wound up in a fight. If we were not fighting some stranger, we were fighting our buddies. That's just the way that military lifestyle is. They pounded that into our heads, that we had to be tough guys.

There were certain areas of West Berlin that were off-limits to American GIs, particularly in the French section of the city where Communism had developed strong roots. Some young West Berliners were interested in Communism as a way of life. When we went to night clubs in the French sector, as soon as they discovered we were American, they started provoking us. That used to lead to fights with some young Germans who wanted to make a political issue of our presence. Otherwise we got along well with them.

Growing up, all of those World War II stereotypes had been pounded into my head: that the Germans were evil, that Germans were no good. So Germans were, in my mind, bad people up until the time I went to Germany. Then I found out that they are human beings.

I developed some beneficial friendships with German people. In our weekend excursions around the city we used to visit different night clubs and drinking establishments. Beer Stubes, I guess they call them. German beer is notably different than American beer. After a while I learned the difference between the beers, the dark beers and light beers, and I developed a particular taste for certain brands. I become a connoisseur of beer. There are so many varieties of beer made in Germany. And there always is an excuse to drink beer. Beer drinking is a way of life.

I used to enjoy going to the different German restaurants in Berlin. I made friends with some of the German people that I worked with on a daily basis or met through my associations with people in the city. I would get invitations to go to their homes for dinner. I developed an appreciation for German cooking. There were little bratwurst stands where one had a selection of bratwurst. There was a certain kind of sauce they used to put on the bratwurst. The Germans are somewhat like Indians—they like to eat wild game. At a German restaurant one can order goose or duck or rabbit. I enjoyed eating those things. And I developed a taste for *schweinhockens,* pork hocks, the way the Germans make them. The food must have been good because I went from 187 pounds to 225 pounds in the year that I was in Berlin.

We used to go out on the town to the night clubs and pick

Reuben Snake, U.S. Army (Green Berets) Radio Repairman/Operator, circa 1955. Photograph courtesy of Darren Snake.

up girls. Berlin was full of party girls. Most of them were refugees from East Germany. I only had one serious relationship with a German girl while I was there. That lasted for several months. Other than that, it was just going to a night club and picking up a girl and partying around with her.

There was a lot of tension in Berlin. We were constantly aware that we were totally surrounded by East German and Russian military units. We were often told that if there was any outbreak of warfare, West Berlin couldn't stand for more than twenty-four hours without being overrun. So it was a constant state of preparedness that we were committed to maintaining all the time.

From Prejudice and Unemployment to Alcohol Abuse

I was stationed in Berlin one year. I came back in February of 1958 and was discharged from the Army at Fort Sheridan, Illinois. That ended my military service. I was encouraged to reenlist but I chose not to. I wanted to do something else with my life. I had ideas of going to college and acquiring a college degree.

When I got out of the service I went to live with my mother and brother in Waterloo, Iowa. My brother was working in a factory that produced farm machinery. It was extremely difficult for me to find employment in that town. I used to go out every day looking for a job. But I just couldn't get hired, even though I had served in the military for over three years and had an honorable discharge. In addition, I had all this electronics training from Haskell Institute and from the Army. That is when I first began to experience the effects of racism and prejudice. I would go to a plant where they were hiring and I'd put in my application and I'd look around and I'd see the White guys that were applying for a job. The next time I came back to apply again, those White guys would be working there.

They would tell me, "Well, we can't use you right now. Come back next week." When I came back again the next week the White guys that were applying for a job at the same time I was would already be working. That's when I began to get a little bit disenchanted with this system that we were living under.

After a few months of job-hunting I told my mother, "I'm going back to the reservation to stay with grandma and see if I can get a job in that part of the country." So I came down here to Nebraska to the reservation in the spring of 1958 and stayed with my grandmother.

It was a situation where my oldest brother, my brother-cousin, and Carl, and two of his brothers were all staying in this little two-room house with my grandmother and one girl cousin. She and grandma slept in the back room and we men all slept on the floor in the front room. None of us could find any work. The only work available was day work for the local farmers.

They used to have what they called the employment log. There was a great big log down by one of the buildings here in Winnebago. Everybody would get up early in the morning and go sit on that log and wait for a local farmer to come by who was interested in hiring somebody for the day. That's the only way we used to get work.

Because I had not lived on a reservation for a number of years, I wasn't well accepted by the local White community, especially the local town marshal, a White man. Even when I was sober he used to throw me in jail. It became a habit for him to pick me up every weekend, whether I was drinking or not. He would just throw me in jail and keep me overnight and then say, "Well, get out of here, and don't bother me any-more." But I wasn't bothering him in the first place. That went on throughout the whole summer of 1958. I must have wound up in that little community jail house about ten times. And it was just because he didn't like me. There was no other reason. I wasn't breaking the law.

Finally one day in August, I told him, "Ben, I've been thinking about it, and I came to the conclusion that you really don't like me, so I'm going to get the hell out of town." He replied, "You know, that's just what I've been waiting for you to say." So then I said, "Well, I said it, so I'm leaving."

That was the kind of experience I had that summer that I got out of the service. That was when I began getting more angry with the system. I couldn't get a decent job. When I came back to the reservation I was set upon by local law enforcement for no other reason than that I wasn't considered a local boy. I was being thrown in jail whether I was drunk or sober. They always tried to convict me of buying alcohol for minors. But they never could prove it. But that was the only excuse they had for throwing me in jail. "Oh, we heard you were buying drinks for these kids." But I never did. It was just their way of bothering and agitating me.

In addition to sitting on that log waiting for the farmers we used to go to Sioux City and put in applications at the different plants and factories up there. But I never did get hired. The same sort of discrimination was affecting a lot of guys. So I told my cousin-brother, who had just graduated from high school, "I'm going to Milwaukee. There's a school there that I want to attend, an electronics technical institute. If I can get the money together, I'm going to school there and maybe after I graduate somebody will hire me."

Members of the local Reformed Church here in Winnebago had been encouraging my cousin-brother to go to a small Reformed Church college in Sioux County, Iowa. So he replied, "Why don't you just forget about Milwaukee and go to school with me?" I said, "Let me think about it." A week later I told him, "Yes, I'll go with you." So we filled out the application papers for the junior college. And we were accepted.

I was flat broke and so was he; when we started college we had sixty-five cents between the two of us. That was all. I had signed up for my GI bill but that check wasn't due to arrive for thirty to sixty days. So we were trying to survive on a college campus in this small town for thirty to sixty days on sixty-five cents. Fortunately we were both ex-football players and this small college gave us each a football scholarship to play on its team. So that scholarship enabled us to get into the dormitory and get into the dining hall without any fees being charged.

The college was Northwestern Junior College, in Orange City, Iowa. It was another tremendous cultural adjustment because Sioux County, Iowa, is populated predominantly with Dutch immigrants. They are all Reformed Church people with very strict standards. Here I was, an ex-GI coming from the city of Berlin where I was used to wild night life, and I ended up stuck in this little town where they considered it a sin to have your laundry hanging out on Sunday morning.

When I started taking courses at this junior college I was twenty-one, which was a couple of years older than most of my classmates. There were few other ex-GIs there, maybe four or five.

My cousin-brother and I were the only Native Americans in the school. In fact we were probably one of four or five minority people. All the rest were White kids. They had a student body of about two hundred and fifty. They had one guy from India, one guy from Yugoslavia, and then I think there was one Black student there. Other than them, my cousin-brother and I were the only different people. In fact the students got all confused when we had our social get together the first week we were there. All these White kids came up to me and asked: "What part of India are you from?" "No, no, no," I said. "I'm not that kind of Indian. I'm the one from the Winnebago Reservation."

As usual, the other students were ignorant about Indians. They were all operating on stereotypical images. Many of them were friendly, but once again there was a certain effort expended to keep us at arm's length. I was never invited to their homes and I became a real problem for them because I wouldn't go to church on Sunday. My cousin-brother used to get up and go to church, but I wouldn't. I'd just stay in bed. Pretty soon the word got around: Reuben Snake is a nonbeliever. So there was a concerted effort to save my soul.

I was taking education courses, with the hope of becoming a teacher. I also became a pretty good preacher. I took some Bible study courses, studied the life of Christ and the acts of the Apostles. I could deliver a pretty good sermon. But I never went to church. I was more proficient in the Bible than a lot of kids who went to church every Sunday. The faculty as well as the students were putting pressure on me to attend church.

We had one English professor who had been a missionary

in India for over twenty years. He was a good teacher and he formed a writing club. Just to test my skills, I wrote a short story that impressed him. He took me aside and said, "You're studying to be a teacher, right? Well, we've got enough teachers in the world. But we don't have enough writers. Why don't you switch your major to English and I'll help you learn how to write?"

So I began to adjust my courses to get more involved with writing. During the year I was there he gave me a lot of valuable information about how to write. He was the only teacher there that showed concern about my well-being. But after a year, I decided that the lifestyle was just too conservative for me. And I thought, "I don't want to come back to this institution. I'm just going to leave and find something else to do." He was the only one who really tried to say something worthwhile to me.

I was still considered a persona non grata on the Winnebago Reservation by that White town marshal, so I couldn't come back and stay with my grandmother. Instead, I went back to southern Minnesota. That was a bad move. I went back over there and started drinking.

Nobody pushed me into that kind of life. It was just that many of my peers, people that I'd grown up with, were into alcohol. The best way I could get along with them was just to drink with them. We'd stay drunk three or four days at a time. Eventually that led me to get into trouble with the law.

When I got thrown in jail, I talked to the sheriff and told him, "I want to get out and go to work." He made arrangements for me to be hired at a local foundry there in Albert Lea. I used to get out of jail early in the morning and go work all day long and then I'd come back to the jail at night. That went on for about sixty days until my sentence was over and I got out.

I stayed on at the foundry. It was a good-paying job. I managed to get in a lot of overtime and pull a pretty good paycheck. I would share my earnings with my uncle, with my brother and his family, and with some of my younger relatives who were in school. I'd buy them school clothes and things of that sort. I'd get drunk on Friday night and maybe get drunk on Saturday and I'd sober up Sunday and go to work Monday morning. It was okay. It wasn't a difficult time for me but I just wasn't happy working in this foundry. I felt that I was capable of better things.

One day one of my Menominee brothers came to our town and said, "I'm on my way to Arizona. I have a good job down there. I work for a crop-dusting organization. If you go down there with me, you can work with me."

"Well, let's go to Arizona then," I replied. So we left Minnesota and went to the Winnebago Reservation to visit my mother. Then we went to Kansas, where we stopped at the Potawatomi Reservation. We got stuck there. We didn't have any money and we couldn't find jobs. We were staying with my grandpa, actually my mother's brother who lived out in the country. In order to make a contribution to his household, we used to go out hunting every day. We'd hunt deer and grouse and pheasant. That's how we spent a good part of the winter of 1959 and 1960. My brother and I cut a lot of firewood for the old people. We'd organize wood cutting crews and we'd go out into the woods and cut firewood for the old people and then we'd go hunting. At night we'd sit at home with the old man. He and another old Potawatomi man were the two principal singers for the Potawatomi people. When they got together they would bring out the sacred drum that they use in a drum society in the traditional religion of the Potawatomies. They would sing all the songs that go with that. Then the next night they would get together and tie up the water-drum so they would sing peyote songs, Native American Church songs. We enjoyed listening to those old men sing.

My grandpa used to like his beer. He was an excellent snooker player. Every Friday night he'd say, "Come on, boys, let's go downtown." Then we'd go down to Mayetta, the little town on a reservation. The local White farmers would be waiting for him. They'd all be lined up because none of them could ever beat him. They were always trying. They'd get into a snooker game. And he'd run the table on them. And then they'd set them up. They'd say, "We will buy you and your grandsons some beer." He never did lose a game. We'd wind up with a table full of drinks. I used to appreciate grandpa's skill at playing pool.

So that's the routine we enjoyed throughout December, January, and February. We stayed with him there at the Potawatomi Reservation until the spring thaw started in March. Then we set off for Arizona. When we left the reservation we hitchhiked to Kansas City, Missouri, where we underwent another ordeal. We lived on skid row renting a little two-room apartment for eleven dollars a week. You can probably imagine what it looked like. We used to go to slave markets, as they were called. We would sign up early in the morning and they would find temporary employment for us for the day. That's how we survived. We'd go to a car wash, or to a furniture store to load furniture, or to any number of places where they needed daily labor. We would work maybe eight to ten hours and earn just enough to pay our eleven dollars a week for rent and buy ourselves something to eat and drink.

We drank virtually every day after putting in a hard day's work. We got so absorbed in drinking that we quit working. So then they kicked us out of the flophouse where we were staying. After that we used to sleep in abandoned tenement buildings with the rats. We'd go into these vacant buildings and there'd be a lot of old furniture in there and we'd pile up old mattresses and we'd lie down on a couple of mattresses and cover up with one to keep warm. Then we listened to the rats scurrying about us all night long. We were just real skid row bums. We lived like that for about two months. We would go to the various gospel missions in Kansas City to get something to eat. We'd sit there and listen to the sermon for an hour or two and then they'd give us day-old bread and a bowl of soup. After that we'd make our way out to find a place to sleep during the night. That was our routine.

To obtain money to keep drinking we would hit the streets and find the winos who knew how to panhandle. We did a little bit of that panhandling ourselves. I don't regret that experience. I don't think I'd be the person I am today if I had not been through that trouble. Being a bum on skid row is not the most desirable life but the suffering taught me something about life that I still carry with me.

One day in the fall of 1959 I was walking down the street in Kansas City. Next to a kind of big embankment there was a concrete wall and a big high mound of earth. I was walking along when I heard this voice proclaim, "Stop, you Black son of a bitch." I didn't think that the voice was addressed to me so I kept on walking. But I heard it again. "I said stop, you Black son of a bitch, or I'll blow you apart." So then I looked around and I realized I was the only individual on the street. That voice must be talking to me. I stopped and I looked around and I looked up at that hillside. There was a uniformed policeman standing there with a shotgun aimed at me. Then he demanded, "Get over against the wall there." I walked over to the wall and put my hands on the wall and he came down the hillside, jumped down and called in on his walkie-talkie. Right away a squad car pulled up. Two more cops jumped out and they shook me down and began to put the handcuffs on me. They said they were hauling me off to jail. They asked me, "What did you do with your gun? Where did you put that stuff?" And I told them, "I don't know what you're talking about. I don't have any gun. I don't have anything."

About that time another police car pulled up and a man got out. He must have been the owner of the store down the street that had been robbed. The policeman asked him, "Is this that damn nigger that you were looking for, the one that you saw?" He looked right at me and said, "No, that's not him. He's not Black. He's Mexican or something. The guy we're looking for is Black." After he told them I wasn't the man they wanted the cops took the handcuffs off me and warned me, "Get your damn ass off the street and don't give us any trouble." That's just one of the experiences that I had while I was living that skid row street life.

My brother and I experienced a lot of unpleasant things. I can recall another incident which had a tremendous impact on me. In the early winter of 1959 we were in Kansas City at a place that provided sleeping places for homeless men. They offered something to eat and had a recreation room. We were sitting in the recreation room along with about a hundred other guys. They were involved in various activities: putting jigsaw puzzles together, playing cards, playing table tennis, and things of that sort. My brother and I were sitting there, just talking, when we noticed these guys playing cards, a Black man and a White man. They began to argue with one another over something regarding the game. Violence erupted almost immediately. They started fighting and the Black man knocked the White man down. When the White man jumped up he had a knife in his hand and he swung and he sliced this Black man's stomach open and all the blood began to pour out. Everybody there saw it. Our immediate reaction was to clear out quickly because the cops would soon be arriving and we didn't want to be there when they came. It was almost like rats running off a sinking ship. Everybody hit the doorways as fast as they could and scattered toward the four directions. My brother and I were running right along with them. Sure enough, as we ran down a street and through the alleys, we could hear the sirens of the police cars coming. That incident left a strong impression on me. It reminded me that by living this street life we lived close to death. Even though it was probably the low point of my life, I still don't regret the experience. It helped me begin to appreciate what homeless people go through.

My brother eventually got a land lease check from his reservation. So we were stepping in high cotton then. We went down to one of the local clothing stores and got ourselves some new clothes. Then we went into a hotel room and showered up and shaved. After we had cleaned ourselves up and put on our new clothes he told me, "Now that we're looking good we better get the hell out of town." We were still thinking about going to Arizona. But then he said, "Let's call sis up and see what's going on." So we went down to a pay phone and he called my sister in Cleveland, Ohio. She and her family had gone to Cleveland on a government relocation program.[1] When we told her we were trying to get to Arizona she declared, "You guys shouldn't go to Arizona. Come over here to Cleveland. There's a lot of work over here. You can surely find a decent job over here." So we accepted my sister's suggestion.

My brother had enough money to buy us bus tickets to Cleveland. It just so happened that we arrived during the biggest snowstorm Cleveland had experienced in a hundred years. There was something like twenty-four inches of snow in a twenty-four hour period. This was in 1960.

My sister had a big apartment. She and her husband and little children made room for us. Then we began the process of looking for a job. It was enough that our sister was feeding us and giving us a place to sleep. We didn't want to bother her for bus money, so we used to walk. We'd get the morning paper and write down information about a couple of places that were hiring. Then we'd walk to those places. Sometimes it was a long way.

We were looking for regular industrial jobs. Eventually we found work way out on the west side of Cleveland, where they were making Melamine plastic dinnerware. Next we had to learn the bus routes, how to get from east Cleveland to west Cleveland on the street buses. We used to ride the bus across town to go to work every morning and come back in the evening.

We were still dedicated to drinking. We were still basically party animals. We had a cousin who lived in a Polish-American neighborhood called the Flats. One day I told my sister, "After work we're going down there to the Flats to visit Beebe." After work we stopped at a tavern and we picked up a couple of six-packs of beer. Then we went over to my cousin's house. She was happy to see us. Her husband was happy to see us. We sat down and started talking. At that point a young lady came in. It appeared to me that she was really hurting. My cousin introduced me by saying, "This is Kathy McKee; she lives upstairs." I shook hands with her. After a while we started playing canasta and I began visiting with Kathy. Although we were both from the Winnebago Reservation, I had never met her before. I had met her brother when we were kids, but I had never met her.

Kathy had been raised by her uncle and aunt. They were genuinely traditional Winnebago people and Kathy was a real homebody. They rarely took her anyplace. She had been married at the age of eighteen and moved to Cleveland. Her husband was an alcoholic. During one of his drunken rages he had beaten her up badly. So she had separated from him. That's why she was spending time with my cousin. So I got to visiting with her and we started laughing. I really appreciated her personality.

When I met Kathy she had been living in Cleveland less than a year. Later on that summer, Kathy went home. My brother and I remained in Cleveland but then my sister got seriously ill. So my mother came after her and brought her back to the reservation. The doctors had decided that they were going to have to take out one of her kidneys because she might be developing cancer. There she was, back in Winnebago with all of her children, and there we three men (my brother, my brother-in-law, and I) were in Cleveland.

The moment my brother-in-law found out that my sister was sick and wasn't coming back, he started drinking. He soon lost his job. That left my brother and me to pay all the bills. It wasn't long before my brother got into drinking and he stopped contributing. Pretty soon I was the only one going to work and trying to pay the rent and buy the food. After a couple weeks of that I told them, "Hell, why am I doing this? You guys are drinking and enjoying yourselves. I might as well get in there with you." So I quit working and started drinking. That went on for a couple of weeks until the landlady kicked us out. I ended up in the streets of Cleveland, sleeping under railroad tresses.

In the meantime my sister was back in Winnebago undergoing an operation and my mother was taking care of her children. We were on skid row in Cleveland. We were sleeping in abandoned tenement buildings. One night my brother and I were lying down by the railroad tracks. We were covered up with newspapers, trying to keep out the chill, when he sort of stretched his feet out and took off his shoe. The whole top of his sock was gone and his toes were sticking out. Talk about stinky feet! I said, "Man, get down wind from me. I can't stand that smell." There he was wiggling his toes and declaring, "Boy, I haven't seen you characters for a while."

He hadn't had his shoes off for weeks. He had been too busy drinking day in and day out. It was exactly at that moment that I decided to sober up. The next morning when we woke up I told him, "Brother, right here and now I'm going to quit drinking and sober up. I've had enough of this. You can keep on drinking if that is what you want. I'll just stay by you. But I'm not going to drink anymore. Then whenever you decide to sober up, we'll get out of town. We will go someplace else." "All right," he replied.

He continued drinking every day for about another week. I tried to look after him. About a week later, after he'd been drinking quite heavily throughout the day, he said, "Well, I'm going to go sleep it off for a while." So I told him, "I'm going to be sitting here in the park. I'll come along later, sometime after the sun goes down." He told me which building he would be sleeping in. I watched him walk down the street. Then I was sitting there in the park in the center of Cleveland. He must have been gone for about an hour. I was just sitting there observing people and sort of reminiscing about life and suddenly I looked down the street and saw my brother coming back. He wasn't staggering. He was walking real straight and he was walking real quickly. So I got up and I started walking towards him. When we met I asked, "What's happening?" He replied, "Boy, that's it for me. I'm going to sober up and we're going to get out of this town." I asked, "What happened?" He said, "I went into that building over there and I made myself a place to lay down. Right after I lay down, some guy came in. He wasn't aware I was there but he came in and then shortly afterwards two other guys came in behind him and they began to argue. These two guys attacked this first individual and they began to beat him with an iron pipe. After they beat him unconscious, they left. I waited a little bit to make sure they were gone and then I got up and I went over to look at him. He was dead. He wasn't breathing. That sobered me up instantly. I think we'd better get out of town." This incident, which occurred in the early summer of 1960, and the murder we witnessed in Kansas City, illustrate the kind of life that we were living on the streets.

We were going to leave town by ourselves but then my brother-in-law said, "I'll go along with you guys. I don't have any reasons to stay in Cleveland. My wife and kids are back on the reservation. I've had enough of this town." So we went down to the railroad yard and hopped on a freight train heading west. We rode the freight train all night long until we entered the Chicago railroad yards. Then we switched trains and got on another freight train north into Wisconsin. We rode that freight train into Madison and got off there. We went into the Madison train station and tried to clean up as well as we could. Then we went out to the highway and we started hitchhiking towards Wisconsin Dells, about fifty miles north of Madison. There was a large Winnebago community there where we had relatives.

After arriving at Wisconsin Dells we went to my aunt's home. We must have looked pitiful because she just started to cry when she saw me. "Oh, my poor nephew. How come you're looking so sorrowful?" I admitted to my aunt that we had been having some trouble. So she made us shower up and then she got some of her son's and her husband's clothing and said, "You men can change clothes." We put on those clean clothes and then she cooked up a big meal for us. She told us, "You can stay here as long as you like." But because she already had a large family we didn't want to bother her. So we just stayed overnight. The next day we walked into town and started trying to find some way of earning some money. We remained in that area for probably a week or so and then we heard that there were some jobs opening up down along the Wisconsin/Illinois border at one of the canning companies. We decided to hitchhike down to Janesville to see if we could get a job. When we arrived at Janesville, we got hired at the Libby-McNeal Canning Company. As soon as we began working for them I told my brother, "I'm going to work at this job until I earn enough money to buy a car. Then we must get to Arizona." He agreed, "Yeah, that sounds like a good idea." I declared, "During the period of time we are working here, I don't care what you do, but I'm not going to drink. I'm going to save my money." And that's exactly what I did.

I worked some long hours in that canning factory. I averaged about eighty hours a week. After several weeks I had saved enough to go out and buy myself a little car. I found a real nice little car and I bought it. I told my brother, "I'm going to work another week, or maybe two weeks, and earn enough money so we can hit the road." But he was drinking yet again. "Yeah, okay." he said. I worked a couple more weeks and saved three hundred dollars or so. Then I announced, "Let's get out of here." We packed up our stuff, jumped in the car, and took off.

I stated, "I want to go up and say hello to my dad and goodbye, and then we'll take off for Arizona." He agreed. We went over to the Black River Falls Indian Mission to see my dad. While we were there we ran into one of my other cousins. It was his birthday. He and I had been at Fort Bragg together. He was in the Eighty-Second Airborne Division when I was in the Green Berets. So he said, "Hey, brother, it's my birthday. You must have a drink with me." I hadn't been drinking for a couple of months so I refused, "You go ahead and have one." "No, no, you ain't my bro if you don't drink with me." So I gave in, "Well, I'll have one with you." I never should have said that.

One round led to another one and before I knew it I was

off on a big drunk. By the time I sobered up we had just enough money to get to Nebraska. So I told my brother, "Let's leave this place. We'll go to Nebraska and we'll find a job to earn enough money to get to Arizona." He agreed and so we left Wisconsin and drove down to the reservation.

We went to my mother's house. My mother was happy to see us again. She hadn't seen us for over a year. About the second evening I was there I asked her, "Hey, mom, I met a girl out in Cleveland. Her name is Kathy McKee. Does she live around here?" My mom answered by saying, "She lives right across the road. That little white house over there is where she's at."

That evening I walked down across the road and knocked on her door. Kathy's sister came to the door. I asked if Kathy was home and she said, "Yes." So Kathy came and I started talking with her. That was the end of my solitary years. That was the end of hill number one.

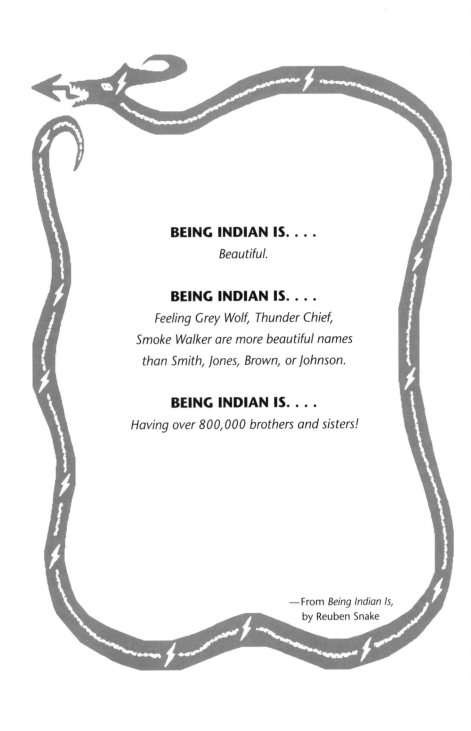

BEING INDIAN IS. . . .
Beautiful.

BEING INDIAN IS. . . .
Feeling Grey Wolf, Thunder Chief,
Smoke Walker are more beautiful names
than Smith, Jones, Brown, or Johnson.

BEING INDIAN IS. . . .
Having over 800,000 brothers and sisters!

—From *Being Indian Is,*
by Reuben Snake

Marriage and Family Life

Everything I've described up to this point in my life has to do with my own personal life, the way that I grew up. Of course, I didn't mention a lot of things. I had the good fortune to have a grandfather, my mother's father, for the first thirteen years of my life. He had a powerful influence on my life, a positive influence. And then my own beloved grandmother, my father's mother, was a very important person in my life. My parents also had a beneficial influence on me. They all tried to teach me things. They all tried to teach me what it was to be a Winnebago man, how I was supposed to think and act as a man in our tribe. So I had those messages from my grandfather and grandmother and my parents and my uncles.

Yet I hadn't actually ever applied that understanding to my life much before I returned to the Winnebago Reservation in the early fall of 1960 and became reacquainted with Katherine McKee, the young lady I had met in Cleveland. After visiting with her almost every day, it occurred to me that it was time for me to think about changing my life. I began to think about becoming more responsible and maybe having my own family. I was twenty-three years old when I proposed to her. I told her that I had come to love her very dearly and that she meant very much to me. I asked her if she would be my wife. So this was the second hill of life that I began to journey on when I asked her to be my wife and we started our life together.

I tried to recall what my grandfather had told me, that a Winnebago man must be responsible and must provide for his wife. I went to work on the reservation for a local White farmer. At that time many farm families were leaving their farms and selling their acreage. This White man was accumulating a lot of land and expanding his farming business. So my Menominee brothers and I began working for him for ten dollars a day. We worked from seven in the morning until maybe six o'clock in the evening for ten dollars a day, six days a week. But I felt very strongly that it was my responsibility to house, clothe, and provide for my wife. This is the way we started our life together.

Kathy had been married previously, as I said, and she had a little girl. I told her that this little girl was going to be my daughter and I promised to love and cherish her. So we started out our family life that way here on this reservation.

In the beginning we lived with my grandmother. Then we stayed with one of my aunts. Then we stayed with Kathy's aunt. It was a real challenge to find our own place to live. There wasn't any public housing available at that time. Most of the housing on the reservation was substandard and just plain inadequate.

My mother became aware of our difficulties. One day she talked to my older brother and me. He was also a young married person. My mother said, "Well, let's go to Omaha. The three of us can go down there and each of us will try to find a job. That way we can improve our life. We'll all get our own place and then you can move your families to Omaha."

That sounded like a sensible plan. So my brother and I went with my mother to Omaha and rented a small apartment. Then my brother and I began seeking jobs. My mother went out too and she soon had a job in a nursing home. Next my brother got a job as a welder at a manufacturing plant. But I was still going down to the slave market, doing different work each day. Eventually my brother's boss observed, "Well, you're a pretty good worker. Do you have any more friends or relatives that can work like you do? If so, bring them around." So my brother told me to report to the plant where he was working. When I applied for the job there I was hired.

That was the beginning of my family life in Omaha. We came back to the reservation, got our families, and moved them down to Omaha. We each rented our own separate apartment and settled down to life in the city. It was interesting work. We worked in the store fixture manufacturing plant. I tried to demonstrate that I was a good worker. And I set many production standards for the company. I was making suggestions to the plant manager on how to change operations to improve efficiency and improve production. I advised them on how to redesign some of the tools and dies in order to eliminate various steps in the manufacturing process. The plant manager was quite favorably impressed with that. He encouraged me to go to school and get an engineering degree so that I could move higher up the ladder in this company. So that's what I did. I enrolled at the University of Omaha and I started night courses in mechanical engineering.

Kathy and I began having children. It seemed like once every year we became parents again. Over a period of several years we were blessed with four daughters and two sons. Having to provide for all these children and my wife increased my responsibility. It made me feel that it was really necessary to get an education and get into a profession that could sustain my family. That was why I began pursuing the degree in mechanical engineering.

The company that I worked for had agreed to help pay for my schooling. Depending on my grade level, they would provide fifty, seventy-five, or a hundred percent of my tuition. I came back to the reservation and went to the Bureau of Indian Affairs and asked for some scholarship assistance. I informed them, "I'm trying to start college and I don't have enough money to see me through." It astonished me that this Bureau of Indian Affairs office, representing three different tribes here in Nebraska, was supporting only ten individuals to go to college. They had plenty of money for vocational/technical training. They had money galore to send people to become nurses, or plumbers, or welders, or auto mechanics, or cosmetologists. But they didn't have any money for us to attend college. They lacked the foresight to see that Indians needed to have college degrees. So after pleading my case, I was given $180 from the Bureau of Indian Affairs to start college. It was barely enough to buy a slide rule and my textbooks.

I was eligible for GI benefits but for some reason or other I just didn't use them. I had utilized my GI bill the year I attended Northwestern Junior College. But I just didn't follow through with that GI bill when I was working for this company in Omaha. After I got started and I began to get some decent grades, the company started paying for my education. I decided that I really didn't need any more support from anybody once my company began paying for my education.

I was taking three courses per semester at night school and working during the day at my regular job. That was my routine for a couple of years. But I still hadn't totally quit drinking. Even though I was working five, six days a week and going to school at night, there were still times when I would go out on a weekend binge.

I really wasn't committed to my own spiritual ways. I wasn't attending the Native American Church on any regular basis. I only came back to the Native American Church when there was a death in the family, or some serious situation. Then I would take a little time out to sit and pray and use medicine. Otherwise I had forgotten that part of my life.

My wife's people, my in-laws, had been drawn into the Mormon Church. Through that connection we were proselytized quite heavily by young Mormon missionaries, both on the reservation and in Omaha. I never paid attention to the missionaries when they came around. I'd always just tell my wife to talk to them and I'd go upstairs and lie down and read.

That went on for several years until one day in 1965. After a rather heavy weekend drinking binge, my wife told me, "You'd better think about sobering up and leaving the alcohol alone." At that particular time I'd gotten into a fight one weekend. My two older brothers were town marshals on the reservation and they had me thrown in jail for my own safety. When they let me out I went back to my family. My two oldest daughters were crying and pleading, "Daddy, please don't drink any more. We don't like to see you looking this way." I had a fat lip and a black eye as a result of the drunken brawl. It touched my heart to hear my little children crying. So I took my wife's words to heart. I told her, "Well, I'm going to put this drinking aside and do something else with my free time."

This was in 1965. I was working from six-thirty in the morning until three in the afternoon. Then I would go to school from six o'clock until nine o'clock or nine-thirty at night. Then our third daughter was born. She was a sickly little girl. She had bronchitis and other health problems which caused our medical bills to escalate. I couldn't keep on going to school. I had to find some other source of income to pay for my daughter's medical expenses. I quit school and got a second job in order to make enough money to take care of my little girl's health. I was working sixteen to eighteen hours a day there for a while.

We didn't even think of having a doctor meeting for her. I wasn't paying attention to the Native American Church at that time. We had gotten involved with the Mormon Church and so it never crossed my mind that my children could be taken care of in the Native American Church. I did have my children named in the Native American Church when they were all very young. That was about the extent of it. My wife and I sponsored a prayer meeting and asked my brother to christen our four youngest children. That's how they got their Winnebago names. Other than that I only came back to the church when something serious was happening.

I became very involved for a brief while with the Mormons. After I stopped drinking and was looking for something else to do, I started associating with these young Mormon missionaries. They asked me to play on an Indian basketball team they were organizing. They soon found out I knew more about basketball than they did, so they asked me to be the coach. I gradually began running all the youth activities for the Lamanite Branch, the all-Indian branch of the Mormon Church. I became the director of all the youth activities for them in Omaha. I organized several basketball teams. I had a large group of boys organized that I used to take to the Boys' Club. I used to take a different group down to the YMCA for swimming. I was constantly on the go. When I got involved in all that it was to overcome whatever temptation I might have for falling back into my drinking ways. I completely immersed myself in all this youth activity. It was really gratifying because these Indian children from the streets of Omaha were getting into drug abuse and alcohol abuse. It was a great challenge to get out there and try to do something with them to keep them away from the drugs and alcohol. Coaching all these teams and organizing all these recreational activities and running all these youth programs for the Indian branch of the Mormon Church was enjoyable. But it was an expensive undertaking. I remember going through about six or seven cars within two years. I was in the habit of hauling kids every evening to the Boys' Club or going to basketball or down to the YMCA. I'd have maybe a dozen kids crammed in my station wagon at one time. I would make two or three trips like that. Those cars didn't last too long.

The Mormons never paid me anything. It was all voluntary on my part. In the summer of 1966, I took a job with the Greater Omaha Community Action Council. Even though I was still working my regular job, Greater Omaha Community Action hired me to be a youth street worker. My hours were from six in the evening to midnight. I was trying to keep the kids off the street. I got paid for that. It wasn't very much. It was enough to keep gas in my car and keep things moving. But that was a very educational experience for me. I was called upon to use all my organizational skills, which were very limited at that time. By associating with the Black community leaders and watching how they did things, I began to learn how to do things. I learned how to make the system react positively to our needs and honed my organizational skills. In the process of getting access to the Boys' Club, the YMCA, the Community Action Agency, and other social service programs, I learned how to talk to people to get something done for Indian children. That was very important in my future work.

After I had been involved in youth work for a couple of years, I got to know an outstanding gentleman by the name of Eugene Crawford. Eugene was a Sioux Indian, originally from a reservation in South Dakota. He was what they called a visiting teacher, which was a glorified name for a truant officer in the Omaha public school system.

One time when he was visiting with me he said, "Hey, Snake, we ought to get organized. We ought to create our own Indian center here in the city of Omaha to meet all the needs of our people. There are several thousand Indians living here. But Omaha has no real Indian organization." I told Gene, "Yes, that sounds like a worthwhile endeavor." So we set about trying to organize the community, to draft some by-laws and articles of incorporation and create an Indian center.

We were aware that groups of Indians in other cities, such as Chicago, San Francisco, and Los Angeles, had created Indian centers. So we asked some people who had lived in Chicago and Los Angeles, "How did the Indian center operate where you lived before?" We gathered information wherever we could find it. Then we drafted articles of incorporation and some by-laws and eventually an Indian center was created. And it still exists today. The foundation for this center was laid by Mr. Crawford and me. Other people carried on the work later.

One day our two oldest girls came home from school and the oldest one stated, "Daddy, the teacher said something today. She said that Indians have weird beliefs. What was she talking about, daddy?" It dawned on my wife and me that we had been shortchanging our children. We hadn't been teaching them what we knew. My wife was one of those individuals who grew up in the traditional way of our people. She was very fluent in the Winnebago language and she had grown up around the Medicine Lodge Society. Her elders and her family had taught her all they knew about this Winnebago life, but we had just never taken time to tell our children about any of this. So when our daughter came home with this question, "How come the teacher said that Indians have weird beliefs?" we were unprepared to give an answer. We discussed it and agreed that we should be trying to teach our children what Winnebagos really believe in and how they lived their life. So we were thinking about that issue when my brother, my older brother, called me up and reported, "There's great things happening here on the reservation. This war on poverty has arrived on our reservation. There's an Office of Economic Opportunity setting up programs here. They're setting up Department of Labor work programs and Head Start programs and establishing all these kinds of things. We need some help. We need some young people to be here to develop and operate these programs. I'm having a hard time." At that particular time, my brother was the youngest member of the tribal council and he said, "Why don't you consider moving back to our reservation and helping us out?"

Cultural Revitalization and Political Activism

It was near the end of 1967 when my brother approached me about coming back to the reservation. By that time the Indian community of Omaha was pretty well organized and the Omaha Indian center was becoming a reality. In late 1967 we left Omaha and the job that I had been working for six years or more, and returned to the reservation.

I went down to this local community action agency and applied for a job and was hired as the director of youth work programs under the Department of Labor. It was what they called the Neighborhood Youth Core. The federal government provided the funding for part-time employment for children over the age of fourteen. I gradually developed work sites and program activities with the Bureau of Indian Affairs and the Indian Health Service and the public school. We even went off the reservation after a while. We became a multi-county community action agency. I developed programs in non-Indian areas where poor non-Indians resided. I worked with county and city officials to create a part-time employment program for children from such non-Indian areas.

The children of non-Indians were also participating as part-time employees. At one time I had about 270 young people working in a five-county area. I had to drive around and keep track of all the time records and listen to their supervisors' complaints and resolve whatever problems they might have in their part-time work. I was also supposed to furnish counseling and other things that went along with the Department of Labor guidelines.

I was in a middle management position within the community action agency. But after some changes occurred in the organization I quit being the Neighborhood Youth Core director and I became the Head Start director and became responsible for the management and administration of five different Head Start centers on the Winnebago and Omaha reservations and in surrounding communities. Working with Head Start on behalf of early childhood development obliged me to improve my skills. So I enrolled in courses at one of the state colleges, including business and administration, child psychology, and everything connected with early childhood development. I was moving up in the community action agency. My own children were all enrolled in the public school system on the Winnebago Reservation.

One of my elders, whom I used to call "grandpa," was the head of the only remaining cultural organization on our reservation. It was called the All Nations Club. They used to have regular weekly meetings when all the families that belonged to the club got together and celebrated birthdays and things of that nature. They would put their drum out there and they would sing and dance and tell old Winnebago stories. One day my grandpa told me, "Grandson, I've been observing you. You seem to be developing a real sense of responsibility. I notice that you don't drink, and I see that you look after your family. It seems that you're trying to do something worthwhile with your life. I'm getting to the age where it's hard for me to run this organization. I want you to take over my job and be the leader of this club."

I replied, "Grandpa, I'd really be happy to do that for you if the rest of the membership agrees."

At the next weekly meeting, my grandpa said he was considering asking me to become the leader of their club. Then one of the other elders, one of my uncles, a very wise old man who wasn't afraid to speak his mind, said, "That man you are speaking about doesn't know anything. Why don't we ask him to sit around this drum with us for a while and when he finally learns something then maybe he could be the leader." So that's the way it was put to me. If I was willing to devote my time to learning these things, then they would consider making me the leader of their club. So I said, "Yes, that sounds like something I would like to do."

After that my family and I used to get together with this group every Wednesday night. We'd go to somebody's home and enjoy a meal together. Then they would put the drum out and begin to sing. The women would get up and dance the traditional dances. We'd take a break and all the men would comment on the various songs, explaining who made this song, what was the meaning of this song, and when it was appropriate to use that particular song. Those conversations helped me learn something about my culture. After about a year of participating in those weekly events I could hit that drum with those old men and I could even hum along with them and sing some of the songs, and so they decided I was worthy of being their leader. They made me the president of the All Nations Club. That was really satisfying to me because it gave me an opportunity to learn from these old men all the things that I needed to know about our culture, and our language.

This learning process at the All Nations Club went on while I was working at the community action agency. I had them organized to the point where we would get requests from various communities for some kind of interaction with the Indian people. I would invite the old men to go along and get some of the younger people to dance. We'd go out and make cultural presentations in various communities around this part of the state. That was a very valuable activity because we created friendships in different communities. Non-Indians were happy to see Indians come over and share some of our culture with them.

I took another step up the ladder in the community action agency after being the Neighborhood Youth Core director and the Head Start director. The board invited me to assume the position of program planner for the agency, which meant I would work with all elements of the agency. There were senior citizen programs and work programs and community centers and a vast assortment of program activities. As the program planner I was required to go around to all those communities and help them plan and design the programs they felt were necessary to alleviate poverty and its effects.

Some of the programs were designed to work with children, the young people that were in the Department of Labor Neighborhood Youth Core. We also developed counseling programs. We brought in Indian Health Service psychiatric social workers and school counselors. We also brought in tribal elders for the counseling program. In Head Start we designed cultural activities for little children. We started introducing them to their native language. This was something that had not been done before. We started teaching them how to speak their language, and started teaching them about Native American music and dance. We developed a broad array of things. Community centers became an integral part of our effort. We would go to certain communities and find a property to develop a community center where people could come and participate in social events on a regular basis.

This project represented a kind of resurgence of Native American culture. My wife had been raised very traditionally. The uncle who raised her was one of the very last active participants and leaders of the Medicine Lodge Society. My wife had acquired all this background but had subordinated that part of her life to adapt to living with me. Because I was the head of our family, what I was doing shaped what she was doing. So it was her wish to come back to Winnebago from Omaha on weekends. She would tell me, "They're having a hand game over here. Let's go over here where they are having a dance." None of that used to interest me. That was her life. Of course she wanted to participate in what she understood about our culture. But it didn't have any effect on me. I hadn't wanted to be part of that until that old man asked me to become the leader of the cultural organization. He encouraged me to accept the fact that I am a Winnebago. I am a Ho Chunk. I realized that I needed to know all about our customs and pass them on to our children.

This older gentleman, whose name was Wilbur Sharpback,

worked as a janitor at the local hospital. He believed in the Native American Church but he didn't attend our meetings very often. He was considered the principal singer of our tribe. He knew all the traditional songs and was the leading singer at our annual celebration. He knew more about our traditional music than just about anybody else. He was a very kindhearted, caring man who really treasured the culture of our people. And he genuinely wanted others to learn the music so we could carry on our tradition.

Winnebagos say that we're a singing people. We have music for any and every occasion, songs connected with celebrations, songs of mourning, and healing songs. Wilbur Sharpback knew all the songs. He was afraid that after he passed on nobody else would be singing our songs. For that reason it was really important for him to try to educate younger people about their music. That's probably the primary reason he tried to get me involved. I never did properly learn all the music. I can differentiate between the different kinds of music and I know something about some of the songs that were used.

The effort to revive one's culture is not unique to Native American people. People who are dominated by other groups undergo phases wherein their culture is oppressed and suppressed. But then, maybe every fourth generation or so, there's a reaction to that domination and an effort is made to revive the culture. So it was just about the right time for Indian people to be doing this. There were still enough people around who knew the old ways and knew the language. It was the right time for this resurgence of Indianness all across the country. So that is what started happening in the late 1960s and throughout the seventies, and it is still being carried on today. It was not only the Winnebagos who were going through this cultural resurgence. It was happening all across the country.

I was absorbed in community action work in addition to being deeply involved in this cultural organization. I was also busy with my family trying to provide the kind of strength that my wife and children needed. This period of my life lasted through 1969. During that time I began to ponder how I ended up being the way that I am and how my wife turned out the way that she is. I was well aware that there were different modes of acculturation and assimilation within our Indian community. Some people had totally rejected their Indian values and adopted Euro-American beliefs. But there were also intensely traditional people like my grandfather and other people who really wanted to preserve their culture.

I began to look at historical documents. I began reading about what had happened. I started locating books about the Winnebago people and other Indian groups. I began to understand what had happened to us as a consequence of Europeans coming over here and subjugating our people and thrusting their values upon us. They denied us our culture and our ways. I began to see the pattern that had been put in place from the very beginning. And when I understood that, I became terribly angry that people would do that to other people.

I felt that if there was anything I could do to turn this process around, I was going to do it. That was my frame of mind at the time when an incident occurred. Some young Indian men from the neighboring Omaha Reservation accosted a young couple and raped the young woman. There was considerable reaction to this event in Walthill, the White community. A petition was circulated that condemned all Indian people, not just the perpetrators of the crime. It was a blanket condemnation of Indian people. When that was published in the local newspapers, my brother called me up. At that time, my brother was the vice-chairman of the tribe and the mayor of our little town. He asked me, "What are we going to do about this? We can't let something like this continue to circulate. We've always been subjected to this nonsense but we have to do something about it." So I said, "I'll come over and see you."

I drove over to the Winnebago Reservation, from my office in Walthill. I sat down with my brother and read this petition that condemned all Indian people. It called us people who lived off welfare and had no sense of responsibility. It alleged that we were never made to pay for our crimes and that type of junk. I told my brother, "Well, this White man really worships money. Money is all-important to him. That town where this petition was circulated exists primarily because Indians go there and spend their money. Indians buy all their groceries and some of their clothing there. They go into the bars and the gas stations. If the Indian money wasn't spent there that town would probably fold up. In order to educate these people to the fact that we're no longer going to put up with this kind of racist attitude, we ought to organize a boycott of that town. We should stop all the Indian money from going in there." So my brother replied, "Let's get some people together and talk about this."

At that particular time we had a group of younger activists, forward-thinking people who wanted to change things. We got these people together and we said, "Look, we're talking about a boycott of Walthill. What do you think about that?" I advised them, "Well, it's going to take a lot of hard work because for many Indian people, that's the only place they go to shop. If we are to succeed in stopping them from shopping there we're going to have to provide them with alternatives. It's going to take a lot of effort but I'm ready if you're ready."

We all decided that it was worth the effort to organize a boycott of Walthill. So that's what we set about doing. We had meetings with members of the Winnebago Tribe. We told them what we were going to do and they were all for it. Then we went down to the Omaha Reservation and talked to a large number of Omaha tribal members and they were totally supportive of the idea. Then we called in the media to explain that we were going to have this boycott against Walthill because of its racist attitude. So then we implemented the boycott. It didn't take very long. It took two or three weeks. Sure enough, when the Indian money stopped flowing into the town, these people began to realize which side their bread was buttered on. Then some efforts at reconciliation were made. The town mayor came to the community action agency and apologized for circulating the petition. He said that a lot of people signed it in the heat of the moment and they weren't really rednecks. They wanted to get along with us. They were sorry that it was published in the newspaper and so on. The community action agency organized a series of meetings between the tribal governments of the two tribes and the village board of Walthill and other community leaders. They would try to find a way to have an amiable settlement of this whole issue and try to improve race relations.

Right then I began to see what was possible through organization. I realized what we can accomplish if we set our minds on doing something. The economic boycott did work. We did change people's ways of treating us. Maybe we didn't change their attitudes. But at least they became more respectful of us and didn't continue saying these things publicly. Because of that boycott activity I was branded a militant Indian.

This boycott occurred in late 1969 and early 1970. After that I felt very uncomfortable working in that community due to the fact that everybody said, "Oh, there's that Reuben Snake, that militant SOB. He's the one that caused all this problem. If he'd just kept his mouth shut we wouldn't have had to go through all this." I used to get anonymous phone calls. Callers would say, "You Goddamn communist son of a bitch" and other insulting things. But I weighed 350 pounds, so not too many people wanted to challenge me face to face.

The American Indian Movement

had been following in the media the techniques Martin Luther King was using to raise the consciousness of this country about the plight of Black Americans. King's efforts inspired some of my thinking about what was necessary for Indians because what Black people were saying was happening to them was happening to us too. And nobody was paying attention. They were paying attention to what the Blacks were saying but they weren't paying attention to the Indian people. We felt we also had serious civil and human rights issues that needed to be addressed.

After the Walthill boycott, I made a turn into activism. I thought, "Well, this is the way we could be active in order to straighten out a lot of things." It just so happened, right at that particular time, that the American Indian Movement (AIM) was growing. There were AIM chapters springing up in various urban communities and even on reservations across the country. The founders of the American Indian Movement wanted to bring some cohesiveness and unity into the organization. So they had a national organizational meeting in the fall of 1970 in Saint Paul, Minnesota. There were some Winnebago people in attendance at this first national AIM conference. And they called me up and said, "Maybe you ought to come over here and listen to what these people are saying."

Prior to that time I had not known personally any of the leaders of the AIM. I had been reading about Dennis Banks and Clyde Bellecourt and Russell Means. One of the three original founders, Jim Mitchell, had been a classmate of mine at Haskell. I got along well with him. So I was thinking, "Well,

113

BEING INDIAN IS. . . .

*Never making quick evaluations of people,
but reserving judgment until their actions show
what kind of people they really are.*

BEING INDIAN IS. . . .

*Having at least a dozen missionaries from
12 different faiths trying to save your
heathen soul every year.*

BEING INDIAN IS. . . .

*Having a Christian missionary tell you
it is wrong to believe in more than one
Divine Being, then listen to him tell you
about God, Jesus Christ, the Holy Ghost,
the Virgin Mary, St. Joseph, St. Patrick,
St. Christopher, St. Francis, etc., etc.*

—From *Being Indian Is,*
by Reuben Snake

if he's involved in this organization, there must be something to it." That was the only contact that I had with the organization.

My family and I drove up to Saint Paul to attend this conference. About the second day they held an election of national officers for the movement. Russell Means was elected the chairman. Then they were looking for a vice-chairman. This one Winnebago said, "There's Reuben Snake standing in the back of the room over there. He's the one that organized the boycott in Walthill, Nebraska." So they called me forward. Dennis Banks asked me if I had an interest in serving as an officer of the movement. I answered that I could probably do that for a year or so. So I was elected the vice-chairman of the American Indian Movement at their first national organizational meeting.

I didn't consider myself to be a militant Indian. But by accepting that position I became one. I always refer to myself as a militant teddy bear, because I really didn't feel that I could carry out that role but I thought that I could contribute something. That's how I became active in the American Indian Movement.

I took a position with the community action agency in Rapid City, South Dakota, and relocated my family there in the spring of 1970. In Rapid City we had difficulty finding housing. Eventually I found a house on the southeast side of town, in a predominantly White neighborhood. Most Indian people lived on the north side of Rapid City. At that time there was one Mormon Church in Rapid City. They had two Sunday services, one at nine in the morning and one at eleven o'clock. All the people from the south side would attend church at nine a.m. All the people from the north side would go to church at eleven a.m. One day I was approached by some of the leaders of the church because my family and I were the only Indian family that was attending church at nine o'clock in the morning. So these church leaders said, "Brother Snake, don't you think you'd be more comfortable coming to church at eleven o'clock rather than at nine?" I asked them, "Why would I be more comfortable?" "Well, all your people come to church at eleven." So then I replied, "What do you mean, my people? I thought we were all Mormons together here." They told me, "You must know what we're talking about here. You're a Lamanite. Don't you think you'd be more comfortable with the other Lamanite brethren?" And I knew Lamanite was a euphemism for Indian so I said, "No, we're all supposed to be Mormons. We're all reading out of the same book and practicing the same ways, but you gave me something to think about."

I went home and I talked it over with my wife. I said, "It's almost impossible to be an Indian and a Mormon at the same time. Mormonism teaches us that we're supposed to be working towards a certain goal. If we achieve that goal, we're not going to be brown any more, we're going to be White. That's their teaching. I think there's a lot of racism involved here. Moreover, just because we're their sole Indian family coming to church at nine o'clock in the morning they want us to switch over to attend church with the rest of the Indians. That's racism in and of itself too. So I think I've been pushed to the point where I have to make a choice. And I'd rather be an Indian than a Mormon."

The following week when I went to church I told the elders of the church, "I've come to the conclusion that I can't be an Indian and a Mormon at the same time. So I'm going to go back to being an Indian." That was terribly upsetting to them. They began to preach at me and tell me I was turning my back on God. I replied, "No, I'm not turning my back on God. I'm just leaving this institution because I think you are basically racist people." They told me they were going to pray for my soul. I said that I would pray for their souls too. That incident in the spring of 1970 was the end of my involvement with Mormonism.

When I first got involved deeply with the American Indian Movement I wasn't really active in the Native American Church. I was only going to prayer meetings when I had to, when something serious happened to one of my relatives.

After I renounced Mormonism I didn't attend any White man's church. I was somewhat disenchanted with the movement people. They talked so much about Indian spirituality and they picked my brother, Leonard Crowdog, a Rosebud Sioux Indian medicine man, as their spiritual leader, but they never seemed to pay attention to him. He would get up and offer advice, but they'd go off and do what they wanted to do. It bothered me that these guys wanted this movement to have a spiritual emphasis but they weren't paying attention to it themselves.

I left Rapid City in 1971 and returned to the Winnebago Reservation. I was overseeing the education programs for the Nebraska Indian Inter-Tribal Development Corporation. I had been one of the principal organizers of a major conference which brought about the change in the distribution of Johnson O'Malley funds. Johnson O'Malley money was earmarked for supplementary and compensatory education programs for Indian children throughout the United States.[1] Yet most of the public school districts utilizing the money never did include Indian people in discussing how it was to be used. The public school district just counted the heads of the Indian school children and applied for the Johnson O'Malley money. They spent it the way that they wanted to spend it.

There had been an investigation. The NAACP Legal Defense and Education Fund had hired some Indian people to investigate how Johnson O'Malley monies were utilized in public school districts throughout the United States. It was a real horror story. None of the money was being used for the benefit of Indian children. My brother and I began an investigation here in the state of Nebraska. We discovered some atrocious things. Even though eighty percent of the children riding the school buses were White, every year Johnson O'Malley money was used to buy new school buses. There was no attempt to include Native American studies in the school curriculum. That money wasn't paying for anything Indian. So following the NAACP report and the investigation of Johnson O'Malley

117

—From *Being Indian Is*, by Reuben Snake.
Drawing by Wesley Green, Jr.

BEING INDIAN IS. . . .

Having high salaried BIA, PHS, OEO, HEW, and DOL
white-collar bureaucrats tell you how much money
is spent on Indians these days.

money that my brother and I directed here in the state of Nebraska, we convened a meeting at the Winnebago Reservation and brought together about 250 tribal leaders from throughout the upper Midwest: North and South Dakota, Nebraska, Iowa, and Minnesota. Then we invited the Assistant Secretary of the Interior to come to the reservation to hear our complaints. The assistant secretary said, "Well, now that you said whatever you wanted to say, what the hell do you want me to do?" Our answer to him was, "We want control of that Johnson O'Malley money. We are talking about tens of millions of dollars that are being poured into public school coffers, without any significant benefit to Indian children." He responded, "If that's what you want, that's what I'll give you." Because of that, the Nebraska Indian Inter-Tribal Development Corporation became the first Indian organization in the United States to control Johnson O'Malley funds. The government took the money away from the state and gave it to the Inter-Tribal Development Corporation. We distributed the money to five different public school districts.

I was hired to be the education director for the distribution of this money. I started working with the various public school boards. I told them, "Things aren't going to be the way they used to be. We're going to design programs to meet the needs of Indian children and not your needs." That really upset them. Some of them even wanted to pick a fight with me because they were being told that they couldn't do what they wanted to do with that money anymore.

We set about changing things. We set up tutorial programs for Indian children. We set up extracurricular activities for the Indian children. We implemented a great deal of projects that had never been done before for Indian children with the Johnson O'Malley money. I ran these programs for Nebraska Indian Inter-Tribal Development Corporation up through 1971.

Nebraska Inter-Tribal Development Corporation was a non-profit organization that was created by the three tribes of Nebraska: the Winnebagos, the Omahas, and the Santees.

It was initially designed to overcome the problems of economic development that the three tribes were experiencing. They needed to learn how to gain access to capital and how to design economic projects that were economically feasible and would generate income. The Nebraska Inter-Tribal Development Corporation gradually became more or less a social services-oriented institution concerned with the administration of the Johnson O'Malley monies, WIC programs, which provide services for women, infants and children, and programs such as transportation for senior citizens. Although it became a very good deliverer of social service programs, the Inter-Tribal Development Corporation never really did accomplish what it was designed to do—to change the economic base of the reservations.

I remained involved with this organization for a year or more. During that time I brought in some people from Albuquerque who had set up a new organization to train Indian people in the use of the federal education money that was available to help Indian children get through the educational system. In the process of helping us, the director of the organization said, "Whenever you get tired of doing what you're doing, why don't you come to work for us? We could use you as a trainer." So, after my mother passed away in 1971, I felt like it was time to move on to something different.

In August of 1971 my family and I relocated to Albuquerque, New Mexico, and I began working for this organization called Indian Education Training. We had a staff of about eight or nine people. Four of us did all of the travel to the various corners of the United States to train Indian groups. Between August of 1972 and July of 1974 I made eighty field trips to twenty-seven different states. I was constantly flying somewhere. That was another enlightening experience, training all these Indian people in the utilization of federal education money. I also got to confront racist school boards and try to re-educate and sensitize them. Doing that was really challenging, rewarding work. In the meantime we maintained our involvement with the American Indian

Movement and became involved in some of their major demonstrations.

In the summer of 1972, Russell Means resigned as the chairman of the board. The executive committee declared that they would appoint me national chairman of AIM at the next annual convention. So throughout 1972 and into 1973 I was actually the national chairman of the American Indian Movement. We organized various kinds of major demonstrations, including the takeover of the Minneapolis Naval Air Station.

We decided that demonstration was necessary at a gathering of the movement in Minneapolis, when we learned that the Minneapolis Naval Air Station was closing down and that the base would be declared excess property. We knew there were some regulations within the federal guidelines that made Indian tribes eligible for excess property. So we applied to the Defense Department to acquire the Minneapolis Naval Air Station so that we could set up a national office of the American Indian Movement and design social programs and other programs that could be housed there. Of course, the response of the Defense Department was negative. They didn't want to support a radical organization like the American Indian Movement. We convened a meeting late at night and said, "Well, if they don't want to turn it over to us, let's just go and occupy the damn place and take it over ourselves." That is exactly what we did. We went in, maybe a hundred and fifty of us, scaled the fences and took over the security posts and declared the Minneapolis Naval Air Station as AIM Headquarters. We found ourselves in a confrontation with local law enforcement over that occupation. After several days, they persuaded us to leave. But we raised the consciousness of a lot of people. There was a little pushing and shoving between AIM members and local law enforcement officials, but nobody was really hurt.

Another of our major activities concerned the fishing rights of the Chippewa people. We had a very large AIM encampment near Bemidji, Minnesota, where local White people were fishing in the Indian lakes. The Chippewas wanted the lakes open only to Indian fisherman. We had a big confrontation over that, to protect Chippewa fishing rights as guaranteed by treaty.

Then there was the occupation of Mount Rushmore. The Oglala Sioux wanted to publicize the fact that the Black Hills had been stolen from them. The Black Hills have always been sacred to the Lakota people but they were stolen shortly after gold was discovered there.[2] No payment had ever been received so they wanted the return of their land. We organized a takeover of Mount Rushmore that received national and international media coverage.

There was also the death of Raymond Yellowthunder in Gordon, Nebraska. Raymond Yellowthunder was an Oglala Sioux Indian who had been accosted by non-Indians, stripped, and shoved naked into an American Legion dance hall in Gordon, Nebraska. The perpetrators were drunk. Raymond died as a result of the abuse. His elderly sisters notified the local AIM leadership about what had happened to their brother. AIM called for a national meeting on the Pine Ridge Reservation. About eleven hundred people attended to protest Raymond Yellowthunder's death. We formed a large caravan to drive from Pine Ridge down to Gordon, Nebraska.

We took over the local American Legion post and we virtually occupied the whole town. Once again we were confronted by the law. But once again we did some consciousness raising about the abuse and mistreatment of Indian people.

The people who caused Mr. Yellowthunder's death were eventually convicted of third-degree manslaughter and given a two- or three-year sentence. It wasn't very significant.

These are only some of the major AIM activities in which I was involved while I lived and worked in Albuquerque. Everything we did was geared to establishing the civil and human rights of Indian people within this country. We didn't do something just to show off or just to agitate people. Everything we did had a purpose.

During the summer of 1972 Vernon Bellecourt called for a planning meeting in Denver, Colorado. I went to Denver as the chairman of the movement. Vernon told us that we had to do something to raise the consciousness of the entire country about Indian people. He suggested that we have a march, a walk from the West Coast to the East Coast. We would time this walk to coincide with the national elections. Four days of planning in Denver gave birth to the "Trail of Broken Treaties," the name by which our march was known. Robert Burnette, who had been the chairman of the Rosebud Sioux tribe and the former executive director of the National Congress of American Indians, and I were elected co-chairman of the Trail of Broken Treaties.

We each assumed responsibilities for that walk. Mr. Burnette would go to Washington, D.C., and make arrangements in the capital so we would all have a place to sleep and eat when we arrived there. He would do all the public relations work and enlist the support of human and civil rights organizations and church organizations. I would help coordinate the activities of the three groups. One caravan would depart from Seattle, one from San Francisco, and another from Los Angeles. We were expected to convene in Minneapolis, Minnesota, at a certain date. All three groups would come together there and then travel to Washington as one group.

I was doing my best to help coordinate these events. I was working with Clyde and Vernon Bellecourt, Russell Means, and Dennis Banks to insure that these caravans kept moving across the country. Eventually all three caravans came together at Minneapolis. We had a big national meeting in Saint Paul. I was the chairman of this meeting. We started putting different task forces together to write position papers. And we spent a whole week in Saint Paul coming up with a twenty-point position paper that we were going to deliver to President Richard Nixon and whoever else we could reach. Right at the end of this large national meeting of the movement, my father-in-law suffered a stroke. I told the leadership that I had to go home to be with my wife and look after my father-in-law's needs, but that when I was sure that everything was all right with him I would journey out to Washington and catch up with the group there. We returned to the reservation and the Trail of Broken Treaties continued on from the twin cities to Washington D.C., in late October, 1972.

My brothers and other relatives were participants in the Trail. I watched them on TV as they took over the Bureau of Indian Affairs building. And I thought, "Oh, now, we're really into it. Now we're up to our necks." I was certain that the occupation of the BIA building would bring about a major armed conflict with law enforcement. My father-in-law was in very serious condition, so I couldn't leave. I had to stay by my wife and stay by him. I never did get to Washington, but I tried to maintain contact with the group as best I could. And eventually, after they had confiscated a lot of paper work and disrupted the Bureau, the movement left town and came back west. But that twenty-point position paper had been delivered to the powers that be. It concerned all the needs of Indian people. We examined all the issues related to our sovereignty and economic development and education and health and jobs. Our situation had been written about and presented to the Administration and to various people in Congress. In that respect we accomplished our goal of making people more aware of our needs.

Harassment and Surveillance

rom the time that I became involved with the American Indian Movement up until 1974 when we moved to Sioux
City, my family and I were subjected to a lot of FBI surveillance because of my involvement with the movement. I
was regarded as a militant Indian who had organized a lot of
demonstrations. I had been involved in a number of Indian
movement confrontations over various human and civil
rights issues, and here in Nebraska I'd organized the boycott
of Walthill. We had organized public demonstrations against
discriminatory law enforcement practices. We had demonstrated against the Bureau of Indian Affairs for their failure to
meet our housing needs. We had demonstrated against the
Catholic Church for unfair labor practices because they were
hiring a construction firm that paid White college students
more than they did Indian workers. Because I had participated
for years in confrontations and because I was considered a
militant and a radical, the FBI evidently considered me a
threat to the American system. I was under constant surveillance. Wherever I traveled, I could always recognize two FBI
agents who were assigned to me.

I never had been charged with breaking any law. We had
confrontations with various law enforcement people in different situations, but nobody had ever arrested me and
charged me with anything illegal. Yet I wasn't terribly surprised when I noticed FBI agents following me. I knew that
most of the AIM leadership was under constant surveillance.
I was somewhat irritated because they came to my home and
talked to me. They began to harass my family when I was ab-
sent. It was an unpleasant situation for me and my family.

There were many other AIM leaders who were subjected to the same kind of surveillance. Until that point in my life, I had believed that the Federal Bureau of Investigation was a real upstanding, straight-arrow organization. I came to realize that they were operating on some rather shady principles themselves, especially in their handling of the kind of situations that we were confronting. They didn't support our cause to any great extent. One response to all this civil disturbance that was being generated by Black people and other ethnic minorities in the '60s and '70s, was the creation of a distinct unit within the Federal Bureau of Investigation called "community relations" or "community service." FBI agents with particular ethnic backgrounds were used as mediators or negotiators with the so-called dissident element in our society. Some of these agents proved to be pretty good guys. We developed a relationship with one of the FBI community relations officers out of the Kansas City office. He was pretty responsive to us. He tried to take seriously the issues we explained to him. In that respect we had an impact on the agency. They created a special unit to demonstrate more sensitivity to what was happening.

There were actually two occupations of Mount Rushmore. The first occurred in the fall of 1970. I was involved with that one. Then about two years later the movement came back and occupied the mountain again. But the first occupation of Mount Rushmore was the major occupation.

I also organized an event to honor the survivors of the 1890 massacre at Wounded Knee, South Dakota. My grandmother on my mother's side was half French and half Sioux, from the Rosebud Reservation. So I have a real affinity, a real kinship with the Sioux people, and when I moved to Rapid City I tried to learn something about that side of my family. In the process of doing that I was made aware that there were thirteen living survivors of the Wounded Knee Massacre. I talked with some people about it and I told them, "We really ought to honor these thirteen survivors of the Wounded Knee Massacre because it's a very important historical event in the life of Indian people." Some of the Sioux relatives agreed with that, so we began to organize a major honoring ceremony for the thirteen survivors. This was in 1970, eighty years after the massacre. All these survivors had been little children during the massacre. Now they were all elders. We managed to bring eleven of the thirteen survivors to Rapid City from wherever they lived. We celebrated this occasion during the Christmas holidays because that's when the massacre occurred. We had a big dance with several drum groups and lots of elders present. We had a big feast and a big giveaway. Honoring the eleven survivors of Wounded Knee really helped strengthen our identity as Indian people, particularly Sioux people.

That was done at one of the busiest times of my life. I was constantly into one activity or another. With the community action agency in Rapid City I worked as the assistant director, under the executive director. My responsibility was in training, reporting, and planning. I spent a lot of time working on community development projects with the Sioux people in the city. We were organizing around health issues and jobs issues and housing. It was a real full-time job for me, the year that I worked in Rapid City.

I came back from South Dakota to Nebraska, to work for the Nebraska Inter-Tribal Development Corporation. I left Nebraska for Albuquerque in August of 1972 after my mother passed away. I lived in Albuquerque until July of 1974. During my years in Albuquerque I made eighty field trips to twenty-seven different states. I was also involved in all that AIM activity. I came to know virtually every Indian leader in the nation and developed personal friendships with many outstanding Indian leaders from around the country.

During this time I was becoming more committed to the Native American Church. Since giving up drinking in 1965 I had been looking for spiritual fulfillment. I couldn't find it in Mormonism, so I was coming back to the Native American Church. I began attending meetings more regularly during the early 1970s. My renewed interest was also influenced by my older brother, who was slowly dying of scleroderma. He had contracted this disease shortly after the Second World War. We used to go to prayer meetings so that he could use medicine and feel better. Anyway, little by little I was being drawn back into the Native American Church.

I had designed a program and won a contract with the Department of Education for the establishment of a program with the Sioux City (Iowa) American Indian Center. The Indian Center's board of directors invited me to come and run the program. They said, "You designed this program the way that we told you to do it, so we feel that you're capable of running it the way we want you to run it. We'd like for you to come and work with us." I resigned my job in Albuquerque and moved my family back to Sioux City, twenty miles north of the Winnebago Reservation.

We settled down in Sioux City in July of 1974 and I began to manage the educational program for the Sioux City American Indian Center. When I took the position, I told them that I would give them three years of my life. I told them that I would try to build their center into something meaningful. At the time that I was employed by them, they had a director and a part-time secretary and operated on a budget of about thirty thousand dollars a year. When I came on board, we had a hundred thousand dollar federal education contract, and I set about designing and developing other programs for the Indian center. Within that three-year time period I had committed myself to, we grew to a staff of seventeen people with over a quarter million dollars in funding.

There was an intense effort by the FBI to buy me out or to get me to be an informant during the Wounded Knee occupation. Some agents came to my house and said, "Mr. Snake, we realize that you're involved with the movement, but we also understand that you're not a promoter of armed confrontation. We know that you want to do things in a peaceable way. So we're here to ask for your support and your help." I told them that I couldn't do anything for them because as the chairman of the American Indian Movement I was still obliged to support the efforts of the people in the movement and what they were doing.

Sometime afterward a couple of guys came knocking on my door professing to be former Vietnam soldiers. One of them, who was in a wheelchair, said he was an Indian. They claimed that they wanted to help out at Wounded Knee in whatever way they could. They asked me to get them into Wounded Knee. They were willing to run guns. Of course, I was suspicious of them because they didn't appear to be genuine activists. I had been around the movement long enough to recognize most of the people in the movement, to know the activist type of people. I thanked them for their offer of help. Then I told them I'd be contacting them and I sent them away. But I never did call them. This type of activity let me and my family know that we were under constant surveillance. They were trying to find a way to use us to get at the people in Wounded Knee.

When the occupation at Wounded Knee took place we were still living in Albuquerque. I was working to train Indian educators. Most of the FBI harassment of my family took place in Albuquerque. Although the harassment stopped, the surveillance didn't. After Wounded Knee there were still FBI people that followed me around to my public speaking engagements. I was one of many young Indian activists who got invited to colleges and universities to talk about these issues. I used to travel extensively to different parts of the country to deliver the message of the movement. I was aware that there were some FBI people around. They stopped harassing me, but they were still there.

There were some pretty strong allegations of corrupt tribal government made by Russell Means and other AIM leaders. I understand that they were attempting to expose the corruptness of the Oglala Sioux tribal government and trying to force the federal government to have greater respect for the traditional leadership of American Indian tribes. The standard practice of the non-Indian system had been to ignore traditional tribal leaders and to hand-pick tribal leaders who were willing to work with the White man. So governmental systems were designed and implemented on reservations. Tribal councils patterned after the White American model of democratic government were created.

As a result, most of the traditional democratic tribal government processes and the traditional tribal leaders were totally ignored. That caused a rather serious problem in a lot of Indian communities where there was still a very strong traditional element. They looked at the system and noticed that the people in control of their system, the tribal government, were the beneficiaries of all the federal money. The tribal government people hired their friends and relatives and set up the programs they felt were necessary. They spent the money the way they wanted to with very little, if any, involvement of traditional people. This became a bone of contention. A lot of traditional people used to say, "What good are all these programs? They're sure not helping us out. We have to change the government to make it be more responsive to us." These are the kinds of factors that led up to the Wounded Knee occupation in 1973.[1]

Not too long after the occupation of Wounded Knee by the American Indian Movement had begun, Richard Wilson, the chairman of the Oglala Sioux tribe, invited the executive officers of the National Congress of American Indians and the National Tribal Chairmen's Association to his reservation for a joint meeting to help him to determine what should be done about this situation at Wounded Knee. Most of the executive officers of the two national Indian organizations came to Pine Ridge. He wanted them to discuss how he should respond to the threat of armed insurrection on his reservation. That meeting was convened at Villamous Hall in Pine Ridge, South Dakota. It just so happened that the chairman of my tribe, the Winnebago of Nebraska, was appointed to be the chairman of this meeting. My brother was the vice-chairman of the Winnebago tribe. So he called me in Albuquerque and he said, "Brother, it might be worthwhile for you to come over here and try to talk to these people because if things get out of hand and both of these national organizations are supportive of Dickie Wilson, there might be a lot of violence and unnecessary deaths at Wounded Knee. Maybe you could come over here and try to help them find a reasonable solution." I promised I would try to do that. My wife and I flew to Rapid City and were picked up by one of our Sioux relatives, who drove us down to Pine Ridge. On the way there he said, "Don't expect me to hang around outside because I'm considered an AIM supporter. If they see me, they're sure to try to hurt me. I'll drive by occasionally to see if you're done. When I see you outside then I'll know it's time to pick you up and leave." He dropped us off at Villamous Hall, where this large gathering was taking place. We met our tribal chairman, my brother, my sister who was on the tribal council, and some other Winnebagos. One of those Winnebagos was Dickie Wilson's mother-in-law. She was really happy to see all of us. During the coffee break she got Dickie Wilson to come over and sit down with us. He was right in the middle of the Winnebago delegation, laughing and talking to us, when we had our pictures taken. I was sitting right next to him. Of course, he didn't realize who I was, that I was the chairman of the American Indian Movement. He got up and went about his business. Then we got in line for lunch.

While we were standing in line for lunch, a lady who I recognized as the editor of the local Oglala newspaper came up and asked me, "Aren't you Reuben Snake?" I replied, "Yes, madam." She continued, "Aren't you involved in the American Indian Movement. Aren't you one of the leaders?" I said, "Yes, madam, I am." Then she demanded to know what I was doing at this gathering and why I wasn't out at Wounded Knee. I explained to her that I had come with the hope of being able to address the people present, that I wanted to help them find some way to resolve the situation without anybody being hurt. She didn't receive that idea too well.

As we continued walking through the lunch line she went and informed Mr. Wilson that one of the AIM leaders was present. She referred to me. While we were sitting down to eat our lunch some of Mr. Wilson's so-called goons came over and demanded that I come down out of the stands where I was sitting. They wanted to pick a fight. "Let's get it on, let's have it over and done with here and now." I told them that I wasn't there looking for trouble. I wasn't there to pick a fight. I was there to try and devise some solution to the problem without anybody being hurt. They declared, "You are not welcome here. You better leave." I stated, "The chairman of this gathering is my tribal chairman. If he tells me to leave, I'll leave."

They went over to Dickie Wilson and told him who I was and what I had said. He sent word back that he didn't want me there. So my wife and I decided it was time to leave. As we got up to leave, members of the goon squad, both men and women, began lining up at the door, forming a gauntlet. They started saying, "Let's kill these no good sons of bitches." These were the kind of threats we heard as we left the hall.

Several of them began moving towards their cars. We assumed that they were going to get their guns. There was no place for us to go. My Sioux friend wasn't waiting for us. We were in a rather precarious situation. Suddenly, around the corner came the Winnebago tribal van with my sister driving and my brother sitting next to her. They came to a screeching halt beside my wife and me and urged us to get in. We jumped in and they peeled out of there. As we were racing down the highway they said, "We're going to get you out of town before something bad happens to you." We were leaving Pine Ridge as fast as we could when we saw my Sioux friend coming down the road. We signaled to him and he turned around in the middle of the road and followed us. We stopped, jumped out, and threw our bags into his car. Then we sped away. My sister and brother led Wilson's goons off on a different route so that they wouldn't chase us.

There were cars coming along to look for us. But we managed to get out of Pine Ridge without anything happening. That was the most serious incident in which we were involved during the confrontation at Wounded Knee. It could have been more serious but we managed to get out before anything terrible happened.

There were numerous deaths on the Pine Ridge Reservation before and after the Wounded Knee occupation. A lot of people died mysteriously. Yet nobody was ever charged with anything. There were probably sixty people killed on that reservation within only a year or two. It was truly a tragic situation. A great deal of public animosity was generated by the publicity surrounding the deaths of two FBI agents. That publicity only strengthened the negative image people already had of Indians. They would say, "Look at what those Indians are doing to us." But nobody ever addressed the fact that some sixty Indian people had been killed and nobody had ever been brought to justice. The FBI turned a blind eye toward that.

There may have been some financial motive involved in this dispute, but it was primarily a power struggle between the established Indian Reorganization Act tribal government and the traditional people. The traditional people were struggling to gain greater access to the tribal government. There are huge mineral deposits on the Pine Ridge Reservation that could be used by various industries. There was probably some fear that if the tribal council lost control, that if the traditional people got more politically involved, they would stop the development and exploration of the various mineral deposits in order to preserve the land. Although it wasn't publicized, it seems likely that corporate America wanted to have unrestricted access to these minerals.

The injustices of the system that we were living in then still exist today. The media, being what it is, never picked up on the message that we were trying to deliver. When the confrontation occurred at Wounded Knee they looked at the superficial aspects of what was happening, the spectacle of the confrontation. They focused on our challenge to the system. They wrote about the confrontation. They didn't write about the problems that we were talking about. When we talked about the death of Raymond Yellowthunder, they didn't pay much attention. They focused attention on the Indians occupying the town of Gordon, Nebraska. We were at Mount Rushmore to establish the fact that the Black Hills had been stolen. No money has ever been paid for the Black Hills. But the media never brought that message to the American public. Instead, they just said, "Here are all these militant young Indians occupying this sacred shrine of democracy." The media never did respond adequately to what we were saying. That's been the situation all along, because the media is the White man's institution. All the reporters, all the journalists, all the editors, and all the producers are non-Indians. They inevitably tell the story from their point of view, not the Indian's perspective.

The alternative news sources, publications such as *Mother Earth News*, did a pretty good job of reporting what was happening. The mainstream media totally ignored what we were trying to say, and played up the most sensational aspects of what we were doing.

Ordained Roadman and Tribal Chairman

After 1972 I began attending Native American Church prayer meetings more frequently. While I was living in New Mexico I was going to prayer meetings among the people at Taos Pueblo and on different parts of the Navajo reservation.

When I started running the education programs for the Sioux City Indian Center, I hired one of my Sioux brothers as the cultural activities coordinator. He was studying to be a traditional medicine man. He was learning all the traditional things about Yuwipi ceremonies and sun dances and things of that nature, but he was also a Roadman in the Native American Church. He and I agreed that in order to achieve success in our program, we should have a prayer meeting. We organized a prayer meeting up in Vermillion, where he lived.

The gentleman I am speaking about is my brother, Asa Primeaux, from the Yankton Sioux tribe. My involvement with brother Asa motivated me to become even more active in the Native American Church. We began to have regular Native American Church devotional services, services where we brought our elders together to sing, pray, and talk to us. We also had regular prayer meetings quite frequently.

I had only one Snake Clan father left who was active in the Native American Church. I had gone to visit this Snake Clan elder a number of times. One time he and his wife told me, "Well, we've been thinking about it, son. We looked at all the nephews. We looked at all the sons that we have in this Snake Clan and we picked you. You're the one that seems the most interested, and you're the one who seems to need the most help. So what we're going to do is have a Native American

Church meeting and we're going to turn these instruments that we've been taking care of, the prayer staff and drum and all these sacred things, over to you. We feel that's the best thing we could do for you. There's no other way we can help you except by putting these instruments in your care and keeping. And if you take care of them properly, they're going to take care of you. They're going to help you along in life."

This event happened on October 26, 1974. My clan father, Michael WhiteSnake, and his wife, Madeleine, sponsored a Native American Church meeting. They invited some of my family elders. I had an aunt, the oldest living member of my clan, and they invited her and her husband. I had another adopted father, Moses Hensley, and there were a number of other elders from my tribe and the neighboring Omaha tribe and then some of my Sioux relatives. They all came to this prayer meeting to pray for me so that I would be able to take care of these instruments in the proper way and to pray that I could improve my life through this Native American Church.

That began another change in my life. My clan father told me that I had to live a certain lifestyle after that. I had to show compassion and respect towards everyone. I couldn't be picking and choosing who my friends were. I had to treat everybody alike. I had to respond to every request that was made of me for prayers. I had to wait on the people and do what they wanted me to do in the way of conducting prayer meetings. I had to do whatever it was I could to help them along in life. He spent a long time telling me the importance of these instruments in my life and the importance of being the kind of Roadman that I should be in the church. I had to make a commitment, to decide that I was going to change my ways again for the better and try to do all these things that my clan father told me to do. I was to have respect for people and to have compassion for people and to honor people and to do their bidding and to pray for them and to treat everybody equally. To do all these things, I had to make up my mind that that's the way I was going to be.

I knew it would require that I change some of my activities in order to fulfill this responsibility. I had to give up some of the things that I liked to do, like going to movies, or maybe taking time out for playing cards with the boys, and other things of that sort. I couldn't do them anymore. I realized that these diversions were just time-consuming. I could be using that time to improve myself. I could concentrate on improving my character.

I felt that it was a tremendous blessing from the Creator to have been chosen by my clan father to take over these instruments, to have been "ordained" as a Roadman in the Native American Church. I admired him because he was a World War II combat veteran. He fought in both the European and Pacific theaters. After that he had come home and married. He had no natural son of his own, just one daughter. He became very active in the Native American Church and was our local church president here on the reservation for a time. He conducted a lot of prayer meetings for different families. I realized that he had said many, many prayers with these instruments that he was turning over to me.

I felt an obligation to continue with those prayers. I know that he had the very best of intentions in giving me these instruments. He wanted me to become a praying person and develop my character. He wanted everything to be beneficial for me and my family once we took these instruments. So I really felt blessed when he turned these instruments over to me and told me to take good care of them and that they would take good care of me. That statement has proven to be true. Since 1974, when these instruments came into my possession, a lot of wonderful things have happened to me and to my family. So what my clan father said was true, "If you take care of them, they're going to take care of you." I always considered it to be a real blessing to have these things in my life and to become deeply immersed in the Native American Church. After receiving these instruments I started going to a prayer meeting virtually every weekend. I was not doing anything except concentrating on the Native American Church. That was because of the advice that my clan father had given to me: "If you're going to do something, you must do it right. Do one thing at a time and make sure that you're doing that right." For the next ten years, from 1974 on, there were probably only two or three weekends when I did not go to meetings. Often I went to prayer meetings during the week, sometimes to funerals or to pray for somebody who was ill.

I kept track of all the prayer meetings I attended. I used to average about sixty meetings a year.

We are taught that the Native American Church way of life is family-oriented. All members of the family must be actively involved. That's the way it was with us. When my two youngest children, my son Darren and my son Michael, were four and five years old, I began to teach them how to sing the songs of the Native American Church, to teach them how to tie up the drum, and to introduce them to all the elements of the church. My wife used to encourage our daughters. From the time our children were young we would all go sit up in a prayer meeting together and pray together and worship God together. Worship had a lot to do with creating good feelings between all members of our family.

Being a Roadman had a definite effect on my leadership abilities. I became extremely active in the Native American Church in 1974 and in 1976 we decided to move back to the reservation. Immediately after we moved back many people started talking to me about running for the tribal council because a number of the council people were still into alcohol abuse. People used to say, "We really need some sober leadership in the tribe. You've shown us that you're a sober, serious-thinking person. That's why we'd like for you to run for the tribal council." I considered their requests for some time after we moved back to the reservation. Finally, in the fall of 1977, I ran for the tribal council. I was elected and then was made the chairman of the Winnebago tribe. I had my responsibilities as a Roadman of the Native American Church, duties which kept me busy throughout the week. I would go to a prayer service virtually every weekend. Perhaps every other weekend somebody would ask me to conduct a prayer meeting.

To conduct a meeting one has to be prepared. A Roadman has to be able to go out and do everything that's necessary to have this prayer meeting: cut the firewood and put up the tepee and fix the altar and do various things in preparation for the service, the ceremony. I had to develop new skills. I had to learn how to put up a tepee. I had to learn what kind of firewood was best for this sacred fireplace. We can't just go out and grab any old piece of wood for the sacred fireplace. It has to be in a specific condition in order to burn brightly and cleanly. We have to look for a certain kind of wood. So there were many things for me to learn. I was concentrating on all that when I was elected to the tribal council and then became the chairman of the tribe.

Reuben Snake, Winnebago Reservation, Nebraska, November 1992. Photograph courtesy of Jay Fikes.

Restoring Winnebago
Self-Sufficiency

When I became tribal chairman, all of my previous involvements with national Indian leaders began to pay off. I had been to most parts of Indian country and knew most of the leaders. I came to know a lot of federal bureaucrats and some of the national politicians. Once I became the tribal chairman, I sat down with some of my relatives and I said, "We've been doing real great work here with our tribal government; we've been accomplishing lots of things. One of the things we haven't done is to create a long-range development program which will move us towards social and economic self-sufficiency. That's what I want to do, put together a plan that's going to take us to the point where we will be totally self-reliant. That way we won't have to depend on federal grants and contracts for anything. That way we can create an economic system on our reservation so we can generate our own income and have our own money. That way nobody can tell us what to do. Today when we go to the government for a federal grant or a contract, we have to abide by their guidelines and do things the way that they want us to do them. That usually doesn't meet our needs. So we need to develop a long-range self-sufficiency program."

As tribal chairman my greatest emphasis was on developing this plan to become economically and socially self-reliant. It was a tremendous undertaking. It took a lot of intelligence and many kinds of people to develop this plan. Then we had to structure it in a realistic way. It had to be something that would really work.

I had to go out and find the resources to implement the program. We were a very poor tribe. Our income was derived from federal grants and contracts and some revenue from tribal land leases. These leases didn't include any mineral extraction. They were just leases of farm land to individual farmers and to various agribusiness enterprises; we never found sufficient mineral resources on the reservation to make that type of development worthwhile. We also had small contracts with local lumber companies for logging some of our timber. The Bureau of Indian Affairs would negotiate contracts with the local lumber companies for logging out walnut. We have a pretty good stand of walnut on the reservation. Of course, this didn't generate a whole lot of income. It was about a hundred and forty or fifty thousand dollars total, annually. The rest of our tribal budget came from federal grants and contracts. The amount available annually to our tribe was between two and three million dollars, depending on what was happening on the national level with federal appropriations and our ability to write the right kind of program applications.

My belief in self-sufficiency was accepted by most of the tribal leadership. There was, as there always is, some opposition claiming, "You guys are just full of bullshit. You can't really do this. It will never happen." There was some of that kind of talk in the community but almost everybody thought it was possible for us to become a self-sufficient tribe. That's the goal we set about achieving during my tenure as tribal chairman. To do so, I had to go out and develop the resources.

I went to a national Indian organization called Americans for Indian Opportunity that had been founded by Mrs. LaDonna Harris, the former wife of Senator Fred Harris of Oklahoma. She had received a grant to work with three Indian tribes on management and administration, to evaluate the status of the tribe and determine what direction they should take. She designated our tribe as one of the tribes her organization would support. She brought her staff over and they analyzed our situation and suggested some very useful things. One of their recommendations was to examine the federal guidelines under which most of our programs were being funded. We discovered that they actually took authority away from our tribal council. Our tribal organization was governed more by federal program guidelines than by the planning and development efforts generated from within the tribe. LaDonna's organization persuaded us that in order to turn things around we had to bring all of these different programs together and create a centralized tribal system of management. We could no longer let the federal guidelines control us.

It took us about a year to centralize all of our programs and to create various departments to oversee them. We devised an entirely different kind of organizational structure as a result of our working with Americans for Indian Opportunity. We began to understand where the money came from and who was responsible to whom for the administration of each program, the dispensation of the funding, and the accountability of the funding. Going through this process really sharpened our skills in government.

I had developed relationships with officials in various federal agencies, including Housing and Urban Development, the Economic Development Administration, the Office of Economic Opportunity, the Department of Transportation, and the Department of Labor. I contacted the bureaucrats in these federal agencies to generate income for the tribe through grants and contracts. I was also trying to meet people from private philanthropic organizations like the Carnegie Foundation, the Ford Foundation, and the Donner Foundation, seeking a way to get some of their money coming into our tribe. Doing that was like pulling teeth. It was really hard to convince those people that they should take an interest in Indian activities.

We did manage to get some grants from the Campaign for Human Development of the Catholic Church. They gave us a grant of $40,000 a year for three years to help us with our water rights struggle and to develop our water conservation programs. We also got a small grant from the First Nations Development Institute to expand our self-sufficiency in the areas of food production and our canning operation.

At the same time we were searching for other kinds of resources to help us cope with the social ills in our community. We wanted to know how to deal with alcohol and drug abuse, how to treat the incidence of diabetes, how to handle the lack of jobs. We included all these issues in designing our self-sufficiency plan and gradually built up our tribal organization. We began to make use of educated, talented young Winnebagos by employing them in programs and electing them to the tribal council. These younger people began returning to the reservation with college degrees in social work, in education, and even in law. We developed all these things in 1977, after I was elected. Eventually we developed some of the programs that our tribal membership wanted. They wanted a wake and a burial program. So we created a wake and burial program. They wanted a revolving credit program. So we created a revolving credit program. They wanted a land acquisition program to regain control of some of the land on the reservation that we had lost. So we set up a program utilizing tribal funds, and Farmer's Home Administration loaned us funds to start buying back land from non-Indians to add to the tribal land base.

We structured our efforts to become self-sufficient into four categories. One category was cultural enhancement and cultural revitalization of our Winnebago culture, reviving our music and our language. The second concerned coping with problems of alcoholism and health, such as diabetes. The third program involved protecting the sovereignty of our tribe as an Indian nation. We had to assert ourselves with the various other governments that we came into contact with: the county, state, and federal governments. The fourth category was economic development. In order to be truly self-sufficient we had to develop our economic base so that we were generating our own income and creating our own jobs instead of relying upon federal or state governments for grants and contracts. It was all very challenging and I really enjoyed working on all these projects.

Right about that time my children were getting to the age

where they were having children of their own. We became grandparents on December 15, 1978, when our oldest daughter gave birth to a little boy. I had the honor of naming him so I gave him my name, both my English name and my Winnebago name, *Kikawa Unga*. My wife and I sponsored a Native American Church prayer meeting to pray for our little grandson to have a long, healthy, and happy life. That was the beginning of another stage of my life, in 1978 when I became a grandparent.

Among the Ho Chunk people becoming a grandparent has great significance. To be a credible spokesman for the people you have to have certain credentials. You have to be a protector and a provider and a defender of the people. And you have to be a grandparent. That's what our elders said: "Before you stand up and talk you should have lived long enough to have grandchildren, so that you know what life is all about before you open your mouth. Then you're going to say something worthwhile." That's the importance we place on being a grandparent.

Becoming a grandfather had a real impact on me personally because I had been told by one of my relatives, "Even though you really love your children and you think that you can't love anybody more than you love your children, when your grandchildren come along you're going to discover something entirely new about yourself. You're going to be able to love your grandchildren even more." I found that was true when my little grandson came along. It opened up a whole new area of attachment and involvement and love and caring in my life. Having that grandchild had a beneficial impact on my personality.

Being a grandparent probably gave me more of a compassionate feeling for people. We are told, "If you want your offspring to be well and be happy and to get along in this world, you have to treat everybody with respect. That way they'll treat your offspring with respect." I thought about my children and my grandchildren. I wanted them to be treated kindly by my people so I made up my mind that

that's the way I had to be towards everybody: to treat them with respect and honor.

I went to some of my elders and talked to them about the kind of qualities it took to be a leader of the people. These are some of the things that they told me. Native American leaders must have certain qualities. A leader has got to have some guts, to have some machismo. A leader has got to have something inside that moves him to stand up and say what needs to be said, because we just can't be wishy-washy about things in the Indian world. When people are hurting, when there's all kind of things happening to our people, we just can't let the system run over us. A leader must have some bravery and be willing to challenge the system and try to change it for the better. Throughout these years of my leadership, I've tried to stand up and say the things that have to be said in the places where they need to be said and to the people that need to hear them. That's one of the attributes of a leader, to have a brave heart, but along with this is to have humility. A leader must also have some kind of vision for the future. Most of us are caught up in the day-to-day struggle for survival. We don't like to think way down the road. We don't like to think in that way. We just want to take care of what needs to be taken care of now. Those who really want some permanent change to occur must have some kind of vision. A leader has to look at things and see how they are and then think about how they could be. So that takes some effort too, to develop a sense of vision. The Iroquois people like to say, "Think seven generations ahead."

Then our old people say, "If you are going to be a leader, you have to have a thickness of seven skins because people are going to be shooting slings and arrows at you, even the very people that asked you to be a leader. They're going to be talking about you and saying hurtful things about you." So a leader has to develop that kind of attitude, to decide to put up with all of this and not to react in a negative way to all the negative things that are said about one as a leader. Along with that a leader has to have equal respect for everyone, regardless of who they are. One should respect every individual. One should not treat some people a certain way and treat other people a different way. A leader is going to treat everybody alike. These are just some of the things that my elders told me when I went to them after I had assumed the leadership of our tribe.

Let me mention something which was crucial to my development as a leader. I lived with my brothers and my sister in the mission home in Neillsville, Wisconsin. This type of institution requires one to find one's place in the pecking order right away. One has to go to "Duke City" with some of the boys in order to establish one's self. I was five years old. I was in the first grade. I was a new kid in the school. My older brothers, who were at the school too, told me, "Well, you take care of everybody you can take care of and if they get too big, then we'll take care of them for you." In the first several weeks I got into several fist fights and wrestling matches with first-, second-, and third-graders. Pretty soon I found my place and everything kind of settled down.

In the course of establishing myself in the pecking order, I had come to know some of these boys fairly well. They gradually started gravitating towards me and would say, "Well, Reuben what are we going to do today? Or what should we do about this?" I began to realize, "Hey, these guys are asking me, asking me what should be done." That impressed me because at five years of age I was probably the youngest individual there. I had first-, second-, and third-grade guys following my orders. "Well, let's do this. Okay, we'll do it this way, then." I began to see that I had something going for me, that I had a gift. I could utilize that gift to get people organized and get people to do things. That was the beginning of my leadership activities, way back there as a little boy.

As the Winnebago tribal chairman I was involved in many activities. We started an oral history and language program to address the cultural concerns of our people. We devised a means of teaching the language utilizing a device called a micro-phonograph, which allowed us to put things down on a small plastic disk. We also had a little hand-held device that we put on the disk to play back whatever one has said. We bought some of these machines, interviewed our elders, and made a bunch of these little disks. From those we compiled a Winnebago dictionary and books of phrases. We incorporated them into the Head Start system, the public school system, and, to a limited extent, in our community college.

I was involved in the creation of our community college back in the early 1970s. Around 1972 we started making plans to create our own community college. By around 1975 we managed to have a community college program in place. At first, it was a subsidiary of one of the state institutions over in Norfolk, Nebraska. It didn't become an independent school until around 1978 or 1979. After I assumed the chairmanship of the tribe, we got our community college accredited. It became its own free-standing entity, Nebraska Indian Community College, and is controlled by the three tribes of Nebraska: the Omaha, the Santee, and the Winnebago. Each tribe appoints three members to the board of trustees. The college has sites on the Omaha and Santee reservations but the headquarters is on our reservation. The combined enrollment is about two hundred and fifty students, full-time and part-time. Education is a very important part of our effort to become self-sufficient.

The language teaching project has yet to be completed. We did introduce Winnebago language courses into the school system and into the college system. But we were never able, due to the lack of funding, to buy a sufficient quantity of these devices to implement a broad program of language instruction.

In the area of social development we developed a master contract with the Indian Health Service. Prior to this contract, the Indian Health Service administered all of the health programs for the tribe. In order to fulfill our self-sufficiency effort, the tribe contracted all these programmatic activities from the IHS and set up a tribal health department with programs for home health care, community health representatives, emergency medical service, and alcohol and drug abuse treatment. All these health programs were controlled by the tribe and not the federal government. We even went to a master contract with the Bureau of Indian Affairs. They turned over the administration and management of various bureau-funded programs to the tribe.

Another area we were committed to defend was sovereignty. We got involved in a major lawsuit with the Nebraska Public Power District, which was challenging the sovereignty of the tribe. Nebraska Public Power District wanted to build a 340-kilowatt line across our reservation. They thought they could condemn our land with the approval of the Bureau of Indian Affairs. They wanted to go ahead and build their line, but we showed them that without the approval of the tribal government they weren't able to do that. So we got into a massive lawsuit with the power company. Eventually we arrived at a negotiated settlement. With the settlement money and associated bank loans, we applied for economic development funds from the federal government. We were able to start up a tribal farm, a tribal grocery store, an auto truck service center, and so on.

Protecting our sovereignty led us right into economic development and economic development led to the creation of jobs. We also helped Sioux Indians develop a defense-related industry on our reservation. At its peak it employed probably three dozen of our people. So the grocery store, the tribal farm, the auto truck service center, the canning center, and the defense industry created well over a hundred jobs for our people. We were coordinating all of these things to work together for the realization of our goal of economic self-sufficiency and social self-sufficiency.

The Winnebago Navy was the prototype of our struggle with the Nebraska Public Power District. The Winnebago Navy was created in 1970 when the Army Corps of Engineers was attempting to condemn our land on the east bank of the Missouri River. The Army Corps of Engineers had entered into an agreement with the state of Iowa to build a gigantic water recreation complex directly across the river from our reservation and was attempting to publicly condemn 627 of our acres over there. And we objected to that. We protested, "Here you are going to spend in excess of thirteen million dollars to build this water recreational complex. You're going to condemn our land, and you're not even giving us a piece of the action. That's not fair. So we're going to oppose you on this." So the Winnebago Navy was created to oppose the United States Army Corps of Engineers and the condemnation of our land.

When it became necessary to mobilize the Winnebago Navy to sail across the wide Missouri, we discovered there wasn't one Indian on the Winnebago Reservation who owned a boat. So we talked with some friends down at the University of Nebraska. One of them had a fourteen-foot runabout and another one had a twelve-foot aluminum rowboat. This was the magnificent fleet of the Winnebago Navy. We brought these two worthy vessels to the back waters of the Missouri River on the west bank. I don't know what the eligibility requirements for the Winnebago Navy were, but I noticed that every person that got into the runabout and the row boat weighed at least 250 pounds; I myself weighed 350. We made some large signs that said, "This is Winnebago Indian land by treaty of March 8, 1865. No Trespassing." We loaded up these big signs on the rowboat, attached the rowboat to the back of the runabout, and set sail across the Missouri.

Our fearless leader, Louie LaRose, was standing on the prow of the runabout with a war bonnet on. Of course we Winnebagos are woodland Indians so we never were familiar with wearing war bonnets. War bonnets are a tradition among the plains Indians. Louie forgot to tie the drawstring on the back of his war bonnet so when we hit the main channel, the breeze coming down the river caught his eagle feathers and turned them inside out. Instead of looking like a fierce Winnebago warrior, he wound up looking like a Mormon pioneer woman in a sun bonnet. I was sitting in the back of the aluminum rowboat, holding onto the wooden signs. As we hit the main channel, they had to rev the engine on the runabout. The acceleration pushed the bow of the aluminum boat up out of the water and I began to sink on the back end. So the television cameras took pictures of me. It looked like I was skimming across the water on my butt because the back end of the aluminum row boat was underwater. So that was the great launching of the Winnebago Navy as we sailed across the mighty Missouri to enforce our rights to our land.

Following this grand excursion, our tribal council took the case to federal court. In District Court the ruling was favorable for the tribe. We had effectively blocked the Army Corps of Engineers' efforts to condemn our land. The Army Corps of Engineers appealed to the Eighth Circuit Court, which upheld the Federal District Court judge in declaring that the Army Corps of Engineers had no explicit authority granted by Congress to condemn our land. The Court ruled that until Congress passed such an act authorizing the Army Corps, they couldn't take our land away from us. This is how that situation turned out. Since that time, we've been able to build on that land. In fact that land is the base of our biggest economic enterprise, our gaming operation. We have approximately 627 acres on the east bank of the Missouri river.

Bingo halls were springing up all over the country and everybody thought they were the answer to our economic woes. I really didn't feel that they would be beneficial for us, but eventually the executive director of Nebraska Inter-Tribal Development Corporation came before our tribal council and said that he had had an offer to develop a bingo operation for the Winnebago tribe. He thought that it would be a lucrative business. The tribal government and the majority of the council members voted in favor of establishing a bingo hall. I think it was seven for the bingo hall and one opposed. Because I was the chairman I was not a voting member. After the voting, we began undertaking all the necessary activities to establish a bingo hall operation. Word was sent out that we were looking for a contract manager who knew how to run this kind of business and that we were looking for financial investment. Then we developed the tribal bingo ordinance and submitted a plan to the Bureau of Indian Affairs for their approval. In October of 1984, we opened a very large bingo hall. I think it had a 2,000-seat capacity. It was located at the east end of the reservation, across the Missouri River about three miles off Interstate 29, near Sloan, Iowa.

We got into a predicament because we hadn't done all of the homework necessary to insure that the bingo contract managers would follow the direction of the council. After a while we began to experience difficulties with the managers. They were undertaking to do things without informing the tribal council. Eventually we dismissed them. Discharging them prompted them to file an injunction in federal court and we became embroiled in a rather lengthy lawsuit.

As tribal chairman, I was one of the defendants being sued. That left a very bitter taste in my mouth. Eventually, after I left the chairman's office and other people assumed leadership for the tribe, there was a negotiated out-of-court settlement. Since then the tribe has entered into a contractual agreement with other people. They have opened up a very large casino, but closed the bingo operation because bingo brings in less money than slot machines and other gambling devices. The enormous gambling casino we have today is on the same property, over on the east end of the reservation, and is generating a lot of income for the tribe. The income is used for a variety of tribal activities. There are about five hundred people employed over there, generating money for the tribal treasury and funding programs that are much needed in the community. It has become a success.

If it is used wisely, the revenue from gaming can help us achieve that goal of self-sufficiency we established in 1978. It can generate the kind of economic ventures that will create more jobs and income for the tribe. If it's used wisely, it will enable us to address a lot of the unmet needs of our people. The current tribal council is setting aside money to build a senior citizens' center and a nursing home, something we've needed for a long time. All of our elders are generally sent off the reservation to surrounding communities where nursing homes are available. When we have our own nursing home, we can keep our elders right here on the reservation. There's also a need for youth development programs. There's a need to restore the natural resources of our reservation by bringing in wild turkeys and pheasant and buffalo. Projects like this have been planned and are being put into operation with revenue from our gaming.

I am personally opposed to having the proceeds from gaming used to make per-capita payments because I don't believe that such payments really enhance community life. They only provide a shot in the arm for individuals and families; they get a little money but when the money's gone, they're back in the same situation. But if the gaming money is used wisely, to build up our infrastructure and build up our programs, it's going to produce something beneficial for all our people.

However, I have observed one disadvantage connected with the gaming operation. Because it is the one substantial source of employment, with some five hundred jobs, all of our young married people are working out there. This creates a problem here in the community. The little children of these young parents receive no care and are running around the streets unsupervised. In addition, gaming creates a dilemma for the Native American Church. The busiest times for our gaming enterprise are Friday, Saturday, and Sunday. Weekends are the time that we generally set aside to pray, to have our Native American Church meetings, but many of our members are required to work on the weekend. They can't come to church and practice their religion. We need their help to keep our church going.

Reuben Snake wearing a foxhead at Karl May festival in Bad Segeberg, Federal Republic of Germany, June 1986. Photograph courtesy of Gary Rhine.

The National and International Scene

first attended a conference of the National Congress of American Indians (NCAI) in 1968 in Omaha, Nebraska. I went simply out of curiosity. I had no deep interest in the organization. It wasn't until after the American Indian Movement was organized and I was elected national vice-chairman that I began to get interested in other national Indian organizations. I started attending NCAI conferences and I was even present at the first organizational meeting of the National Tribal Chairman's Association (NTCA).

The National Tribal Chairman's Association was the brainchild of the Nixon Administration. Evidently they felt that the National Congress of American Indians didn't speak adequately for Indian people, or perhaps they wanted more control over a group of Indians. Vice President Spiro Agnew was given the task of organizing the chairmen into a national body, so a meeting was convened in Kansas City, Missouri. I took one of the officers of the Santee Sioux Tribe to that first conference. My only purpose in being there was to act as a chauffeur for this old man. However, I was given credentials on the floor of the convention; I was made a voting member. When the issue was put before all of the tribal council members present, the vote came down: ninety-two against and eighty-nine for the creation of the National Tribal Chairman's Association. All of the tribal chairmen present and the Nixon people present were upset because they had lost the vote. They said that they were going to go ahead and create this organization anyway, and that's exactly what they did, around 1972 or so.

I tried to get involved with these two organizations,

because I felt they were very important to Indian people. During the 1970s, I was elected to serve on the education committee of the NCAI and the education committee of the NTCA. Later on I was elected to a cultural concerns committee at the NCIA. One of the products of the 1972 Trail of Broken Treaties march was the Twenty Points position paper. This comprehensive paper, which covered all aspects of Indian life, had been presented to the Nixon Administration and to various members of Congress. In response to this paper, and in response to pressure from Indian country, the United States Congress formed what came to be known as the American Indian Policy Review Commission, in 1974 or 1975. It was a joint Congressional committee co-chaired by Congressman Lloyd Meads and Senator James Abourezk. Eleven task forces were established to investigate the different issues confronting Indian people including sovereignty, education, health, economic development, all the way to alcohol and drug abuse. The executive director of the commission was a former schoolmate of mine at Neillsville Indian School during the Second World War.

When I called my friend to congratulate him on his appointment as executive director of the policy review commission, he told me, "I need some help, my friend. Would you be willing to serve on the policy review commission?" I said, "Sure, I will do anything I can do to help you." He talked it over with Congressman Meads and Senator Abourezk and they agreed. I was appointed to be the chairman of the alcohol and drug abuse task force of the American Indian Policy Review Commission. I was given a budget and told that my task force had one year to define all the problems of drug abuse and alcohol abuse among all Indian tribes and to prepare a report for the commission. This report would enable them to consider appropriate legislation. Two other Indian individuals were appointed to the task force with me. We began to devise a series of hearings. We sent out surveys requesting information about what the tribes needed in the way of alcohol and drug abuse programs. Working on this problem at

—From *Being Indian Is,* by Reuben Snake.
Drawing by Wesley Green, Jr.

BEING INDIAN IS. . . .

Meeting at least two dozen anthropologists before you are 21.

the national level was exciting. Eventually the report was completed and given to the commission. Then it was shared with the national Indian organizations. In response to our report, at its fall 1976 convention, the National Congress of American Indians passed a resolution declaring war on alcohol and drug abuse.

In 1980 I began another phase of activism. I had some friends who were employed at the top level of the Bureau of Indian Affairs. They called me up and asked if I was interested in becoming a delegate to the Eighth Congress of the Inter-American Indian Institute, a hemisphere-wide organization that is a subsidiary of the Organization of American States. They were convening the Eighth Congress at Mérida, in Mexico, in the fall of 1980. Although the Institute had been created back in 1940, for the first time in its history it was actually inviting real live Indians to the congress. Before that time, anthropologists, linguists, archaeologists, and social scientists made up the membership of this Inter-American Indian Institute. Official government representatives had been speaking on behalf of the various Indian populations within their respective countries. They had never ever had any real live Indians present at these congresses. Their Eighth Congress, in 1980, was the first time they were going to have some real Indians show up.

I was one of fifteen Indians selected by the State Department and the Department of the Interior to represent the Indian people of the United States at this very important gathering in Mérida. We were all flown to Washington, D.C., and given the standard propaganda by the State Department about how well things were going for Indian people in the nations throughout the Western Hemisphere. We knew differently. We had been communicating with various groups from throughout the Americas and were aware of the many atrocities that were still being perpetrated against Indians in Central and South America. So the State Department's point of view was taken with a grain of salt. Eventually the U.S. delegation was flown down. We all came separately. I flew from

Sioux City, Iowa, to New Orleans and took a flight from New Orleans to Mérida.

I had quite an adventure just getting from the Mérida airport to the hotel where I was supposed to stay. Of course, I don't speak Spanish and the welcoming delegation was at the wrong end of the airport when I arrived. So I never found out who was supposed to be welcoming me. Then I had to hire a taxi cab. Bartering to arrive at the price of the ride from the airport to the hotel was a lot of fun. He wanted to charge me fifty dollars and eventually I got him down to five dollars.

This was my very first trip into old Mexico and, except for my military service, my first journey outside the United States. I spent a really wonderful week in Mérida getting to know Indians from Central and South America. There were over a hundred Indians representing the different tribes throughout Central and South America at the conference. We had a good time getting to know each other and sharing our ideas.

One of the most significant things that happened was that the Sandinistas in Nicaragua sent a colonel over to represent the interests of Nicaraguan Indians. We were all well aware that the Sandinistas were killing Indians and enslaving them, putting them in internment camps and destroying their traditional villages. We knew all this, but the colonel stood there and told us lies about the good relationships the Sandinistas were enjoying with the Indian people. Then he made a statement about North American Indians. He claimed, "The United States government has sent some token Indians to this conference. Even though they have long hair and they're wearing beads, they're still only tokens of the United States government." His remark upset me terribly, because I was still considered a member of the American Indian Movement. So I made a public statement at the conference to the effect that I was not a token Indian. I was a member of the most militant Indian organization in the United States of America. And I didn't appreciate this Sandinista colonel's bullshit. My statement hit all the media in Mérida and created quite a stir.

That night there was a big reception sponsored by the Mexican president, Lopez Portillo. There was a lot of hustling and bustling about in the diplomatic ranks about how to bring this militant Indian to the table and have him make peace with the Sandinista colonel. A lot of pressure was put on me by United States State Department personnel and by representatives of the Mexican government and by some members of my own delegation.

They were saying that I should get up and shake hands with this colonel. I refused to do it. I stated, "I will not shake hands with any of them until I'm sure that the Sandinistas have stopped persecuting our people."

The next day, at the general assembly, I stood before the crowd. We had been instructed by the State Department that we were not to make any public statements, that we were not authorized to act on behalf of the United States government. So I told the people assembled, "Even though my government told me not to say anything, and even though my government says I'm not an authorized speaker for our government, I'm going to extend an invitation to you, to attend the ninth congress of this organization, which will be held in the United States of America." I did this because the United States government had shied away from bringing this organization into our country for forty years. The government didn't want to get embroiled in all the civil and human rights problems that would be brought up. They figured that as long as they could keep it out of the country, then they wouldn't have to be involved in it. But I made that statement and pledged, "Whatever's necessary for us to do, we will make sure that the Ninth Congress is held in the United States of America." That got me a standing ovation from all the Indian people present. It upset the State Department people, but I told them they would just have to live with it. That's eventually what happened. The Ninth Congress was held in 1985 in Santa Fe, New Mexico, and I served on the steering committee. That congress at Mérida was the beginning of my international involvement.

In 1982, the World Assembly of First Nations was convened in Regina, Saskatchewan. I was invited to speak on the health needs of Indian people. I stayed a week in Regina at the World Assembly of First Nations and met even more good brothers and sisters, not only Indian people from throughout the Western Hemisphere, but some Sami from Lapland (Finland), some aborigines from Australia, and some Maoris from New Zealand.

Throughout the 1980s I was also becoming more active in the Native American Church. I was invited to conduct Native American Church services here on this reservation, on the neighboring Omaha Reservation, in South Dakota, Iowa, Minnesota, and Wisconsin. I was invited down to Oklahoma to conduct a meeting and out to Colorado, New Mexico, Utah, Nevada, Idaho, and California. I was totally immersed in this Native American Church way of life at that point in time. I was constantly traveling and conducting meetings in various places for different relatives and friends throughout the country.

At the same time I was busy here with the tribe as the chairman, working to achieve the self-sufficiency objective that we had established. Then I began to get involved at the international level in Native American rights and environmental issues. Throughout the 1980s I was invited to sit on the boards of directors of probably fifteen national and international organizations, among them the First Nations Development Institute, the Seventh Generation Fund, the American Indian Law Resource Center, the Native Lands Institute, and the Americans for Indian Opportunity, a whole array of Indian organizations concerned with different issues connected with Indian people. I was terribly busy taking care of business for the Winnebago tribe, taking care of Native American Church business, serving on all these boards and commissions, and then participating in international activity.

In 1985 we were planning the Ninth Congress of the Inter-American Indian Institute to be held in Santa Fe, New Mexico. I was appointed to the steering committee that was established by the U.S. State Department and the Department of the Interior. I really wanted the story of Indians along the Atlantic coast and in Nicaragua to be heard by this group of people. So I called up Brooklyn Riviera, who was at that time the general coordinator of the MISURASATA organization which included representatives of the Sumo, Miskito, and Reva Indians of Nicaragua and asked if he would be willing to come and talk at this Ninth Congress. He said, "If you come and observe our negotiations with the Sandinistas, I'll consider coming and speaking."

He wanted me to observe so that I would have a clear understanding of the relationship between the Sandinistas and his organization. In May of 1985 I flew down to Bogotá, Colombia. The day before I left, my mother-in-law, Neola Walker, who was a member of the tribal council here in Winnebago, came to me and said, "You better not make this trip because I had a dream. I dreamed that you were surrounded by a bunch of little brown people and they took you hostage." Hearing her say that made me a little nervous. I called one of my friends in the Federal Bureau of Investigation and asked him about the situation in Bogotá, Colombia. He replied that it was one of the most dangerous places in the world for American people, that American agents went around armed twenty-four hours a day. They had to be extremely careful. He gave me the names of some agents whom I was to contact in case I had any difficulty whatsoever.

Several South American countries were trying to play the role of mediator between the Sandinistas and the Indian people of Nicaragua. I believe it was at the invitation of the president of Colombia that this negotiation session would take place in Bogotá, a neutral location acceptable to both the Sandinistas as well as the three native peoples of Nicaragua. I was one of perhaps twenty people that had been invited by Mr. Riviera to be observers at this negotiation session between his organization and the Sandinistas. I spoke very little, if any, Spanish. People in Bogotá made us welcome, and tried to help us as best they could. On the morning we were preparing to go to the building where the negotiation session was to take place, they herded us all into the lobby of the hotel where we were and they made us all stand in a group. Then the Colombian secret service checked all the entrances to the hotel. They gave a signal and around the corner came a truckload of Colombian GIs. They all jumped out of their truck and stood on each side of the doorway with automatic weapons in their arms. Then they marched us out into this little VW bus. There were about twenty of us and they were trying to pack us all in there. Of course they couldn't do it, so then we had to hire a couple of taxicabs, and this little caravan of a VW bus and a couple of taxicabs careened through the streets of Bogotá, surrounded by Colombian GIs and jeeps and trucks. We made our way to the Governor's Palace for the negotiation session. When we arrived there, the entire building was ringed with armed Colombian GIs. I began to realize that this was a serious situation. Anything could happen. We entered the building and there were only three or four people who were allowed directly into the negotiation session from our observer's group. The rest of us had to sit out in one of the rooms and wait for them. They took a break for dinner, which was rather fancy.

There was a break for dinner at the Governor's Palace. My American lawyer friend and I made the mistake of sitting at the wrong table. I guess everybody understood the Sandinistas were going to sit on one side and the other people on the other side. But we just walked in and sat down at the table where the Sandinistas were seated. Although that was a little bit embarrassing, we never left. We made it through dinner, and we made it through lunch the next day. But at this particular session, negotiations broke down. The Sandinistas weren't genuinely interested in settling their differences. They just wanted to accuse the MISURASATA organization of subversion and rebellion. There were various accusations thrown back and forth. Both groups walked away from the table at the end of the day without settling anything.

During this time I had continued my involvement with

the National Congress of American Indians and the National Tribal Chairmen's Association. I had attended the NCAI convention in Spokane, Washington, in 1984. At that conference I was asked to consider running for the presidency of the National Congress of American Indians, the oldest, largest, and most prestigious Indian organization in the country. Throughout 1984 and 1985 I thought about it and talked with my wife about it. She said, "Well, if you want to do it, go ahead. I'll try to support you in any way I can." As the time approached for me to begin campaigning to be the president of the NCAI I asked my tribal council if they had any objections. They told me it was fine with them. Then I went to the tribal chairmen's meeting, where the chairmen of all the tribes of the Aberdeen area, which encompasses North and South Dakota and Nebraska, come together on a regular basis. I asked for the endorsement of the Aberdeen area tribal chairmen. They gave it to me by resolution, one hundred percent unanimous endorsement for my candidacy. I think it was in September of 1985, at the annual convention in Tulsa, Oklahoma, that I was elected to be the president of the National Congress of American Indians.

It was a tense situation because I was regarded as an activist, radical Indian. Because I was extremely pro-Indian, the Department of Interior people felt I was going to cause them a lot of headaches as president of NCAI, and so they strongly endorsed a more moderate candidate. As you can guess, they did it all very quietly, not publicly, but behind the scenes. They felt that they could communicate better with their candidate than with me. That made the election a more intriguing situation, but I prevailed and became the president of the National Congress of American Indians.

The Department of Interior people were still upset with me as the Ninth Congress of the Inter-American Indian Institute was approaching. The Interior people were trying to find some way to keep me quiet and to minimize my involvement because I had been pressing the issue of getting real Indians to participate in this congress, not simply the usual government representatives, linguists, archaeologists, and anthropologists. We had put on a concerted drive to contact Indian organizations throughout Central and South America and Canada to send representatives to this Ninth Congress. And when the Ninth Congress convened in Santa Fe, New Mexico, in November of 1985, there must have been close to five hundred Indian people from throughout the Americas participating.

The Institute is a very, very rigid organization, a very conservative organization. They have established rules and procedures that they vigorously enforce during their conferences. It was a difficult time for us. All the Indian people present withdrew to caucus under the leadership of people like Bill Means from the International Treaty Council and other Indian activists. They immediately declared that any federal representative, any representative of any government, was not allowed in there. I was a member of the U.S. steering committee so I thought they were talking about me, and I got up to leave. My dear friend LaDonna Harris asked for the floor and informed them, "By doing what you just did, by asking all the governmental representatives to leave, you're throwing out the one man that made it possible for all of you to be here. This is Mr. Reuben Snake. He was the one that really carried on the struggle to see that all you Indian people were invited to this conference. And now you're throwing him out of your caucus." So they invited me back. When LaDonna's remarks were translated into the Spanish tongue for the South American Indians, they wanted to know what my last name, Snake, meant. They were informed, and I was immediately given a title, *El Grande Anaconda* ("the great anaconda").

We had quite a congress in Santa Fe. The people on the Navajo Reservation who were engaged in a struggle to remain at Black Mesa and who opposed the relocation program taking place in the joint use area, sent a large delegation. Naturally, the Hopis also came in force. The media was fascinated by these two groups bringing their problems before this international organization. One of the most significant issues which was raised at this momentous gathering concerned the importation of the sacred medicine, peyote, from Mexico into the United States. Because the supply of peyote in the United States is limited to Texas and was gradually declining, there wasn't enough medicine available to satisfy the needs of all of the members of the Native American Church. We began a dialogue between the Mexican government and the United States government with the hope of reaching an international agreement whereby Indians of the Native American Church could go into old Mexico and harvest the peyote and bring it back across the border. One thing led to another and pretty soon we had identified seven different sacred plants being utilized by different Indian groups throughout the Americas. Those groups were enduring the same kind of difficulties we faced with our use of peyote. They were using the sacred mushrooms, and the coca leaf and Ayahuasca from Brazil and Peru. So instead of passing a resolution concerning only peyote, the resolution that was finally drafted called for an international conference on how the governments of these various nations could support Indians and help them retain their cultures and their spiritual ways by providing for the movement of these sacred plants from one country to another, wherever the indigenous religions that use them were being practiced. A resolution calling for an international conference to address this issue was adopted at this Ninth Congress.

There were many other problems. Indian people were being slaughtered in Guatemala, Nicaragua, and other countries. Naturally, the United States didn't want that fact brought out. They were trying to keep a lid on it. We were trying to make it public. Because I was among those trying to get this message out, I was branded as a threat to the peace and tranquility of the conference. Once again, FBI agents were assigned to watch my family and me as well as my nephew, Douglas Long, who was then the president of the Native American Church of North America. He was traveling with us and we were constantly under surveillance by the Federal

Bureau of Investigation during this week-long conference in Santa Fe.

During the Santa Fe conference I was put off and stalled and sort of diverted by Department of Interior people who were participants in this conference. But eventually I managed to bring a representative group. During the conference, the steering committee had breakfast every morning to talk about how things were going. So at one of these breakfast sessions I persuaded the people in charge to hear from a representative group of Indians from Guatemala and Nicaragua and other places. They allowed a small delegation of ten of them to come into the breakfast and to state their case. I think that hearing what these people had to say about what was happening to them had a tremendous impact on the U.S. governmental representatives. That event helped make the conference more amenable and more open to the Indian people.

By the end of the conference the Indian group had drafted a number of resolutions that were put before the voting body. Only the governmental representatives could vote so all these resolutions were laid in their hands and they adopted most of them with very little change. In that manner the goal we were trying to accomplish there was achieved. The real story of the plight of the Indian people in Central and South America was brought out.

I was also invited to a major international conference in Vancouver, British Columbia. The Canadian government was attempting to find ways of dealing with economic problems facing the Indian communities in their country. They looked to the United States Indians to provide some role models. Participating in this international gathering on Indian economic development in the United States and Canada added to my experience at the international level.

During this time of political activism I was also active as a Roadman in the Native American Church. The Iroquois people have a particular wampum belt that shows the connectedness, the interdependence, between spirituality and political life. This connection is something I have found to be true. When I sit in a prayer meeting I pray for the well-being of my people and I pray that we will obtain all the things that we need. I pray for adequate housing, for decent education, for economic opportunity and other things, but I just can't pray and let it go at that. I have to go out and do something about it. That's why I got so deeply involved in all these projects, because I was trying to make my prayers effective. It wasn't enough to just be praying about them; these were issues that I was moved to do something about. That's what led to my involvement in all these things. The 1980s were the busiest time of my life. Like I said, I was elected to serve on these different boards and commissions throughout the United States and even internationally.

During the latter part of the 1980s I was approached by some people who have since become very dear friends of mine. They represented the Center for International Cooperation, a non-governmental organization of the United Nations, based in Maryland. Through their efforts and the efforts of the Americans for Indian Opportunity and a couple of other major environmental organizations, a conference called "Earth Walk" was convened near Sydney, Australia. The purpose of this conference was to have indigenous people from different places in the world speak to these environmentally conscious groups of people about how to have respect for the earth, how to treat the earth in a manner which could stop the pollution of the earth and the air and the water, and how to start turning things around and improve our situation. So I was one of a handful of Indian people invited from North America.

In 1989 I flew down to Sydney, Australia, and opened the conference by conducting a pipe ceremony. We had a whole week there to discuss all the issues. It was very interesting to come into contact with powerful environmental groups such as Greenpeace and Earth Repair Action. I was pleased to see them sitting and listening to the elders of the various indigenous populations. We had Indians from North America, aborigines from Australia, Maoris from New Zealand, tribal leaders from the continent of Africa, and Arabs from the Middle East. It was a good cross-section of indigenous people from different corners of the world who came to share their understanding of the world with these environmental groups.

Probably the most positive outcome of the conference was the adoption of a resolution that the representatives would take back to their respective countries to inspire more respect for the earth and to implement programs and activities to stop the pollution of the earth. The primary message proclaimed by this gathering was to teach people that the earth is our mother and provides for all of us and takes care of our daily needs, and that therefore we should have respect for the earth and try to do something about improving our relationship with the earth. That effort to have all nations adopt this resolution is still being carried on.

Another event which took place there was organized by Chief Jake Swamp, of the Mohawk people, one of the nations of the Iroquois Confederacy. He was charged with the responsibility of planting trees of peace throughout the world. He had a tree planting ceremony at the Earth Walk conference and prayed for peace and understanding in the world.

Somewhere around 1985 I was approached by a German immigrant from the city of Lincoln, Nebraska. He told me about an event that occurs in northern Germany, in a place called Bad Segeberg. Every summer the city produces a Hollywood-type show based on the writings of Karl May. Karl May was a German who never set foot in the United States but had a very romantic image of Indian people and wrote all these fantastic stories about Indians, particularly Chief Winnetou, the great Apache chief.[1] One of the major economic activities in that town was to perform a summer-long pageant in their outdoor amphitheater. They had never invited a Native American to participate. So this German immigrant from Lincoln asked if I would have any interest in creating some intercultural activity and perhaps an opportunity for some economic activities to go along with it.

We made arrangements to fly to Germany. When we arrived there we were met by the *bergermeister,* the mayor of the town, and a number of other dignitaries. They wined and dined us for a couple of days, explained their whole operation, and extended an invitation for me to return with a small group of Indian people to participate in their summer-long activities. I agreed to do that. When I came back to Winnebago I spoke to some of my relatives. The result was that in the summer of 1986 I took my son and one of my brothers and three young ladies over to Bad Segeberg, Germany. That amphitheater was jam-packed. There were about ten thousand people, all quite thrilled that real live Indians had appeared at their Karl May festival. Media people from all the different magazines and newspapers and television stations came to cover the occasion of Winnebagos showing up in Germany. We had positive experiences while we were there for this cultural exchange.

There really was no place to fit real Indian culture into the performance, but just prior to the opening of every show we would go down into the arena and put on a fifteen minute presentation of our culture, including singing and dancing. The Germans were willing to construct a building for genuine Indian arts and crafts. They had been selling beadwork made in Hong Kong. They built a whole new building, called the Nebraska House. It houses a lot of genuine Native American arts and crafts. We were invited to bring all of the arts and crafts that we could possibly bring for sale there. It put some money into the pockets of Indian people and established a relationship between the state of Nebraska, the Winnebago tribe, and the German people. That relationship is still growing today.

Since then the German people from Bad Segeberg have been making an annual trip to Nebraska. Each year they send a delegation over here to further strengthen our ties and to look at other ways of improving the intercultural activity and improving economic opportunity for both of us.

One of the results of this activity was that I was honored

by the state of Nebraska for my work at the international level. My efforts attracted more Germans to Nebraska, bringing us their tourist dollars. For that reason I was recently honored by the state of Nebraska.

I think Germans admire Native Americans because we exemplify their concept of free spirits. Prior to the coming of the White man, we Indian people were able to travel across the face of the land without any oppression and without creating problems for anybody. We were just free people, living our lives the way that we wanted. Perhaps the Germans were envious of that. Perhaps they wanted to be that way too.

Many Germans became engrossed in the different aspects of American Indian culture. They read books on Indian lore and learned how to do beadwork and leatherwork and how to make tepees and various other things. German people are well known for their technical accuracy when they undertake to do something. It was impressive to be in Germany and see them wearing Indian clothing such as leather shirts, leather leggings adorned with beadwork, and feathered headdresses that they had made for themselves. It was impressive because they had never been taught by an Indian; they just learned all this out of a book.

Reuben Snake relaxes with young relatives after celebrating his twenty-fifth anniversary of marriage to Kathy Snake. Photograph courtesy of Kifaru Productions.

Coping with Heart Attacks

Eventually all of this activity, conducting numerous Native American Church services all over the country, running the tribal government, serving on all these different boards and commissions, and doing all this international travel took a toll on me. In October of 1986 I suffered a major heart attack. Up until that time I was doing everything at full bore. About two weeks after my initial heart attack I suffered total cardiac arrest. That really slowed me down. The doctor told me I couldn't keep on going at the pace that I was used to going. I had to start cutting back on a lot of things.

There wasn't any particular incident that created severe stress. I suppose it was just everything heaped together that was causing all the stress. I had been invited to speak at an Aberdeen area tribal chairmen's meeting. The Aberdeen tribal chairmen were impressed with the efforts of the Winnebago tribe to develop a tribal grocery store, a tribal auto truck service center, a tribal farm, and various other enterprises. They wanted to hear from me how we had developed our economy.

I got on the airplane to fly to Bismarck, North Dakota, where the meeting was being held. When I got to the Minneapolis airport I began to have the sensation that something was going wrong, but I tried to ignore it. I went on from Minneapolis to Bismarck, but by the time I got to Bismarck I knew there was something seriously wrong. I spent the whole night and part of the morning just lying in bed. Then I went to the meeting that afternoon and I did my workshop. That evening I got on an airplane and flew back to Sioux City, Iowa.

By the time I got back home to Winnebago I knew that I was experiencing a heart attack. I thought I could just be macho about it, that I didn't have to go to the hospital. So I just stayed home suffering pains in my back and my arms throughout the night. Finally the next morning I made up my mind, "Well, you better go see what's going on with you." So I got ready and went down to the hospital, which is not far from my house. When I told the doctor, "I think I'm having problems with my heart," they hooked me up and did an EKG on me. They reported, "You're having a heart attack. We better rush you to Sioux City."

During my first heart attack I never lost consciousness. It wasn't until sometime later, when I was in Wisconsin, that I had total cardiac arrest. My wife had told the tribal council and everybody she knew that I needed rest. I was staying at home and people were coming to my house to ask for my help: "I need to get a loan" or "I need to have some help to get this housing." I hated to refuse them. My wife insisted, "You can't be doing this. You can't just keep on doing the things you're doing. You've got to rest. I'm going to get you away from here." So she loaded up the car and took me off to Wisconsin. She said, "They'll take care of you up there. You can just rest and relax and visit your family and when you're all rested up, then we'll come home." So that's the way it was.

We were staying with my younger brother, Roger, in his home. On the morning of November 22, 1986, I suffered total cardiac arrest. I had to be rushed to the hospital. Then they flew me back from Wisconsin to Sioux City. I was put into the hospital there and after thorough examination they suggested that I go to the University of Nebraska. After further tests, they recommended that I undergo open heart surgery. So I had open heart surgery in the latter part of 1986.

My heart problems were not totally unexpected. I had suffered from various symptoms. I was very overweight. I knew, probably two years before the actual heart attack, that I was having trouble. But I have a stubborn mentality and I thought, "Well, I'm man enough to overcome anything." I

174

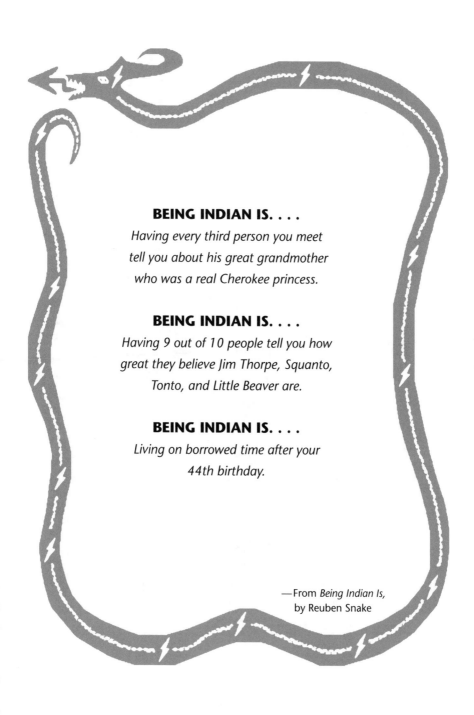

BEING INDIAN IS. . . .

Having every third person you meet tell you about his great grandmother who was a real Cherokee princess.

BEING INDIAN IS. . . .

Having 9 out of 10 people tell you how great they believe Jim Thorpe, Squanto, Tonto, and Little Beaver are.

BEING INDIAN IS. . . .

Living on borrowed time after your 44th birthday.

—From *Being Indian Is,*
by Reuben Snake

Reuben Snake, Winnebago Reservation, Nebraska, November 1992.
Photograph by Ginger Miles.

never paid attention when I used to get this angina and different symptoms of that sort. As far back as 1985, I suffered a bout of phlebitis. At that time the doctor advised me that I probably had a heart problem.

After I underwent surgery, I was put on various medications. I was taking about thirty pills a day for a brief while. That really bothered me. I thought, "Who has to live in this way, to survive by taking thirty or so pills every damn day?" I was really frustrated by the fact that I couldn't keep on doing everything I was doing. I had to scale back on a lot of my activities. I felt that I was doing important work and that it was essential for me to keep on doing that work. I have, since that time, found out it's really not so essential.

I was still the president of the National Congress of American Indians up through 1987. I was asked if I was going to run for re-election and I chose not to run due to my poor health. I only served the one term, from 1985 to 1987, as president of National Congress of American Indians.

My drive to achieve was based on a personal commitment. I had told the Creator back in 1974 that if He would help me, if He would bless me with the good things of life, and if I could be happy with my family, I would devote my time and energy to serving His people. It was my personal commitment, not a cultural imperative, that motivated me to do all these things. I was trying to live up to that commitment I made to God, to the Great Spirit, that I would wait on His people and do what had to be done to help them.

I continued serving as tribal chairman even after my heart attack. After my open heart surgery I was incapacitated for a while. I didn't go to the tribal office, I stayed at home throughout the early part of 1987, and turned the reigns of government over to the vice-chairman and the rest of the council. In May of 1987 I felt strong enough to come back and try to do things. When I did come back to work, I limited my time. Whereas before I was spending maybe ten to twelve hours a day on tribal issues, I reduced that to maybe six to eight hours a day. In 1988, when my term was up, I chose to not be the chairman anymore. I was re-elected to the tribal council, but I said I didn't want to be the chairman or hold any of the executive officer positions.

I also decided to cut back on my traveling. I let people know that I wouldn't be traveling hither and yon to conduct Native American Church meetings. Formerly my wife and my son and maybe my nephew and my grandchildren would get into the van and off we would go to take care of a prayer meeting in California, or maybe Colorado or New Mexico. I just couldn't drive that way anymore. I tried to let the people on the various boards and commissions know that I wouldn't be present at every meeting that they held. I still wanted to be involved but I wouldn't be flying all over the country either. So I just tried to scale everything back and slow down.

The heart attack had a profound impact on my family. They all were terribly concerned about my well-being. My daughters used to cry and say, "Dad, we don't want to lose you." My wife was always there, constantly trying to make me comfortable. Sometimes we used to laugh about certain things that were happening. The first morning that I decided to go back to work, she put me in the shower, and she cleaned me up, just like a little kid. She dressed me, combed my hair, and put my clothes and jacket on me. She put an orange in one pocket and a banana in the other, exactly like sending a little kid off to school. Then she pushed me out the door and said, "Now, go to work." That's how attentive she was to me. She's still that way today. She still waits on me all the time, trying to make me feel comfortable and make me feel good. My children did their best to give me their moral support. I always was thankful that I had a wife and children. But my heart attack drew us a lot closer together. I became even more appreciative of them and more grateful for their presence in my life. I think the whole experience brought us closer together as a family.

My heart problems also forced me to cut back on my activities as a Roadman in the Native American Church. Ever since October of 1974, when I was given those instruments

Reuben Snake receives ribbon shirt in giveaway ceremony at the annual Winnebago Homecoming celebration, circa 1988. Photograph courtesy of Darren Snake.

by my clan father, Michael WhiteSnake, I had been totally involved in the Native American Church. I remember the very first meeting that I conducted on December 7, 1974, in the foothills of the Rocky Mountains, south of Denver, Colorado. One of my relatives that lived in that area had invited me out to conduct a memorial service for her mother. The plan was to have this prayer meeting at some Sioux relative's home where prayer meetings were held on a regular basis. Evidently the information hadn't been conveyed, because the Sioux relatives were gone and their home was locked up. Eventually we went out in the foothills at a place south of Denver called Morrison, Colorado. We put up a tepee on December 7. The snow was about two feet deep on the ground. With the wind chill factor it was fifty-five degrees below zero. My introduction to being a Roadman was to cope with the physical challenge of putting up this tepee in the middle of all of this cold weather, high winds, and deep snow, and then conduct my first prayer meeting. It was a bitterly cold night and all the people who came to support me really had to suffer through that experience of sitting up in a tepee on a night where the temperature was fifty-five below zero with the wind chill factor. It was very strengthening to go through that experience.

Since I've been a Roadman of the Native American Church I've baptized somewhere around a hundred and forty people in ceremonies I have conducted throughout the country. Probably one of the most memorable of these baptismal events occurred around 1984 when my adopted father, Moses Hensley, the son of Albert Hensley, came to me to say that he and his sisters had been having a discussion about a memorial service for their father. They asked me to conduct a memorial service for his father. The primary goal was to bring Albert Hensley's offspring, his grandchildren and great-grandchildren, to the fireplace to have them named and baptized. At that particular prayer meeting I baptized and christened nineteen of Albert Hensley's grandchildren and great-grandchildren. That was a very great honor for me. The memory of that meeting has stayed with me all this time and brought me very close to the Hensley family.

Another experience I had was in making a relationship with Louis Ballard. I call him "brother." He's a very prominent musician, well known for his symphonies and other compositions. He takes Indian themes and transforms them into symphonies. He has performed all over the world.

Louis is a Quapaw and a Cherokee Indian. After I got to know him, I believe it was around 1978, he invited me to come and pray for his Quapaw people, who were beginning to lose touch with the Native American Church. There were just a handful of Quapaws who were actively participating in the Native American Church. They didn't hold meetings anymore in their community of Quapaw, Oklahoma. So my brother wanted me to come and pray and light the fire and bring the traditions back to the Quapaw people. I organized a trip to Oklahoma with some of my Winnebago relatives, my Sioux relatives, and my Omaha relatives. Twenty-four of us traveled down to Quapaw and had a prayer meeting with this handful of Quapaws. There were also some Shawnees who were related to the Quapaws who came and sat up in the meeting. That experience was very meaningful to me because two eagles showed up while we were putting up the tepee. I felt they were like spirit messengers coming to tell us that what we were doing was good. And my brother, Louis, was very, very pleased with the outcome of the meeting. After that the church came alive again for the Quapaw people. They began having prayer meetings at their community and started drawing people back to the church.

We traveled all over the country fulfilling people's requests for prayers. Conducting meetings among different groups was very, very uplifting. I remember conducting a Native American Church wedding service for my nephew and his young Ute bride on the Ute Reservation in Wide Rocks, Utah. I remember conducting a prayer meeting in Washo country, south of Lake Tahoe. I even conducted prayer meetings as far west as the San Francisco Bay Area. Over the years I had many truly positive experiences and developed a lot of friendships and relationships with people representing many different tribes from here in the Midwest clear out west to California. When I had this heart attack I couldn't travel to these distant points anymore to conduct these services. Having to curtail my activity as a Roadman is something I feel bad about. I wish that I could still do it because I really enjoy those relationships with all those different people and now I don't get to see them as often as I used to.

When I first went back to work at the Winnebago tribal council I had to go real slowly. I tried to delegate as much responsibility and authority as I could to various tribal council people so they could carry on with the attainment of the goals and objectives of our self-sufficiency program. Gradually over time the tribal council, the vice-chairman, secretary, treasurer, and other council members assumed greater responsibility for developing these activities, and gave me some rest.

The Native American Church and the Four Hills of Life

My involvement in environmental issues has been growing steadily since 1989, when I attended the Earth Walk international conference on the environment down in Australia. In 1990 we planned an Earth Day activity here on this reservation. We were right in the middle of getting that off the ground on April 18, 1990, when we received word through the media that the United States Supreme Court had reached its decision in the now-infamous case *Employment Division of Oregon v. Smith*. In that case the Court ruled that there was no constitutional protection for the sacramental use of peyote by bona fide Native American Church members. Al Smith was a Klamath Indian who had been fired from a private alcohol and drug abuse treatment program because he admitted participating in a Native American Church ceremony. His employers had designated peyote as a drug. They claimed that when Smith used peyote in a Native American Church meeting, he violated the rules of their organization. Al Smith filed for unemployment benefits and was upheld by the Appeals Court in the State of Oregon. He was upheld all the way to the State Supreme Court in Oregon, but Oregon's attorney general took the case to the United States Supreme Court. The Supreme Court's decision was shocking, not only because it jeopardizes Native Americans, but because of its detrimental effect on the whole religious life of the American people. There have been more than eighteen cases so far which have been controlled by the Smith ruling. These cases have abridged the religious freedom of the Amish people and of Moslems, Jews, and others.

It would seem impossible that the Supreme Court justices

could have reached that decision if they had actually attended a prayer meeting of the Native American Church. People often have strong negative stereotypes about those of us who use this divine medicine. They regard us as dope addicts and imagine that we are into some kind of weird or strange occult activity. But when they come to the meetings of the Native American Church, when they sit in the circle and witness this poor humble way of life, they change their minds. I've seen that happen to a lot of people who came out of curiosity, including doctors and lawyers. They have generally learned something that changes their mind. Then they begin to appreciate where we're coming from. I think that if any members of the Supreme Court could have had that kind of experience that such a ruling wouldn't have been handed down. But the current Supreme Court, being the ultra-conservative institution that it is, based their decision on hearsay.

At any rate, we were preparing for the Earth Day activity when this ruling came down. Various media people called to ask me what my feelings and thoughts were because they knew that I was a Native American Church person. I was also called by the president of the Native American Church of the Omaha tribe. They were having their annual church meeting on that very day, so I went down to the Omaha Reservation and talked to them and they elected me to be their official spokesperson, to look for some means to correct this grievous error. The Omahas hoped I could help devise some kind of legislative initiative that would be passed by the Congress and would protect our use of the sacred medicine peyote. The following week the membership of the Native American Church of the Winnebago tribe of Nebraska also chose me to be their official spokesperson.

The Native American Church of North America called an emergency meeting of its Executive Committee. I went to Denver to attend this meeting and present my ideas to the Church officers. I announced that I was going to organize a Native American Religious Freedom Project to educate the

AIRFA Hearings, Portland, Oregon, March 1992. Senate Committee on Indian Affairs, hearings on amending the American Indian Religious Freedom Act of 1978. *(Left to right)* Ola Cassadore, Traditional Leader, San Carlos Apache Reservation; Reuben Snake, Religious Leader (Native American Church), Winnebago Reservation; Peterson Zah, President, Navajo Nation; *(standing)* Walter Echo-Hawk, Senior Staff Attorney, Native American Rights Fund. (The other two gentlemen are unknown to me.) Photograph © Chuck Williams.

American public about the significance of this ruling and to teach them what the Native American Church truly stands for, to explain our theology, philosophy, and history. I received the endorsement of the Native American Church of North America.

From April of 1990 until now I have been immersed in this effort to work on the Native American Religious Freedom Project and to enact national legislation that strengthens the American Indian Religious Freedom Act. This legislation has been proposed for the protection of the people that utilize this Holy Medicine and for other religious issues confronting Indian people, issues concerning sacred sites and the use of animal parts and the human rights of incarcerated Native Americans. These are the religious freedom issues that have been addressed by the amendments. In May 1993, Senator Inouye of the Senate Committee on Indian Affairs introduced a bill (S. 1021) containing these amendments into the United States Senate. We are very hopeful that sometime in the not too distant future Congress will adopt these amendments giving us some protection for our spiritual ways.

My life story can help younger Native Americans learn that it is possible for anybody to overcome their problems. They can understand that these problems are generated by all that has happened to Indian people. Many laws, such as the Indian Citizenship Act, the Indian Reorganization Act, and the General Land Allotment Act, were initiated on the part of well-meaning non-Indian people. All their legislation and activities have actually turned out to be detrimental to Indians, causing us to lose control of our land and our lives, and to be governed by paternalistic governmental agencies such as the Bureau of Indian Affairs. All the problems that these institutions have generated for Indian people can be overcome. But Indian people must make a commitment.

That's what I preach to younger people today: sacrifice. In the old days our ancestors had, as a regular part of life, a sacrifice for the well-being of the people. Whether that was sun dancing or something else, sacrifices were made on behalf of

Reuben Snake *(center)* leads an informal prayer meeting at his home for the success of the documentary film, *The Peyote Road,* January 1992. To his left is Johnny White Cloud, an Oto-Missouri peyote Roadman, and on his right is James Botsford. The film was made as part of the campaign to restore religious freedom to the Native American Church. Photograph by Phil Cousineau.

Reuben Snake, January 1992, during the filming of *The Peyote Road*. Photograph courtesy of Kifaru Productions.

Reuben Snake during an interview for the documentary film, *The Peyote Road,* in Santa Fe, New Mexico. Photograph courtesy of Kifaru Productions.

the people. It has to be that way again today if we intend to overcome all these problems. We have to learn what sacrifice means. We have to give up the good times. We have to give up the alcohol and all the party times. We have to get serious about our lives and concentrate on the good things that are there for us to have if we just get ourselves together and go after them.

I also believe one must try to develop one's mind in order to discipline oneself. Self-discipline is necessary; nobody else is going to discipline a person so that person does things right. Each of us is going to have to do that for himself or herself. That doesn't mean one has to be assimilated. One can go out and acquire the tools provided by the White man's education. One can learn how to become a lawyer, a doctor, an engineer, a teacher, a social worker, or whatever. But one must take that teaching and bring it back to one's people. It should be brought back to our people and used among our people. Today a lot of young Indian people have become disconnected with their own culture. They go out and they get an education and they just gravitate into the mainstream. They move to some urban area, get themselves a job, and then they forget about being Indian. But many others get the credentials and come back to their home communities and try to make a difference.

I believe that the foundation of all of our lives should be our spirituality. No matter what one plans to do with one's life, one should develop a spiritual relationship with the Creator and the Divine Creation. To do so means one has to learn from the elders; one has to take time and get connected with one's elders and listen to those elders. They're going to say things to us and show us things that are vital for us to develop our spirituality.

There wasn't any particular individual who motivated me to get back into the Native American Church. If I was to designate anybody it would be my brother Sterling Snake, who was about five years older than I. As I told you, he had contracted scleroderma as a young man serving in the South

Pacific. During his lifetime he went to several hundred Native American Church meetings to help himself cope with life. After I got out of the service, there were times when I'd go to prayer meetings with him. He would talk to me and tell me how much this medicine meant to him and how it could improve one's life. In addition to him, there were many elders that I associated with from time to time who impressed me with their sincerity and their humility and their wisdom. I heard them say, "The medicine is the teacher and it teaches us all about life. So if you really want to understand life you have to come sit down around the light of this Holy Fire and eat this medicine and open up your mind to the Creation and to the Creator."

As I've come along through life, I've tried to pay attention to what the old people say. I hear them talking about the four hills of life that we all have to walk. They say we're on a journey. We're climbing these four hills. They talk about this first hill being your own personal self. From the time we are born until we grow to adulthood, we are going through life's experience and we are supposed to be learning something about our place in the Divine Creation. That first hill of life has to do with the individual, how one develops all of the personal gifts that the Creator has given each of us. Sometime after one reaches that stage of adulthood, each of us will meet another human being, a person of the opposite sex, some person we will be drawn to and whom we will ask to share our life. That's the beginning of the second hill of life. From then on one is no longer responsible merely for one's self. One is no longer required only to look after one's own personal needs. Now one has a life to make. From then on as we walk down this road of life we have to make adjustments and be considerate of this other individual. We must shape our thinking and mold our thinking in that manner as we walk down this road with another human being. As we go along together as man and wife we are going to be blessed with children. These children are going to come into our lives and that's going to increase our responsibility because we are taught that when we bring life into this world we have to be responsible for that life. We have to do our best to bring this person up, to make sure they are walking in a right way and walking on the good road. So we have to devote time and energy to that end so that this person is not going to go astray. So that's the second hill of life that consists of being dedicated to our mate and to our children.

Then one reaches a certain age where one's children grow up to be the same size that we are. They're going to know something about life if we did our job adequately and well. They're going to do the same thing that we did. They're going to get married and eventually have children. When our children have children, that's the beginning of the third hill of life. These grandchildren of ours are going to become very special to us. We are going to want the very best for them. Because we have lived as long as we have, we're going to be able to share life's experience with them. We're going to be able to help their parents in that way. We're going to be able to tell these little people the meaning of life and how to walk this road of life to avoid all the pitfalls and the dangers of life and to have a good and happy life.

Our grandchildren are going to walk in the footsteps of their parents who are going to be walking in our footsteps. So we are walking down this road of life, climbing these hills of life, and our offspring are coming along behind us. They'll find a mate and they'll get married and they'll have children. And when our grandchildren start having children, when we have great-grandchildren, then they say that's the fourth hill of life that we are ascending. By then the Great Spirit will have crowned us with the gift of life, by turning all the hairs on our heads white. Just like the great bald eagle, we'll be white-headed. That's a blessing from the Creator. And one is going to continue to lay down footsteps, the footprints in which one's children, grandchildren, and now one's great-grandchildren, are going to be walking. As one lays down these footprints one has to be very careful to insure that one does not lead one's offspring astray. That's what the

BEING INDIAN IS. . . .
Respecting your elders who have earned it.

BEING INDIAN IS. . . .
Having the greatest grandparents in the world.

BEING INDIAN IS. . . .
*Watching your daughter give away her only
pair of overshoes to her friend because she
has to walk six blocks to school and her
friend lives in the country.*

BEING INDIAN IS. . . .
*Feeding anyone and everyone who comes
to your door hungry, with whatever you have.*

—From *Being Indian Is,*
by Reuben Snake

elders say. One must stay close to the Holy Fireplace and practice these spiritual ways.

We must have compassion and respect and honor for our fellow humans. All these virtues are needed in order for our offspring to have a full and rewarding and happy life. This is what our old people have talked about, the four hills of life. The four hills symbolize that we are making an ascent into the spirit world. We are going uphill all the time. Sometime after we have fulfilled all of our duties and obligations, we will go on into the spirit world. It's like ascending into heaven. That's what we are working towards.

When I reflect back upon my life I feel that's what I'm doing today. I feel a certain amount of regret over my early life, a period when I didn't pay attention to what the old people were saying. I went and did what I wanted to do. I could see my mistakes in my children.

My biggest mistake was being involved with alcohol. I was admonished early on not to become involved with alcohol but I drank anyway. Even though I knew it wasn't good for me, I went ahead and did it. Drinking led to a lot of other things, like getting into drunken brawls and other damaging things and winding up on skid row. All that damage was due to abuse of alcohol. That's why I say I have some regrets about that because I see it in my children. I tell them over and over and my wife tells them over and over that drinking is not good. Nevertheless, some of them do it. When I think about it I realize, "That's exactly the way you were. You didn't pay attention when they said that to you. Now look, you're saying that to your children and they're not paying attention to you." That is what I'm talking about when I refer to what the elders tell us, "When you put these footprints down, be very careful because your children are going to follow along. They're not going to do what you say, they're going to do what you do."

If one can put aside the alcohol and concentrate on spiritual development, one will find life is very fulfilling. That person is going to be a lot happier and is going to get along better in life. That's what I discovered. I didn't become immediately a financial success. I didn't have all the money in the world. I didn't have all the material things, but I found happiness.

I always use this old cliché when I talk to young people. "Happiness is not doing what you like to do but learning to like what you have to do." There's a lot of truth to that. If you can learn to like the spiritual side of your life, which is what we should be doing, then you're going to feel a lot better. Life becomes very rewarding if one learns to like going to Native American Church meetings, or whatever spiritual pathway one is following. If it is not just an obligation, not just a duty to save one's soul, if it becomes something that one really enjoys doing, then life becomes very rewarding.

Kathy Snake poses with husband Reuben Snake, circa 1982. Photograph courtesy of Kifaru Productions.

Kinship and the Spirit World

According to what I understand from our elders, we were in the spirit world prior to being born on this earth. Then we are born into this earthly plane and we walk this earthly road of life. Our lives seem to be devoted to getting back into the spirit world. Some people refer to it as "the happy hunting ground," some people call it "God's holy kingdom." In my mind, it's a place where there's all that one could possibly imagine to make one happy.

I had an experience one time when one of my elderly aunts passed away. She had lost a son many years earlier, when he was just fifteen years old. I hadn't really thought about him for a long, long time. I was just a little boy when he died. But I really cherished this aunt of mine. She was like a mother to me. She used to treat me very kindly. When she died I couldn't go to her funeral service. I was at home and I was praying. I was living in Omaha at the time. I prayed for her eternal happiness. Now that she had left this earthly plane, I prayed that she would be happy in the spirit world. I went to bed with that thought in mind. While I was sleeping, I had this dream. I saw a lady sitting on a hillside covered with beautiful grass. I could hear birds singing and there was a light that filled the heavens. That light just made everything look real nice. This lady was sitting under the shade of a tree and she was wearing a traditional Winnebago dress. She was brushing her hair. In my dream I looked at her real closely and determined that it was my aunt sitting there. And she looked very happy. She looked young. She looked full of life.

All of a sudden I could hear the pounding of hooves off in the distance. Then up over the hill came this horse with a young Indian riding it. This man and his horse rode right up to where my aunt was sitting under this tree. In my dream I thought, "Now who is this? Who is this on the horse?" When he jumped off that horse and I looked at him, I could see it was my cousin, who had died many years before. He smiled at his mother and he picked her up and put her on the horse. Then they rode on up the hill and disappeared from my sight. Now that to me is what the spirit world is all about.

Having that kind of experience has made me a strong believer in the ways of our people. As I mentioned, while I was growing up I was subjected to a lot of proselytizing by very White Christian representatives. Of course, they never talked about these kinds of experiences with me. They talked to me about the saving grace of Jesus Christ, and how, if I followed Jesus Christ, I would be rewarded with eternal life and God's heavenly kingdom. They talked about eternal life, but they could never really graphically portray for me what it was all about. But my own people have done that for me. My own elders have taught me this way so that I could have these dreams, so that I could see into the spirit world with my spiritual eye, so that I could comprehend the goodness and the vitality of life that is there. I could never get that insight from any place other than from my own cultural background, my own elders.

My experiences have shown me that the family has an enormously different meaning among Native Americans. Having lived a good part of my life in a non-Indian environment, I noticed that families are confined to the nuclear relationship: father, mother, son, and daughter. It doesn't go much beyond that. Whereas in the Indian world, right from the very beginning of our lives, we are taught how we are related to everyone around us. Somebody might be considered a third or fourth cousin, but within our kinship system they are regarded as our uncle or our aunt or our brother or our sister or our niece or our nephew. That emphasis on having close kinship ties is reinforced throughout our lives. We are taught to respect these relationships.

Let me give you an example from my life. There's a very elderly lady who was told in her childhood that the male members of the Snake Clan were her grandfathers and that she should always respect male members of the Snake Clan and call them *Choka,* grandfather. So even though she's around ninety years old and I'm only fifty, she still calls me "grandfather" because she was told to. She was advised to treat me just like she would treat her own grandfather. When I came to her home, for any reason, she would always sit me down at the table and put food before me and give me something nice to drink, perhaps cold water to drink, and sit down and chat with me. Maybe she would present me with some Indian tobacco or some other gift. This is the way that she treated her own grandfather so this is the way she was taught to treat me.

These are the kind of teachings that are handed down from generation to generation: that we're all related, all connected in one way or another, and we should have respect for people who are related and honor them and take care of them. So in regard to this elderly lady who calls me "grandpa," whenever she wants something, all she has to do is tell us what she wants and we're going to do it for her. That is what makes Indian life a whole lot different than existence in the rest of our society. We try to honor these family ties and to honor these relationships from generation to generation so that we can all live harmoniously together.

I feel sad that a large segment of our tribal society has drifted away from these cultural teachings. For them, others are just "Joe," "Sam," or "Harry." We are no longer treated as a "grandpa" or an "uncle," or as a "brother." Many of our people have accepted the values of the dominant society and they don't honor those family relationships anymore. But for those of us that do, it's really good. It really is fulfilling.

My grandmother, my father's mother, had several sisters and only one of them is alive today. All the rest of her family has passed on. She's the oldest living member of our tribe today. She'll be ninety-eight years old in July. She's the one who assumed the responsibility for all of her sisters' offspring.

We are a large family now, being the offspring of the Greywolf sisters. So Minnie Greywolf Littlebear is the last remaining grandmother that we have. She's the one who concerns herself with our well-being, prays for us, and does other things for us. For example, when I had developed occlusion in my heart and was in the hospital in Omaha, I was told I had to go on dialysis and that if this blood clot in my heart got into my lungs or into my brain, I would die. So I wasn't feeling too good. I was right on the edge of being depressed when this grandmother came. My relatives brought her over to the hospital in Omaha. It surprised me to see her because it was early in the morning and she was a long way from her home on the reservation. She said to me, "Well, Grandson, I was thinking about you so I made some of this special food for you." You know the corn that we Indian people have is regarded as a gift from the Great Spirit. There's certain ways that we have to prepare the corn. There's a process of grinding and parching and cooking this corn. When it is all done we call it *warooj*. She had brought some of that *warooj*. So she said, "I want you to eat this, Grandson, because it will do you good." And sure enough, when I ate that *warooj*, it lifted me out of my state of near depression. It revived my spirits and I actually felt physically better.

My interest in Winnebago culture was rekindled when my daughters came home from school in Omaha and stated that the teacher had told them that Indians had weird beliefs. My daughters wanted to understand what that teacher meant. This indicated to my wife and me that we hadn't paid enough attention to teaching our children about the culture, the history, and the heritage that they enjoyed as Indian children, as Ho Chunk children.

That was during the period when I was actively involved with the Mormon Church. But I felt uncomfortable with the way that the Mormons portrayed the original people of this land, the so-called Lamanite people. I didn't feel comfortable with the patronizing manner that Mormons had towards Indian people. They seemed to be a real nice group of people.

They were hospitable, kind, sharing, and very loving. Yet underneath all that there was distinct feeling of superiority, so to speak, in their treatment of Indians. The way the Mormons talked about Indian cultures was pretty negative. That's what motivated me to start reading and studying the history of Indian/White relationships in this country. It was during the mid-1960s that changes were beginning to occur. There was a resurgence of Indianness. More and more Indian groups were being organized. Indian centers were being established.

When I was working with Eugene Crawford to create an Indian center in Omaha, I organized a number of educational and fund-raising activities. We put on variety shows that I had created and designed. We put on a pageant. I wrote the pageant and we staged it at the auditorium in one of the local high schools. We incorporated about sixteen different dances that the Winnebago do: harvest dances, eagle dancing, and various other Winnebago dances went into this pageant. I got elders together to talk about the songs, to teach how these songs fit into our culture. That pageant was a step back into the cultural world of my people.

Then there was an amazing spiritual experience I had in Utah. I have an uncle who is the descendant of four different chiefs of the Winnebago, Iowa, Oto, and Omaha tribes. During my lifetime I had the good fortune to get to know him pretty well, and he told me about his early childhood. When he was four years old, his grandmother had turned him over to his great-grandfather for a fasting experience. Because of that he had a dream that he explained to his great-grandfather. His great-grandfather told him that the dream was an answer to his grandmother's prayer. That dream represented what she wanted for him to have, a blessing from the Great Spirit. So his grandfather told this little boy that in days to come he was going to grow into manhood. He would have to teach the younger generation. This old man's prediction was made way back around 1920, prior to the days of jet aircraft. He was speaking of great big silver birds flying across the heavens and roaring like dragons. He was talking about great stone roads, which we now understand to be the interstate highway system. He was talking about all these things that the boy had seen in his dream. He told this little boy, "When life gets to be the way it was in your dream, our people are going to be in a state of confusion. They're not going to know who they are. They're not going to know their roots. When that time comes, you're going to have to teach them. You're going to have to talk to them and tell them who they are and where they come from."

My uncle grew up with that kind of background. When I was getting seriously involved in trying to discover my roots, to learn something about my spiritual background, I chose him to be one of my mentors because I was tremendously impressed with him. One time he told me an old Winnebago story that concerned the Great Salt Lake. He made it clear that he wanted to go there some day to see this Great Salt Lake because of what had happened to our people there. I told him, "Someday if I can arrange it we'll go over there, Uncle." Eventually I was invited to Utah to carry out a number of speaking engagements in various colleges, universities, and public schools. I called my uncle and I told him that I would like him to accompany me on this trip. He and his wife made arrangements to fly to Salt Lake City with me. I flew out of Omaha and they flew out of the Twin Cities. We met in Denver, got on a plane together, and flew on to Salt Lake City. While we were flying in the sky high above the clouds he told me an old story that his great-grandfather had told him. "Hundreds and hundreds of years ago, long before the coming of the White man, a great sickness came among our people. Many people were dying. All the people were in mourning. They were wailing and they were heartbroken. They pleaded with the Great Spirit to help them, to let them know that all the relatives that had gone on were in a good place. Shortly thereafter the holy people of our tribe received a vision. In it they found themselves standing on the mountaintops looking down through four layers of clouds at a great body of water. They realized that they had to go and find this place. So four holy men were selected to be the guides and leaders of this expedition. A certain number of people were chosen to follow each one of these four men. They set out from the Western Great Lakes and began the journey westward, in search of the spirit world. They came across the Great Plains and across the Rocky Mountains, traveling until they got to the mountains overlooking the Great Salt Lake. When they arrived at the mountaintop there they could look down and see four layers of clouds below them. From there they could also see this great body of water. They realized that this was the place that they had been shown in the vision. So they went down to the Great Salt Lake and made some offerings. Then each of the four holy men took their followers and they went to the four sides of the Great Salt Lake. They climbed to the hilltops and mountaintops and they fasted for fourteen days and fourteen nights, pleading with the Creator to let them see their relatives and to communicate with their relatives. Here is what eventually happened.

"Each one of them had an experience and communicated with the spirits of the deceased relatives. So after fourteen days and nights they came back together. Then they sat and talked about what they had experienced. They decided it was time to make a covenant with the Creator. They promised that they would always bury their dead in the ground, based on one of the revelations they had. Prior to that time they had been taking care of their deceased in different ways such as placing them on scaffolds or burying them in caves. They discovered that this wasn't the right thing to do because other people would come and open up these corpses and they would extract the heart or the liver or some other organ and they would use it to make bad medicine against our people. So these holy men said, 'We will inter our dead from now on. We won't leave them above the ground.' That was the covenant that they made with the Creator. They departed from the Great Salt Lake and returned eastward to their people." This is the story my uncle was telling me as we flew to Salt Lake City.

When we arrived in Salt Lake City, we discovered that there had been a drought for quite some time. All the animals in the national and state preserves were dying due to lack of water. The buffalo herds, the wild burros and many other animals were dying off for lack of water. On one occasion we were taken to see some reservoirs. The reservoirs were drying up. They were less than a third full. We saw all these effects of the drought with our own eyes.

I went about fulfilling all my speaking engagements. The students at the University of Utah declared that they wanted to have a spiritual awakening. That was the main purpose for inviting me. They asked my uncle if he would conduct a Native American Church ceremony for them so that they could be spiritually awakened. He agreed to do that.

We went to the Goshute Reservation in Skull Valley, about seventy-five miles west and south of Salt Lake City. We put up a tepee there and about twenty students, including several Eskimo students from Alaska, came to pray with us. There were probably eight Winnebagos in our group and about twenty of them. We filled the tepee. During the course of this prayer ceremony my uncle laid a pipe on the altar. He said that his two brothers had fashioned this pipe just for this purpose, because he was coming to visit this place where our ancestors had fasted many, many generations before. My uncle wanted to make an offering unto the Great Spirit on behalf of these departed ancestors and the prayers that they had made for their descendants. He had requested that this pipe be made especially for that purpose.

Early the next morning, when he was preparing to call for morning water, his wife was standing outside with the water pail, waiting to enter the tepee. She spoke through the tepee flap at the eastern entrance, "You had better hurry because something is going to happen here." So my uncle began to blow on his eagle-bone whistle and right at the instant that he blew on his eagle-bone whistle something amazing happened: the sky just turned pink all around us. There was a great flash of lightning and then there was a great crash of thunder, and then all the rain started to fall. And my aunt brought in her water and knelt before the holy altar and she said her prayer. All during the time that she was praying it was raining. When she concluded her prayer, it stopped raining. Then my uncle went into the ritual of lighting the pipe. He took the pipe outside the tepee and invited some of us to come with him. We left the tepee and we stood outside the tepee facing east. We could see all around on the mountaintops the rain clouds were gathered and the rain was falling in the mountains. My uncle made a prayer of thanksgiving with this pipe. He was thanking the Great Spirit for hearing us and sending the rain down to us.

It just so happened there was an elderly Arapaho man in this group. Later on that morning he said to us, "I was called upon by a lot of different groups here in Salt Lake Valley to have ceremonies and pray for rain. No matter what I did, even though I did it with all sincerity and with all faith in God, it never did rain. But what you did here this morning proves to me the truth of your words, that your ancestors were here in times past and that their spirits are here yet today. Because you talked to the Creator and you asked Him for this blessing, He sent all this rain down. So that's all the proof that I need that what you say is true."

Ho Chunk people have a distinctly philosophical view of the world. In my opinion, the Ho Chunk people are very positive thinkers. They conduct their lives in a manner which maintains that positive outlook on life. Ho Chunk people used to perform ceremonies, carried on today in the Medicine Lodge Society, which coincide with the changing of the seasons. These four nights and four days of ceremony are celebrated in the spring, the summer, the fall and the winter. These ceremonies are designed to bring balance and harmony into our lives from season to season. They put us in rhythm with what's going on in the Creation. To my mind this is much better than trying to change the Creation to fit our needs. The Judeo-Christian concept of having dominion over the earth, and the Greek philosophy of controlling everything, don't fit the Winnebago or Indian way of thinking. We believe it's much better just to adjust your mind to be at peace with the Creation instead of trying to change everything. That's one of the fundamental differences between Indian thinking and non-Indian thinking.

The concept of family also differs remarkably. In the non-Indian society families are generally confined to nuclear units, whereas in our world, there is an extended kinship system. We are related to everybody. There is no word for "cousin" in the Winnebago language because there is no such relationship. Those who are one's cousins, according to the White man's standards, are defined in our kinship system as brothers or sisters or aunts or uncles. Kinship even extends beyond my tribe into other tribes. For instance, my grandfather made a relationship with an Omaha family a long time ago, maybe seventy years or so ago. Because of this relationship, there's an Omaha lady who calls me her "son." And so I took my Omaha mother with me to Oklahoma one time when I was invited to conduct a prayer meeting. When we arrived in Oklahoma she introduced me to some relatives that she had made among the Shawnee people during her lifetime. She had made some relationship with the Tinner brothers and she called them "brothers." When they found out that I was her son, they told me, "You're going to be our nephew." That's what I'm talking about, establishing these relationships, reaching out to people of various tribes. It's really fulfilling, rewarding, and satisfying to have those kinds of relationships. Because of them I can travel just about anywhere in the United States and I know that I have Indian relatives there that I can count on for whatever I need in the way of support, or to visit, or just to have a good time.

Another procedure we use to cope with difficult times in life is fasting. Many people, even my own Indian people, go through this life relying upon the White man's medicine. Sometimes they descend into a state of depression and then they consult a psychiatric counselor, and the counselor advises the use of various kinds of medication to help them control their moods so that they won't get depressed. We Indian people believe that isn't necessary. If there is something that we really need straightened out in our lives, then we can make a commitment to fast for spiritual guidance and direction. We can conduct a vision quest. We believe that the answer to our problems will come to us, whatever it is that we are seeking. It will help us straighten out our lives and resolve our problems.

Within the Siouan-speaking tribes, there are what we call the *herooshga* organizations. They all have this warrior society concept. In the Winnebago tribe, the warriors, *wank-washoshera,* are highly respected individuals.[1] We preserve that lifestyle and we come together to carry on the traditional *herooshga* activities, singing and dancing and putting feathers on people. For instance, we might tell a young lady, who could be our niece or our granddaughter, about our war exploits. And then we bestow a feather upon her. We place a feather upon her as a sign of our sacrifice, to remember some brave deed that we might have performed on the field of combat. The activity which has come to be known as a "pow-wow," represents a very distinct way of life. It is vitally important that we sing and we dance in order to maintain our peaceful, harmonious relationship with the Creation.

Reuben Snake leads the 1992 Sunrise Ceremony in Central Park. Photograph courtesy of the Repatriation Foundation.

Faith, Humility, Healing, and Rising Up to Serve God

I would like to describe the vision that appeared during one of our ancient four-day-long ceremonies. This is a story that I heard from some Ho Chunk elders a long time ago, when I was growing up. My elders told me this story after we had sat up all night in a Native American Church prayer meeting. It is about our original ancestors, who were living way down south. These ancestors of ours were using this divine medicine and through that they had developed a relationship with the Creator and the Creation that resulted in their practicing these ceremonies. At one of these ceremonies they heard beautiful music coming from the east and they saw great lights in the heavens. They realized that something wonderful had happened in that part of the Creation, somewhere to the east of them. Years later, in the middle of performing one of these ceremonies, they saw a being descending out of the heavens. It was beautiful and had a kind of sparkle, like gemstones of different kinds. It was descending out of the heavens toward the earth and it was trailing a cloud. A trail of beautiful lights was coming down with it. Then this object landed right among them and was transfigured into a human being. The people thought of this being as a sacred serpent because that's what that trail of beautiful lights looked like as it came down out of heaven. It looked like a serpent descending out of heaven. This spirit, when it became a man, addressed the people. It spoke to them and stated that he was the son of the living God. He had come to visit with them for a brief while, to share with them some of his knowledge of the spirit world. This is exactly what he did. He walked the earth with these people for a short time and then he was again transfigured back into this sacred serpent. Then he ascended back into heaven. But before he left, he said he was going to come back to them someday. I always thought this story referred to the spirit of Christ who came to visit our people, to touch their lives in that manner.

I am convinced that Christ's message is compatible with traditional Winnebago teachings. When Christ was approached by His followers and asked which of all the commandments is the greatest commandment, His response was that there were two great commandments: the first was to love the Lord thy God with all thy might, with all thy strength, and with all thy soul. The second commandment was like unto the first, to love thy neighbor as thyself. That is basically identical to the understanding that Winnebago people have, that the Creator comes first. We have to pay homage to the Creator in our lives. We have to put Him before anything and everything else. We have to show our respect to Him. Then the second commandment, to love thy neighbor as thyself, is one of the basic operating principles in our lives. We must have respect for one another. Our extended kinship system teaches us to treat everybody with kindness, respect, and honor. I feel that Christ's message is something that our people already understood. When the missionaries came and brought the word of Christ we saw the parallels between what Christ said and what we were practicing in our lives. All of the old Winnebago teachings about how to interact properly as human beings are taught in our Medicine Lodge. In the Native American Church we are taught how to have compassion, how to have respect, how to treat each other with honor, how to share with one another. Those are all traditional Winnebago teachings. They were in place long before the coming of Christianity. They are ideas shared by both traditional Winnebagos and Christians.

But within the Native American Church we pray to God in Jesus' name and we emphasize the life of Christ as a model. That is something they don't do in the Medicine Lodge. So in that respect it's totally different.

Escuinapa, Sinaloa, Mexico, March 1992, the occasion of an Inter-Tribal Ceremonial Gathering where native people from over twenty tribes met for four nights of peyote meetings. *(Left to right)* James Botsford, Indian Law Office Director; his wife, Krista, Indian rights lawyer; Donna Goldsmith; Reuben Snake; and The Peyote Road co-director, Fidel Moreno. Photograph by Phil Cousineau.

On the final morning of the Inter-Tribal Gathering in Mexico, Reuben Snake discusses the different origin stories of peyote with a Huichol medicine man, Prisciliano Carrillo Rios of Santa Mariá del Oro. Photograph by Phil Cousineau.

Some people have asked if the Native American Church is a Christian church. Knowing the history of the Christian church, I don't like the term "Christian." I believe in the message of Christ. But I don't accept all that cultural garbage that the White man brought with him when he brought the message of Christ over here. So I don't like to say, "I'm a Christian," because literally hundreds of millions of people have died at the hands of Christians through the Crusades and other "holy wars." So I don't regard that term "Christian" very highly. But I am a believer in Christ. I would say that the Native American Church people are believers in Christ and that they try to pattern their lives after the life of Christ.

I don't see any great conflict between Christianity and traditional Native American religions. It's just like the Old and the New Testament. The Old Testament is supposedly the inspired writings of prophets from the time of the Hebrews, the Israelites. The New Testament deals with the followers of Christ, His disciples, His apostles. But for some reason or other, Christian people have separated them. They believe that by adopting the message of Christ they no longer need to respect the tradition and the law of the Jewish people. So in the Christian world there's not a whole lot of regard given to the Jewish way of life. But we Indian people took the message of Christ and integrated it into our lives. We added it to what we were already doing. For us there's no separation between the old teachings and the message of Christ. I consider that to be very meaningful. Other ethnic groups, in different corners of the world, have done likewise. Northern Europeans are the only ones who have separated Christ from His cultural roots. Everybody else adopts His way and His teachings into their lives. They maintain their roots while they're practicing Christianity.

I feel it is possible to reconcile orthodox Christian doctrines with Ho Chunk beliefs. Early in my life I was upset by the fact that it was said that God cursed Satan by turning him into a reptile, into a serpent, into a snake. Therefore all the Judeo-Christian teachings revile snakes. Once I started studying the Bible, the Old Testament, I noticed a couple of examples which were inconsistent, like the time when Moses came down from the mountain and the people were engaged in idolatry and God was upset with them. He sent fiery serpents among them and they were biting them and killing them. Finally the people all turned to Moses and asked for his help. So Moses told them to put a post in the ground and then under God's direction he got his artisans together and they made a brass serpent and put it on this post. And everybody who came and touched that brass serpent was saved. That's one story that doesn't get told. Instead they all say, "Oh, Satan is a snake." They leave it at that. They don't recognize the healing power. But that's one of the basic teachings of our people: that the serpent, the snake, has healing power. So to read this story told in the Old Testament changed my mind. If people would just pay attention they would see the reality of the situation and conclude that snakes aren't inherently evil.

I was told by my elders about my Snake Clan background and how my clan fits into the life of the Winnebago tribe. I never did fear snakes. I developed a healthy respect for the poisonous ones. Growing up in Wisconsin every now and then we would come across a cottonmouth snake. I knew those cottonmouths could hurt us. But I never had a fear of them. I've been able to handle snakes when I come across them without any fear. We members of the Snake Clan were taught that we should respect them, that we should talk to them and offer them tobacco whenever we came across them.

I have offered them tobacco from time to time. I remember getting ready to have a Native American Church service down here near one of my grandfather's homes. Everybody got excited because this big bullsnake came out of a tree. They got so excited they started jumping around. I just went over and picked up the snake. Then I walked down towards the railroad tracks where I knew that I could put him down without him coming back. When I put him down, I took a cigarette and I broke it apart and offered him the tobacco and told him, "Well, Grandpa, you upset these people over here, so don't come back. Just go on your way and everything will be all right."

Of course some beliefs differ. The Winnebago idea of an afterlife does not resemble the Christian concept of hell. Winnebagos speak about good and evil spirits in the universe. They tell me that we can fall prey to evil spirits and they can lie and make life miserable for us. But I've never heard a traditional Winnebago refer specifically to hell.

According to my understanding of the teachings of Christ, we will descend into the depths. I talk about this from time to time when the situation is appropriate. The twenty-third Psalm states, "Yea though I walk through the valley of the shadow of death." I interpret that to mean the place where Christ went after He was crucified. He journeyed to the valley of the shadow of death. But he came out of there and was resurrected. So I always say that if we're following in His footsteps, if we're walking in His footsteps, we're going to experience that. We're going to go through that valley of the shadow of death. But the Psalm also says, "For I will fear no evil, for thou art with me." If we maintain our strong belief in God, He will lead us through that valley of the shadow of death and bring us out. Then we'll be able to live eternally in His Holy Kingdom.

Think about the design of the Native American Church fireplace, the Half-Moon fireplace. The design is symbolic of the unending cycle of life. We descend out of the spirit world into this physical plane, this earthly plane, and then, at whatever time is chosen by the Creator, we go back. We go back into the spirit world and evolve into a higher state of being. I believe that the spirit world is around about us all the time. It's just that we, due to our physical limitations, can't see it or feel it. We can sense it if we get our spirit attuned to it. It's not way off there somewhere. It's right here. It's just in a different plane.

I developed this kind of thinking quite a while ago. An event which verified it for me happened while I was conducting a prayer meeting for a young lady friend of ours. She had been told that she would have to undergo a hysterectomy.

She was terribly upset. She was a mother of two little boys and she said, "I want more children. I really don't want to go through this operation." So we sponsored a Native American Church prayer meeting for her. She asked my wife and me to take care of the service. At about four o'clock in the morning I was fixing some medicine for her and praying that the Creator would bless this medicine so that it could do this young lady some good. I was praying that she could be healed of her afflictions so she wouldn't have to undergo this operation, so that she could have more children just like she wanted. All of a sudden all around me, behind me and on each side of me, I could hear voices. They were all talking to God along with me. They were speaking in the Winnebago language and saying, "Bless my daughter, bless my granddaughter." I knew that these spirits of her relatives were there. I really felt good about that because I realized that this young lady was going to be well. When I finished my prayer I burned some incense and I took the medicine to her. I told her, "If you take this medicine, you're going to be all right." She did take it. And sure enough in the morning when we concluded our service she got up and said, "I know that I'm well. I know it." And sure enough, a couple of days later she went back to see her doctor. The doctor told her, "Evidently you don't need an operation." They had re-examined her and found out there was really nothing wrong with her. About a year later she had another little boy. And my wife and I got to be godparents for this new little son of hers.

That's one of the incidents which proved to me that the spirit world is not way off there somewhere. It's just right here. As a consequence of my intense involvement in the Native American Church, with our sacramental use of this divine medicine, peyote, I've learned a lot of things. I believe what our old people say: "Peyote is a great teacher. It will reveal things to you that you never understood before." The greatest teaching that I ever received through the use of this medicine is a sense of humility. I came to understand that we can't be self-righteous, we can't be filled with pride and expect God to hear our prayers. I tell the younger generation all the time that if they bend their will to God, then God will do their will. If you bend your will to God and do what He wants you to do, when you ask Him for something, He'll grant it to you. But in order to get to that point where we can submit ourselves to God, we must have true humility. We have to put aside all our self-righteous pride and all of our human weakness and just get right down to the nitty-gritty and tell God that without Him we are nothing. We are nothing without God in our lives. We have to rely upon Him for all things. And if we truly mean that, then we can ask for a blessing and He'll give it to us.

It was at a prayer meeting I attended when I was eighteen years old that I got my first clear understanding of the virtue of humility. My older brother was dying of scleroderma. I had come home on leave from the service. My mother and step-father and I went to Wisconsin to bring my brother home to Minnesota because the doctors said they couldn't do anything more for him. He was in extreme agony. We couldn't even touch him, his skin was so sensitive. He would cry out in pain if anybody touched him. We brought him back to Minnesota and my mother asked one of our good relatives to pray for him and to give him medicine. So that weekend we took him to this home where we were going to have this Native American Church service. We carried him in on a mattress. He was moaning and groaning and feeling the pain of every movement. We laid him down and I sat down next to him. I told him that I would wait on him throughout the night and do whatever he wanted. The man in charge of the prayer meeting said that he had 150 peyote buttons that he was going to prepare for my bother to take throughout the night. He would fix ten or twelve of these buttons at a time and give them to my brother. My brother was in constant pain until it was almost morning. He was lying there on this mattress and praying. I heard his prayer because I was sitting right next to him. He was praying this way: "You don't have to make me well, God. You don't have to make me well. But just give me another opportunity at life. Let me get up. And let me walk.

And let me do something with my life. Let me be of service. And if you can do that for me, well, I'll be happy. I want to get married, I want to have children. I want to enjoy life like everybody else does."

Lo and behold, early in the morning, while the praying and the singing were going on in the circle, my brother sat up. Then he stood up and walked around the altar, around the holy fireplace, and he stood at the foot of the fireplace and picked up a large red coal from the fireplace. He picked it up with his bare hands. And he was talking, talking to us, saying that God had heard him and God was going to give him another chance at life. And he said, "All you have to do is have faith, to have this kind of faith." And he was holding this red, burning charcoal in his hand. "If you have this kind of faith then God will do for you what you want Him to do." Then he put the live coal back in the fireplace and he came back around and sat down. After that he went to school and acquired a trade. Later on in life he got married, had children, and became the vice-chairman of our tribe and the mayor of our town. He gained a national reputation for his work in health activities of Indian people. I used to marvel at him because everything he said to God in his prayer came to pass in his lifetime. It was a great lesson for me, to see my brother living his prayer.

I eventually learned much more about humility. One day my daughter told me she had seen a bumper sticker that immediately reminded her of me. This particular daughter is the one who likes to tease me so I said, "Oh, yeah, what did the bumper sticker say?" She replied, "It said, don't act so humble, you ain't that great." She made me laugh.

I'm a very egotistical person. I admit that to people all the time. For much of my lifetime I thought, "Well, I have the brains and the ability to do this and to do that if I so desire." After everything I did I told myself, "That's because you've got the brains and you've got the ability, that's why you can do all this." But an occasion came where I was confronted with an obstacle. Because of my over-involvement in so many

—From *Being Indian Is,* by Reuben Snake.
Drawing by Wesley Green, Jr.

BEING INDIAN IS. . . .

To be the best you can possibly be at what you do,
but not to openly compete with your fellowman to your
own aggrandizement and glorification and his shame and humiliation.

things, I had let my family life deteriorate. That neglect had a tremendous impact on my wife, so she left me.

We were separated and I got to thinking about it. "Now what are you going to do with your life? The one person that you truly care for doesn't want you around or doesn't want to be around you and here you are with these children. So what are you going to do now? Are you going to do something different with your life? Are you going to try to make amends and start over again?" I went through a troubling experience then. The only thing I could do was to turn to this medicine. I couldn't find any other way of coping with my problem except through prayer and using this medicine.

I started praying at my sister's home one evening. And this medicine took me through some ordeal. I found myself standing outside in sub-zero weather with just a towel wrapped around me. The water had melted in the yard and frozen over. There I was standing barefooted on the ice with just a towel wrapped around me. I was praying to God. I was wondering, "What am I doing out here? Any person in their right mind would be inside where it's nice and warm." But I remember staying out there for about forty-five minutes, praying to God and telling Him that I was nothing without Him and that I needed to get my life in order. And that morning, I was moved again to do something else. I went and I woke my brother up. I told him what I wanted to do. He said he would help me. Then I woke my two sisters up and they said they would help me. So we went out to where my grandmother used to live and started a fire. And then my brother handed me a small jar filled with ground peyote. He said, "Brother, if you really mean business, if you really want to get wired with God, before you say your prayer you could eat this medicine here. Doing that will help you attain what you're striving for." So I said, "Well, I really mean business. So give me that medicine." He gave it to me and I took this ground medicine in four swallows. That was the greatest challenge I ever faced, to have to focus my mental energies. Because all this medicine going down wanted to just come right back out. It just turned my stomach inside out. So I had to really focus my mind to hold that medicine inside of me so that it would do the thing that it could do. I got down on my knees in front of the fire I had built and I poured my heart out to God. I told Him that I wanted to make amends to my wife and to my children for the way that I had been treating them, and that I wanted us to come back together as a family. I said that if He heard my prayer and granted me my heartfelt desire, I would wait on Him, I would do whatever He asked me to do or whatever He showed me to do from then on.

This occurred in January of 1974. Sure enough, it happened just the way that I asked Him. My wife called and said she'd been thinking about it and that she wanted to come home and wanted to start over and try to build a better life for us and our children. From that moment on everything began to improve. So that's a personal experience that I went through with this medicine to learn humility and relying on God for guidance and direction.

It took me many years to become aware of the fact that I was living up to the meaning of my name, *Kikawa Unga*. I had been told by my grandmother about what she had done for me as a little tiny infant. She told me that she had sponsored this meeting and my great-grandfather, John Painter Senior, had prayed for my life, christened me, and baptized me. But I really didn't pay much attention to my Winnebago name and that ceremony until I was thirty-seven years old. That was the year when my clan father turned his instruments (sacred paraphernalia) over to me. At that time, under the influence of this medicine, I got to reflecting on my life thinking about this prayer that my great-grandfather had said for me. And it came to me that this is what he wanted for me, to retain as much of this Ho Chunk cultural tradition as I could and to try to share it with as many people as I could. And to carry the message of Jesus Christ out into the world. This all came to me, like I say, while I was sitting in a meeting, using this medicine at a time when I was making a definite transition from just being an active member to actually becoming a

Roadman, a leader in the Native American Church. I've had an opportunity to visit with some of my family elders since then and that's kind of the way that they see it for me. They say, "Well, that's what your great-grandfather prayed for you for, just the kind of thing that you're doing."

Let me explain the significance of naming. In our Winnebago tribe, one is born with an Indian name that depends on the order of birth. We have a certain name for first-born sons, second-born, third-born, and fourth-born sons. The same sort of birth-order naming applies to the little girls. So one is simply born and receives an Indian name without any effort. But then as we progress through life, one of our relatives is going to have a compassionate feeling for one of us. This is the way my grandmother felt for me.[1]

So she sponsored a ceremony and asked an elder to come and pray for me and to baptize me in the Native American Church. Then they christened me with a Winnebago name. This particular elder knew something about my family history. He thought about all of the people in my family tree. Then he picked a person that he admired in my family tree, somebody that he knew had lived a long and useful life on this earth. He took that name and gave it to me, to wear as a coat of armor. As they say, that name will protect the person from the world. They also say that at some point in time, the Creator-of-all-things will call that name, and that person is going to have to answer to that name. One must be prepared, because when the Creator calls one's name, then one is going back into the spirit world. This is what my grandmother thought about for me. That's why she selected my great-grandfather to think of a Winnebago name. He came up with *Kikawa Unga,* an old Snake Clan name which means "to rise up." The ceremony where he christened me was held on Easter Sunday morning, so my great-grandfather recited the story of Jesus Christ's crucifixion and resurrection. He said that he was naming me after the resurrection of Christ and that I would rise up as Christ did and carry God's message. So that's the significance of my name.

Reuben Snake Speaks About the Native American Church

While I was tape-recording Reuben Snake's life story, Peter Canby, the journalist and author of The Heart of the Sky, *had traveled to South Dakota to observe a Native American Church ceremony in preparation for an essay he was writing. Upon returning to Winnebago from his visit with the Yankton Sioux, Peter Canby asked Reuben Snake many questions about the Native American Church and the meeting he had just attended. With Mr. Canby's permission, I selected and edited excerpts from Reuben Snake's answers. During this interview I also asked several questions. Reuben's insights about the meaning of ceremonies he had conducted for twenty years as a Roadman are evident in this chapter.*

I was born into the Native American Church. One of the basic tenets of our faith is that peyote is a teacher, that when you use this divine medicine it's going to teach you many things about life. That is something I always understood.

I became especially involved in the Native American Church at the time when there was a resurgence of Indianness going on throughout the country, through the creation of various organizations such as the American Indian Movement and Survival of American Indians and the National Indian Youth Council. Many young Indians of my age were on the verge of being acculturated, and then they realized they were losing something. What motivated me was essentially my involvement in the Indian movement. I wasn't a sun dancer. I didn't go to Yuwipi ceremonies. I was a Native American Church person. If I was going to be actively involved in this movement I had to relearn my heritage. So I started going back to the Native American Church. During the time that I was in New Mexico I attended prayer meetings with the Taos Pueblo people and in several different places on the Navajo Reservation. I was attending a prayer meeting two or three times per month while I was living in New Mexico.

When we moved back to Sioux City, Iowa, in 1974 I hired one of my Yankton Sioux brothers by the name of Asa Primeaux as my cultural activities coordinator to help me start instilling this Indianness in these young Indian people who had grown up on the streets of Sioux City. They had no real roots, no real ties to their culture. We invited Native American Church elders to come to Sioux City so the younger people could hear these old men sing and talk. That's what really spurred my interest and my involvement in the church, and I started going to prayer meetings every weekend.

Let me explain the way songs are used in the Native American Church ceremony. There are sets of songs. There's a song to begin the ceremony. There's a song to call for midnight water. There's a morning water song. There's a closing song. The Half-Moon ceremonial ways that you were exposed to always use those four songs during the course of the night. There are songs that go along with that and there are songs that go along with the occasion of the meeting. At the memorial service you attended there were, no doubt, songs sung to memorialize people. There are songs of healing. There are birthday songs. There's a wide variety of songs, depending on the purpose of the particular meeting. We try not to repeat ourselves. We each try to sing a different song. To your untrained ear it sounds like the songs are the same, but they are actually different.

There is a beginning song in every Half-Moon meeting. Any Roadman will sing that song, but the three songs he uses after that are his choice, whatever songs he feels appropriate to go with that. Then there's a midnight water song, the first song we use at midnight, when we are calling for water. Then you sing three other songs which are songs of your choice.

Every tribe has its own music. We associate with one another to the degree that we learn each other's songs. I'm a Winnebago and when I go over to Sioux country to pray with them, out of respect for them and to honor them, I'm going to sing their kind of songs. If I go there (to Sioux country) I'll sing: *"Wakan Tanka a ya non a nee yo ne no."* I sing that way, using *Wakan Tanka* instead of *Ma'oonna* (the Winnebago word). This is because *Wakan Tanka* is what they say when they talk to God.

In the prayer circle, the purpose of the music is to bring our minds together, to fuse our minds into one thought. Maybe we're there for the healing of some individual. If so, we're going to sing our healing songs. Every individual sitting in that circle, if he knows what he's doing, is going to be able to build on the previous singer's music. After one person sings four particular songs then the person sitting next to him will say to himself, "Well, now I'm going to use these four songs to back him up." And it just goes around the circle. In the beginning one uses simple short songs that are primarily vocables: "ha you which in na, ha you which in na, ha you which in na, ha you which in na, ha you which in na." Then when one begins to eat this medicine and begins to strive for that unity of thought, one starts introducing some more powerful music. By the time daylight comes, this music has really taken hold of us. We are all able to harmonize with one another and we are all able to concentrate on the purpose of the meeting. We can all sing the healing song together and feel that Holy Spirit in there then. It builds up, layer by layer. The music and the drum sound is what carries one to that unity of thought.

Most people start out learning the really simple songs. We learn a set of them. We start using them and then as we go along we begin to hear this other music and we think, "I could learn that song, I can sing that song." We get a little more involved and pretty soon we are singing Bible verses. Our people, the old Winnebago men from times past, used to take the verses right out of the Bible and make a song out of them. There is one that we use for baptisms. The whole song tells the baptism of Jesus Christ. That song is what God said, you know. It says, "This is my beloved son in whom I am well pleased. Hear ye him." That's what the song is saying.

Although songs are sung in different languages, people tend to learn the songs in the other languages and also what they mean. My son is much more adept at this than I am. He sings all kinds of songs, Kiowa and Comanche, Cheyenne and Ponca, Navajo and Sioux and Apache. Even though we don't speak those languages, we still know what the songs mean.

There's an old story that goes along with the creation of the water-drum. This is what we were told by the elders: "When you enter the tepee, it's like re-entering the womb of your mother. The tepee poles symbolize her ribs and the fireplace in the center signifies her blood that kept you warm and alive in her womb. The drum represents your mother's heartbeat, because that's the first sound that you heard when you were in her womb." That sound, boom-boom, boom-boom, boom-boom, boom-boom, is the first sound you heard. That's what this water-drum signifies to us; it is the heartbeat of our mother. It also symbolizes the voice of God. This is what the old people said: "When somebody starts beating on this drum, people all around, for a long distance away, know that something sacred is going to take place. So they start gravitating toward that drum. That drum sound is like God calling you. When you get over by that drum, you are going to come in contact with something sacred and something holy." That's how important a drum is to us.

The water-drums are very traditional. They used to be used a long time ago, and they still are, by the traditional long-house people, the Medicine Lodge people. In those days they used a hollowed-out tree stump for a water-drum. The tree stump was covered with an animal hide and then water would be poured into it. Today we have the modern convenience of cast iron or aluminum or brass kettles. The water-drum is a very old instrument. It wasn't one that was just adapted to the Native American Church.

Although having water inside the drum basically has to do

with the sound, we also have this understanding, about the time that the Creator-of-all-things became a physical being. They say that He looked around and He understood that He was the only being in creation and this gave Him a certain feeling so that a tear rolled out of His eye and down His face and fell out into the void. Then He looked at this and when He looked at it lightning flashed from His eyes and pierced this teardrop. That was the beginning of this universe, that teardrop and that flash of lightning. We say that those are the two gifts that the Creator gave to humankind, the water and the fire. When lightning hits the earth, it causes fire. We really revere those two elements. When we put this water-drum together, we put some live coals into the water inside the drum. Those two elements are there for us, the water and the fire are contained in this drum. These are the things that sustain us in our everyday life.

Let me explain the significance of the water bird, which is a recurrent symbol in the Native American Church. There are two kinds of water birds. One is an anhinga and the other is a cormorant. We use the anhinga feathers. The anhinga is a diving bird. There's an old Creek Indian legend which tells of the significance of this bird. The original Creek homeland was located around a place where seven springs came out of the earth and formed a big clear pool of water. They say that water was the beginning of life and they call it *porch* in the Creek language. In this large pool there were different plants growing under the water, ferns and plants like that. Those water birds, those anhingas, used to come there and dive. Those Indians, being students of nature, were always observing. They noticed that the anhingas would take the ferns and feed them to their young and to the sick birds. The sick birds would get well. It is for that reason that the Creek Indians really respect this water bird, because he showed them how to use good medicine from underneath the water. That's how highly this water bird is regarded throughout the Native American Church. It has healing powers, it brings one good medicine.

You may have noticed the feathered fans that everybody

has in the Native American Church. There are certain birds that we regard as sacred, the eagle being the most sacred of them all. An eagle feather is very important in all aspects of our culture. We take the eagle tailfeathers and we make a prayer fan. Another sacred bird is the hawk. We make a prayer fan of his tailfeathers, too. In recent years we assimilated some things from the southern Indians from old Mexico and even further south. The macaw parrot is a sacred bird to them and so you may see some of us with macaw feather fans.

When we pray for one another, the spirit of that eagle, the spirit of that hawk, is holy and sacred. It is going to bring a blessing to you to burn incense and fan you off. (It is) going to put spiritual armor on you.

The eagle is considered more important than other birds because the eagle is the one bird that can fly up into the face of God and pierce the clouds and fly way up into the heavens. He carries our message up to God.

You probably noticed the eagle feather tied to one of the tepee poles when you were with the Yankton Sioux. That feather is on the main pole. In the Native American Church they call that main pole, the one that holds the canvas up, the Jesus Pole. That's why we put the eagle feather on it.

Tobacco is a sacred gift from the Creator to the red man. We believe that He gave it to us to use whenever we are seeking His blessings. If we make an offering of tobacco and He smells the aroma of this tobacco, He knows we are asking for something. He's going to grant us our heartfelt desire when we make this sacred tobacco offering. There are a lot of different ways to offer it. My people, Winnebagos, put it on the ground. Sometimes they put it in the fireplace. The other Siouan-speaking people put the tobacco in a pipe and they make an offering to the Creator with the pipe. In the Native American Church they use corn shucks (husks) to roll a sacred smoke as an offering to the Creator-of-all-things.

According to our belief system fire and water are two gifts which came from the Creator. Out of the eye of God comes fire and water. These are the elements that sustain us on this earth, that make life possible. So we cherish that fire and water. We incorporate fire into everything that we do that is sacred and holy. People from other cultures had that understanding too. The Old Testament talks about God calling Moses to the mountain and speaking to him through the burning bush. The bush wasn't consumed by the flames because it was sacred and holy. They also talk about the pillar of fire that God put between the Israelites and the Egyptians. Just think about all these examples in the Bible about fire.

Today most Christian denominations have reduced the significance of fire to a lit candle. But we keep the fire on the ground and we keep it alive. In my lifetime a lot of young White people have become disenchanted with their spiritual value system. They came around our fireplace looking for that connection with God. They came to sit down around our fireplace because their fire had gone out. Some people are beginning to learn that, like Matthew Fox, the Catholic priest who teaches creation spirituality and wants to bring those things back to life, to have people chanting and dancing and building sacred fires.

My uncle once explained the meaning of the half-moon to me. He said, "Life is an unending cycle. There's no beginning and no ending to life. We existed in the spirit world before we came to this earth. When we leave this earth we're going to go back into the spirit world." At the beginning of time this universe was created through a word of prayer from the Creator of all things. He spoke the words that brought this universe into reality. We put this half-moon down, that crescent moon on the earth inside the tepee. It signifies the earthly portion of this unending circle of life. The other half of it that lies in the spirit world is not a physical thing. So we don't put it down on the earth inside the tepee. We don't make a complete circle because we're coming out of the spirit world. When you walk in the tepee on this side, that's the beginning of the road of life on this earth. On that crescent moon they have a little line drawn on top. That's the road of life, they say.

Each person journeys down this road of life for however long it takes to get back into the spirit world. Then over here at this end of this crescent moon is the end of our earthly journey and our return to the spirit world. That's the symbolism of this crescent moon; it's the road of life here on this earth.

The male and female aspects of our ceremony depend on each tribe itself. The Winnebagos are a strongly patriarchal tribe. We follow the lineage of our fathers. Custom and tradition teaches us that women should sit quietly and not intrude upon the things that are taking place. In our Native American Church meetings, you don't see Winnebago women singing or drumming or talking. I have sisters-in-law who attended a prayer meeting where there was just a handful of people and they were trying to heal somebody. Their grandfather said, "Well, granddaughters, we need your help. Go ahead and sing and you can sing from now on." Women do sing, like that, when they have permission. Among the Sioux people a woman can sing. Navajo women sing. In fact, there are even Navajo women that run the prayer meetings. How women fit into the ceremony depends on whether it is a patriarchal or matriarchal tribe.

Cedar and sage are also essential in Native American Church meetings. We have a prayer staff which to us is a tree, a symbol of the Tree of Everlasting Life. The old people tell us, "When you want to plant a young tree and have it grow up straight, you take a stake and you put it in the ground. Then you put this little cutting next to it and tie it to that stake so that when the wind comes it isn't going to bend and grow up bent over and crooked. It's going to grow up straight." That's what they teach us, that if we are going to grow up straight and true for God, we should be praying around this Native American Church. We should be hanging on to that staff of life, that Staff of Everlasting Life. We know that there's a tree exactly like that in the spirit world: the Tree of Everlasting Life. This evergreen tree signifies that because it's always green. We take the needles off the evergreen tree and the cedar tree and we use them for incense, to symbolize that Tree of Everlasting Life.

There are several different varieties of sage that Indian people use for various medicinal purposes. We make a sage stick and we pass it around with the prayer staff to help us to purify our thoughts, to purify our minds and our hearts and our bodies. The sage stick is handed around before we pass the peyote around, and everybody rubs the sage in their hand and rubs it on their body, for spiritual purification.

At the meeting you attended among the Yankton Sioux you may have sensed that people got into a shared frame of mind and with their minds fused together they were able to contact their "deceased" relatives. A lot of tribes do that. We talk to the Creator and ask Him to send the spirit of our loved ones to be around the circle with us, to bring us a blessing from Him. The Sioux do this regularly, not just at a memorial service. I had occasion to conduct a healing ceremony for my Sioux grandpa, for Newland's father. That's what happened. The Sioux relatives called upon the spirits to return and bring a blessing for this old man. That's actually what happened. The old man was touched and he was made well.

There's a lot of similarity between Native American Church ceremonies and those of Mexican Indians who use peyote. When I went to Mexico and watched the Huichols and the Tarahumara and the Tepehuan do their ceremony, I could see the roots of our Native American Church there. A lot of their ceremony was just modified slightly to fit inside the tepee. There's a little different rhythm when they beat on a drum. And their dance step is a little bit different than ours. There were no striking differences. See that prayer arrow right there? That is what they use in old Mexico. When they burn incense, they bless you with this. We have an eagle feather fan. But it's the very same thing.

The gourd we use has a musical function as well as a spiritual meaning. Most Indian belief systems suggest that when one gets ill it's because one is not in harmony with the Creator and the Creation. That's the significance of the gourd rattle. The old people said, "If you can take this gourd rattle, this water-drum and the God-given voice that you have and put those three things together and create a harmonious sound out of those three things, then balance and harmony are going to come to you." The gourd represents our mind and our heart getting in tune with God. The gourd helps us get in balance and in harmony with the rest of the Creation. The drum symbolizes God's voice. We are using the voice that He gave us and we are shaking this gourd rattle. If we can get all of those in harmony with one another, then we can feel the power of God. We can overcome our difficulties and be well.

Once I went out to Fort Dushain, Utah. My nephew was going to marry a Ute Indian girl, and he wanted me to conduct a Native American Church wedding ceremony. My family and I and some of my relatives journeyed out to Utah. When we got to the home of the mother-in-law-to-be, she introduced us to an elderly Sioux woman. That old Sioux lady was lying on the couch. She didn't look very well; in fact, she was moaning because she wasn't feeling good. The lady of the house said, "Tonight when we have this prayer meeting I'd like to take my auntie (this old Sioux lady). I'd like to take her in there and have her use some of this holy medicine. Maybe it will do her some good." We said that was fine. That evening they brought her in and laid her on a pallet on the ground. We started our service. At that particular time my sons were singing Sioux songs pretty regularly. Along about the third round of singing, when the staff got to one of my sons, he started singing the Sioux songs. This old lady was lying there and she was moaning and she was groaning. When my sons sang that first Sioux song she turned and she looked at him and she sort of smiled. Then he started up with a second Sioux song and she sat up. When he started that third song, she started singing with him. When he sang the fourth Sioux song, she started war whooping. Then she said, "I'm well, I'm well!" Just four songs, four songs made her well because out there among the Utes they weren't using Sioux music. When we brought the Sioux music to her, when my son sang the music, she got well. That's what I have been talking about, what the music does for a person.

Reuben Snake and Elizabeth Sackler co-chaired the Sunrise Ceremony held October 10, 1992, in Central Park, New York City. Reuben Snake was then and Elizabeth Sackler is still a trustee of the American Indian Ritual Objects Repatriation Foundation, an intercultural partnership committed to assisting in the return of sacred ritual objects to American Indian nations and to educating the public about their spiritual and cultural significance.

Reuben Snake introduces Elizabeth Sackler at the luncheon for participants. Photograph courtesy of the Repatriation Foundation.

Sunrise Ceremony, 1992. Participants inside tepee. Photograph courtesy of the Repatriation Foundation.

Sunrise Ceremony, 1992. Reuben Snake being interviewed by WBAI radio reporter before the Sunrise Ceremony. Photograph courtesy of the Repatriation Foundation.

Attendees leaving the 1992 Sunrise Ceremony. Photograph courtesy of the Repatriation Foundation.

Epilogue
by Jay C. Fikes

Reuben Snake's eldest son, Darren, told me that in the months just before his father passed on he had spoken of two unforgettable dreams. On January 24, 1993, a Native American Church meeting was held to doctor Reuben Snake. During that prayer meeting Reuben explained that in a recent dream he had seen himself standing next to a river near a beautiful wooded area. His eldest brother, Peter John, appeared before him, carrying a peace pipe. He invited Reuben to smoke the peace pipe and then travel with him to a gathering. Reuben woke up before they could begin smoking the peace pipe. Reuben mentioned that he felt strange about that dream, that he had awakened from it abruptly, even though he had wanted to smoke that peace pipe and go along with his brother.

Although that meeting to doctor him did make him feel better temporarily, Reuben's health continued to deteriorate slowly. Two weeks before he died, his son went to visit him at the intensive care unit in the hospital in Sioux City. Darren asked his father if they could hold another prayer meeting for him. Reuben told his son that he wanted to wait until he got home from the hospital.

On June 25, 1993, Reuben Snake came home from the hospital. He promptly told Darren and his brothers about the vivid dream he had that morning before leaving the hospital. In the dream his elder brother, Peter John, brought the peace pipe again. This time Reuben smoked it with him. Then they started walking until they came to a large Indian village where there was a gathering. At the gathering Reuben glimpsed something moving, something glittering like gold. Some sort of golden object was sparkling brightly enough to attract Reuben's attention. He walked toward it and found Sterling Snake, his other older brother, holding a golden eagle feather. Sterling fanned Reuben off with the sparkling golden eagle feather. After being fanned off (cleansed and blessed), Reuben woke up and prayed: "God, let me make it home one more time. I want to use that medicine, I want to sit in the tepee, to hear that drumming, to hear that singing and experience all those wonderful things we have in the Native American Church one more time." Then he told Darren that the moment Darren had entered the house and proposed that they have a Native American Church meeting he knew that his prayer had been answered.

Reuben told Darren that he had wanted to ordain him, to officially present him with the staff and sacred instruments at a tepee meeting but that circumstances had prevented it. "Son, I want you to run that meeting. When you finish conducting that meeting you can take that staff and those instruments home with you." Darren felt elated that his father had lived long enough to give him the prayer staff, that prayer staff which had been given to Reuben by Michael WhiteSnake, who had inherited it from its original maker, Thomas Earth. His father explained the history behind that prayer staff, and advised Darren, "These sacred instruments I am giving you are going to take care of you, they are going to provide a way for you, and a home for you. Whenever anybody needs prayers, pray for them." Darren cherished the sacred instruments he was receiving but felt bad accepting those instruments because of the thought that his father was now letting go of the only thing he had relied upon, leaned on, and trusted in to keep him alive.

The sacred instruments Darren received from his father included the prayer staff, a blessed peyote called the "chief peyote," an eagle-bone whistle, a wooden flute, an altar cloth and the eagle feather that is placed on top of it, an eagle-tail fan, a bundle of sage, and a drum. His wife was given the pail in which consecrated water is carried and the set of bowls in which morning foods are offered before being consumed by the congregation.

Darren put the tepee up in his father's backyard while arrangements for Reuben's final Native American Church meeting were completed. Reuben began the meeting seated in a wheelchair. By morning he was able to walk around the fire. During that meeting Reuben spoke to his grandchildren about the folly of acting like those non-Indian youths who become gang members. "If you put God first in your life you won't be a lost person, you won't need to use drugs, alcohol or join gangs." As he spoke to his grandchildren his love for them moved him to tears. He advised them to treasure their Ho Chunk heritage.

Reuben's final prayer meeting went well. Darren, the newly ordained Roadman, returned to his own house. Scarcely two hours after arriving home Darren's younger brother, Michael, arrived there. Michael was crying, saying that "Dad is ready to go." Darren quickly returned to his father's house. When he walked into the house he was immediately fascinated by a beautiful sparkle radiating from his dad's eyes. After assuring his son he was not in the least crazy, Reuben declared, "Let us sing praises to God. I am getting ready to go but I want to see you and your family one more time."

Darren and his brother started singing while preparations for devotions (a short version of the all-night prayer meeting) were made. Reuben sang a favorite Morning Song, one praising God and Jesus Christ. Reuben ate medicine (peyote), drank holy water, and ate morning food once more. When they had finished their devotions Reuben ate what was to be his last meal, some Indian soup and fry bread which he had requested. It was late Sunday night when Darren went to sleep, with some hope that his father might get well again. Darren was soon awakened by his sister, Janet Bass. He heard thunder and lightning nearby while Janet told him that his dad was gone.

As he entered the room where his father had been alive, he heard his mother giving a big war whoop, to celebrate Reuben's passing. According to relatives present there, thunder rolled in from the west, hovered over the house, and then crashed directly behind the house. At the moment when the thunder and lightning shook the earth behind his house, Reuben's spirit left his body. The thunder then returned slowly toward the west.

Darren's report about Reuben's last few hours on earth reminded me that Reuben's earliest memory was of his beloved grandmother praying with tobacco to the spirit of Thunder one spring morning at Big Bear Hollow. After singing his last praises to God and joining his family in prayer, Reuben's life on earth was complete. Darren and I believe that his spirit traveled west with the rolling Thunder.[1]

Kathy reported that her husband's eyes had remained open after he passed away. She is confident that Reuben's eyes were focused on Jesus Christ at the moment his spirit left his body.

Darren said his father's funeral was beautiful. "He was a man greatly loved, not only by his family, but by the people of his community, of his country and of the world. I really believe I am going to see him again; as long as I work for God, I am going to see my dad again in the spirit world."

After his father's funeral Darren dreamed about him. In that dream Reuben showed his son that achieving spiritual maturity would require that he do more than learn how to forgive. He must also learn how to overcome his anger toward those whose behavior annoys or disappoints him, and simultaneously become committed to setting a good example for them. The value of "walking your talk" was the message this dream, and Reuben's life, conveyed eloquently.

Reuben's living faith had transformed his life and improved the lives of many people who knew him.[2] Reuben's life will always remind me of heroes such as Martin Luther King, Gandhi, Crazy Horse, Buddha, Mohammed, and Jesus Christ. Visualizing Jesus Christ as a bodhisattva figure, as the redeemer who suffers for the sake of his friends, must have guided Reuben gracefully through the many obstacles and hardships encountered in his quest for justice.

Reuben kept the faith, remaining committed to following the example set by Jesus Christ. He kept compassion alive while working to achieve justice for Native Americans. When I knew him his body was in pitiful condition. Yet he was still doing all he could possibly do to win religious freedom for the Native American Church. The pain and suffering he endured had strengthened his spirit. His integrity and his passion for justice will continue to inspire me and others who knew him.

Reuben brought tremendous intelligence and humor to his efforts to harmonize Native American beliefs with Christ's message. His words and deeds strengthened my conviction that the best of Christ's teachings can and should be integrated with the best of ancient American Indian spirituality.

Reuben considered the spirit of the eagle his lawyer: "The eagle is the one bird that can fly up into the face of God and pierce the clouds and fly way up into the heavens. He carries our message up to God." For Reuben, putting God first in his life, remaining faithful to the first great commandment, meant cherishing the web of life on earth created through a "word of prayer" by the Creator-of-all-things. I was privileged to witness Reuben calling upon God (the Great Spirit) with his eagle feather and eagle-bone whistle in numerous ceremonies of the Native American Church. Some of his reverence for life will remain with me and others who knew him. His spirit endures.

Reuben Snake participating in a "drumming and singing session" (not a ceremony) during the production of *The Peyote Road* (1992), in Santa Fe, New Mexico. Photograph by Gary Rhine.

Afterword
by Walter Echo-Hawk

R euben A. Snake, Jr., *(Kikawa Unga)* passed away on June 28, 1993. He was buried with full tribal and Native American Church rites by his beloved family and Ho Chunk people on the Winnebago Reservation in Nebraska. His death was a great loss to his family and to the Ho Chunk people; and his passing was deeply mourned by the thousands of Native and non-Native peoples whose lives had been touched by this great man. It is hard to express the meaning of Reuben's life, yet it is fitting that we try to define the wonderful legacy he left us.

Reuben Snake was truly a great man—for any age or race of people. He was at once an accomplished warrior, orator, religious leader, writer, educator, diplomat/statesman, humorist, ambassador, singer, humble servant, and leader. He carried out these roles with courage, pride in his heritage, compassion, and humility about himself on behalf of his beloved Native peoples in the great battles and issues of our day. True to his name, he was able "to rise up"—with tireless self-sacrifice— to meet the challenges of his day, to transcend differences, and to provide vision.

While he experienced a troubled youth quite familiar to many Native Americans, Reuben's quest for Native American justice, freedom, and humanity during his adult life gives us a role model comparable to Nelson Mandela, Martin Luther King, Jr., Chief Joseph, and Chief Seattle. In his latter days, as a profoundly spiritual leader of the Native American Church, he played a key role in defending this ancient American religion (leading to the posthumous passage of federal legislation to protect the religious use of peyote in 1994). He also transcended race and culture, serving as a Native American ambassador to the world at large (leading to his receipt of the World Peace Award in 1993).

To appreciate Reuben's many contributions, it is important to bear in mind the situation of American Indians in the United States during the years of his life, 1937–1993. Ever since the 1890 massacre at Wounded Knee, American Indians had been written off as a defeated people. The Indian Tribes had been conquered and placed on reservations by the late 1880s. Tribal religions were outlawed by the federal government from 1892 until 1934. Federal Indian policy was designed to stamp out all aspects of Indian land holding, subsistence, religion, culture, and language in order to forcibly assimilate Indians into mainstream American culture. This federal policy was not subject to or curbed by recognition of any civil or constitutional rights of Indian people because of their "unique" status as "wards" of the government under American law as interpreted by the Supreme Court.[1] In fact, citizenship was not granted to Indians until the Citizenship Act of 1924 (41 Stat. 350). With respect to Indian lands, federal policy was also intended to "assimilate" them into non-Indian hands. What was essentially theft was done under the guise of "civilizing" the Indians under the General Allotment Act of 1887 (24 Stat. 388). Under the allotment policy, Indian reservation lands were divided up and allotted to individual Indians to abolish traditional Indian ways of communal land-holding, with "surplus" lands being sold or given to non-Indians. This destruction of communal land tenure was supposed to help "civilize" the Indians. Millions of acres of Indian land were lost in a short period. At the same time, the power of the chiefs and traditional tribal governments was replaced by the rule of Bureau of Indian Affairs agents, who on many reservations were selected from various missionary groups. During this period, from about 1892 to Reuben's birth, Indians lived in stark poverty.

In 1934, Congress finally repudiated the failed Allotment Act policy. In a change of course, it enacted the Indian Reorganization Act of 1934 ("IRA") (48 Stat. 984) to "allow" Indian tribes to establish their own forms of government. While the move toward promoting Indian self-government was a step in the right direction, the "IRA" governments—most of which exist today with little change—were not patterned on tradional forms of tribal government but were instead fashioned from a single model in Washington, D.C., and imposed on tribes across the country without regard for their traditional forms of government. The sovereignty and governmental rights of the fledgling IRA governments were not well defined by federal courts nor well recognized by state and federal governments in this early period. Thus, exploitation of Indian property and resources held in trust by the federal government continued unabated on the reservation homelands in a colonial-type situation not unlike apartheid in South Africa.

While the federal ban on tribal religious practices was lifted in 1934, interference with such practices and infringement upon Native religious freedoms continued, particularly in federal and missionary Indian boarding schools, such as the ones attended by Reuben Snake. There, the intent and practice was to "kill the Indian and save the child" by stamping out all aspects of Indian culture and replacing it with what was perceived as more "civilized" White values.

In addition, during this period when Reuben was growing up, brown-skinned Indians (whether assimilated or not) were subject to the same cruel forms of prejudice and discrimination as other minorities in America's "separate but equal" segregated society. The racial caste system remained the de facto law of the land in the United States until the Supreme Court decision in *Brown v. Board of Education*, 347 U.S. 483 (1954). Moreover, the intended improvements of the IRA policies initiated in 1934 were reversed in the virulent federal termination policies of 1953–1961, when Congress enacted a host of laws to promote rapid assimilation of Indians through termination of the federal government's legal, political, and treaty relationship with Indian tribes and the transfer of jurisdiction over Indians and Indian lands to the states. This period was described by one historian as "the most concerted drive against Indian property and Indian survival since the removals following the acts of 1830 and the liquidation of tribes and reservations following 1887."[2]

Thus, when Reuben Snake came of age and reached his Second Hill of Life, the situation of American Indians, sadly, was similar to that of Black South Africans under the apartheid system. However, during the 1960s and 1970s, major changes came to Indian country. Awakened and inspired by the African-American civil rights movement and leaders such as Martin Luther King, Jr., Native people saw that it was possible to change their situation and define for themselves their social aspirations. So a civil rights movement—Indian Style—came to Indian country led by such organizations as the American Indian Movement and the National Indian Youth Council. The aspirations of the Indian civil rights movement were different from those of Black people. For Indians, treaty rights, sovereignty, self-rule, self-determination, and the cultural freedom to be different (Indian) were the primary goals, even though other Fourteenth Amendment freedoms and basic civil rights were also sought.

Reuben A. Snake, Jr., was the national leader of the American Indian Movement during the height of this movement in the early 1970s. His courage and vision were sought in the historic demonstrations and take-overs in the battle to rekindle Indian pride and to change fundamentally the way Americans view Native peoples. Just as Nelson Mandela and Martin Luther King, Jr., led their people during historic periods of social change, Reuben led Native American activists during our critical human rights period in this century—when incidents at Wounded Knee (1973) and the Trail of Broken Treaties and many other events forever changed the way America views its indigenous people and the way Indians view themselves.

Coinciding with the activist movement, Indian tribes went to court in the 1960s and 1970s to win and define their rights as governments and to refine tribal sovereignty, treaty rights and the status of Indian governments in the American political system and constitution. During these decades and into the 1980s, Indian tribes gradually acquired more experience and sophistication as modern governments. An impressive array of tribal government leaders emerged to improve tribal infrastructures and expand the exercise of governmental power in many areas, including economic development and the retention of Native cultural values important to tribal members. When I first met Reuben Snake in 1978, he was one of these outstanding tribal leaders—busily at work as the chairman of the Winnebago Tribe of Nebraska making major strides in bringing to fruition Ho Chunk aspirations for sovereignty and self-rule.

On the national level from the 1970s into the 1990s, Native advocacy in Washington, D.C., became more sophisticated and effective as tribal governments and organizations came into their own on grassroots, local levels, through the leadership of organizations such as the National Congress of American Indians (NCAI). Here was Reuben Snake, again—president of NCAI.

If measured by cultural pride and revival, self-determination and sovereignty, Native America's situation in the United States had improved significantly between 1937 and 1993, the year of Reuben's untimely death. This process was aided in significant measure by the tireless work of Reuben A. Snake, Jr. The self-sacrifices he made as a "humble serpent" and great leader made a difference in the lives of thousands of peoples. Along the way, he touched many people with his humor, his respect for people, his honesty, and his humility.

During his life, he served on many national boards and fought many important fights on a national and international level for Native people. One such fight, discussed below, may have been closest to his heart—the battle for Native American religious freedom and to defend his beloved Native American Church.

In 1990, the Supreme Court ruled in *Employment Division, Oregon v. Smith,* 494 U.S. 872 (1990), that the First Amendment does not protect the religious use of peyote by Indians in Native American Church prayer services. This decision, and its supporting rationale, was shocking in many respects and produced immediate outrage by church and civil libertarian groups across the country. First, the decision was a sweeping retreat from First Amendment legal principles and caselaw protecting freedom of worship for all Americans under the "compelling state interest" test.[3] Legal scholars were upset, because settled caselaw was disturbed. Citizens were disturbed, because the decision weakened religious liberty for all citizens in the United States.[4] Yet, for Indians, the *Smith* decision was devastating. The lack of legal protection for the religious use of peyote created a "loophole" in the First Amendment for Indians[5] and a human rights crisis seen in arrests, prosecutions, court-martials, and employment discrimination against members of the Native American Church. The Native American Church—which is composed of a diverse and autonomous number of organizations and chapters that, until the *Smith* crisis, had never been united on a national basis—was faced with a battle for its very survival: Would this ancient American religious practice become another victim of government suppression—like the Ghost Dance—or would it be able to survive and flourish into the next generation? Once again, Native people turned to Reuben Snake, who, despite failing health, took up this challenge to save his beloved religion. Under his spiritual guidance and stature, the Native American Church was able to transcend its many factions in order to become unified and organized for a long and grueling human rights campaign for the passage of a law to protect this religious way of life. Along the way, Reuben was our Gandhi, our Chief Joseph, and Crazy Horse in one person.

Reuben's untimely death in 1993 came during the latter legislative stages of the movement, which he had set in motion, to protect Native American religious freedom. As the inspirational spiritual leader of the Native American Church and a founder of the legislative movement, his presence was sorely missed by Native American Church leaders who carried on the campaign to its successful, historic conclusion.

On October 6, 1994, President Clinton signed into law the American Indian Religious Freedom Act Amendments of 1994 (Public Law 103–433) to protect the religious use of peyote by Indians. This landmark new law overturned the *Smith* case! Further, it legalizes Indian religious use of the holy sacrament peyote in all fifty states; and it prohibits penalties or discrimination against Indians on the basis of this religious practice. In short, the new law safeguards the spiritual way of life embraced by Reuben and the 250,000 members of the Native American Church. This federal law guarantees that a remarkable, spiritually profound, and very ancient indigenous religion will survive. While Reuben did not live to see the enactment of this law, his spirit was strongly felt by all who worked on the legislation and he undoubtedly guided its passage from the Spirit World.

Leadership for a people in need. This is what Reuben A. Snake, Jr., blessed us with through his example. Many of his teachings on leadership are found in this book and I respectfully quote some at length:

> Native American leaders must have certain qualities. A leader has got to have some guts, to have some machismo. A leader has got to have something inside that moves him to stand up and say what needs to be said . . . [so] a leader must have some bravery and be willing to challenge the system and change it for the better. . . . That's one of the attributes of a leader, to have a brave heart, but along with this is to have humility. A leader must also have some kind of vision for the future. Most of us are caught up in the day-to-day struggle for survival. We don't like to think way down the road. . . . A leader has to look at things and see how they are and then think about how they could be. The Iroquois people like to say, "Think seven generations ahead." . . . Along with that a leader has to have equal respect for everyone, regardless of who they are. One should respect every individual. One should not treat some people in a certain way and treat other people a different way. A leader is going to treat everybody alike.

All the problems that these institutions have generated for Indian people can be overcome. But Indian people must make

249

a commitment. That's what I preach to younger people today: sacrifice. In the old days, our ancestors had, as a regular part of life, a sacrifice for the well-being of the people. Whether that was sun dancing or something else, sacrifices were made on behalf of the people. It has to be that way again if we intend to overcome all these problems.We have to learn what sacrifice means. . . . I also believe one must try to develop one's mind in order to discipline oneself. Self-discipline is necessary; nobody else is going to discipline a person so that person does things right. . . . One can go out and acquire the tools provided by the White man's education. Once can learn how to be a lawyer, a doctor, an engineer, a teacher, a social worker, or whatever. But one must take that teaching and bring it back to one's people. It should be brought back to our people and used among our people. . . . [C]ome back to [your] home communities and try to make a difference. . . .

I believe that the foundation of all of our lives should be our spirituality. No matter what one plans to do with one's life, one should develop a spiritual relationship with the Creator and the Divine Creation. To do so means one has to learn from the elders. . . . They're going to say things to us and show us things that are vital for us to develop our spirituality.

Reuben A. Snake, Jr. *(Kikawa Unga,* "to rise up") left many lessons in leadership, not only for Native Americans living in the twentieth century but for all ages and races of people. The beloved Humble Serpent will be missed, but never forgotten, as Native people continue the struggle to achieve his vision.

Notes

INTRODUCTION

1. The Winnebago Indian language belongs to the Siouan language family. The English name *Winnebago* was adopted from the Algonquian Indian word *Winipeko,* which means "people of the dirty water," commonly identified with the Fox River and Lake Winnebago, located south of Green Bay, Wisconsin (Lurie 1978: 690, 706). The meaning of the self-chosen name, Ho Chunk, could be "great voice," "people of the parent speech," or perhaps "big fish people." Some Winnebago prefer the second meaning because it corresponds to chronicles asserting that their language is the most archaic of all Siouan languages. Others favor the latter meaning, observing that it shows their aboriginal dependence on the large sturgeon once abundant in the waters of their homeland (Lurie 1978: 706; Radin 1970: 5). Another possible meaning of Ho Chunk has been given by Felix White, Sr., a Nebraska Winnebago. White's definition, "voice of praise," suggests that every time Ho Chunk (the language) is spoken it is uttered in praise of the Creator (Danker 1994b).

Nancy Lurie's concise history of early European encounters with the Winnebago and the Winnebagos' subsequent participation in the fur trade is highly recommended (1978). Lurie suggests that today's Winnebago population is composed of diverse sources. Discovering their ancestry is complicated, requiring sound judgment about how they adapted to the ravages of warfare, infectious disease, and the massive influx of Algonquian peoples and remnant Hurons from the East fleeing the Iroquois (Lurie 1978: 692). After years of research Lurie concludes that "much of 'traditional' Winnebago culture is the culture of the fur-trade period" (Lurie 1978: 696).

Lurie notes that before treaty-making began the aboriginal Ho Chunk homeland, centered in Wisconsin and northern Illinois, was encroached upon by refugees of various Indian tribes fleeing toward the west from the east (Lurie 1978: 692). She emphasizes that Winnebago culture was modified extensively to adjust to such refugees, first by fighting with them, later by assimilating them. In order to profit from the trade in fur-bearing mammals, the Winnebago evidently intermarried with and borrowed heavily from Algonquian Indian refugees (Lurie 1978: 692).

2. The American victory in the War of 1812, in which the Winnebago fought as allies of the British, initiated the treaty-making era in which most aboriginal Winnebago territory was ceded to the United States of America. To accomplish this land "transfer," the Winnebago signed eight treaties (Danker 1994a; Jackson 1964), the three most important of which were ratified by the U.S. government in 1829, 1832, and 1837 (Fay 1966, Hughes 1969, Lurie 1966: 112–113, Lurie 1978: 697–699; McKenney and Hall 1933, Turner 1951). A substantial segment of the Winnebago tribe complained that fraud had been used to induce them to sign the 1837 treaty (Lurie 1978: 699). Accordingly, they refused to be forcibly relocated from Wisconsin. The last major removal of Wisconsin Winnebagos occurred in 1874 (Jackson 1964: 242–244; Lurie 1966: 2, 19, 113; Lurie 1978: 702). Hundreds of indomitable Winnebagos managed to remain in Wisconsin.

Lurie (1978: 705) reports that the 1837 land cession was obtained by chicanery and has caused "irreparable social damage in dividing the Winnebago as a people." Nevertheless, Winnebagos from Wisconsin and Nebraska frequently visit and intermarry with one another. The U.S. government's appointed court, the Indian Claims Commission, eventually decided to pay the Winnebago fifty cents per acre, the value of their land in 1837. In 1977 the total payment for the 1837 lands was divided equally between Wisconsin and Nebraska Winnebago. The Wisconsin Winnebago distributed all their money on a per capita basis. The Nebraska Winnebago distributed 70% of their money on a per capita basis and invested the remaining 30% in tribally controlled projects (Blackhawk 1994).

Some 600 Winnebago homesteads were registered after 1881, when legislation authorized Wisconsin Winnebago to take up 40-acre homesteads (Lurie 1978: 702). As of mid-1994 about 4,850 Winnebagos inhabit some 6,500 acres in Wisconsin.

The Winnebago Reservation created in northeastern Nebraska by the treaty of 1865 is located along the Missouri River, just north of the Omaha Indian Reservation. This Nebraska-Winnebago Reservation was established in exchange for land in Crow Creek, South Dakota (Lurie 1966: 112–113, 1978: 700).

In what can be called at best a misguided effort to assimilate American Indians by abolishing their communal land holdings, Congress passed the General Allotment Act, also known as the Dawes Act. The Dawes Act declared that Indians who received allotments were to become United States citizens. On most Indian reservations where this federal law was implemented, each head of family was able to retain only 160 acres and each single person over eighteen would keep eighty acres (Prucha 1990: 171). In Nebraska, however, Winnebago family heads were receiving patents for eighty acres of land before the Dawes Act (Jackson 1964: 241–245). The ultimate result of the

General Allotment Act was a loss of two-thirds of all Indian lands in the United States, from a total of 150 million acres in 1887 to 50 million in 1934, when the Indian Reorganization Act halted the sales of "surplus" Indian land (Grossman 1979: 9).

The Nebraska-Winnebago Reservation included about 100,000 acres prior to the General Allotment Act of 1887. From 1888 to 1934, the amount of reservation land in Nebraska was reduced by almost two-thirds because better land was rapidly sold once individual Winnebagos gained fee simple title to it (Lurie 1966: 19, 1978: 700). To facilitate acquisition of the most fertile Winnebago lands, those comprising the western two-thirds of the reservation in northeastern Nebraska, White farmers cajoled Indians to exchange their trust lands for fee simple patents. Whites successfully lobbied Congress to relax regulations governing sales of Indian allotments (Kneale 1950: 198–205). Around 1910 the Indian Bureau, "apparently dissatisfied with the lack of speed with which the Indian was relieving himself of his land," created "competency commissions" to examine all Indians on a particular reservation and determine which ones could be permitted to continue holding their land in trust (Kneale 1950: 223). As of mid-1994 about 3,800 Winnebagos reside on the 27,000-acre reservation in Nebraska.

3. The Sioux uprising in Minnesota was predictable inasmuch as virtually all their aboriginal land had been surrendered by treaties of 1805, 1837, 1851, and 1858. By 1862 the Sioux in southern Minnesota were confined to a narrow strip of land which provided poor hunting. Indian agency delays in dispensing annuities of money and goods to the Sioux had left them on the brink of starvation during the month prior to their revolt (Babcock 1962; Jackson 1964: 162–164).

Some Winnebagos, led by Little Priest, were alleged to have fought with the Santee during the first few days of their uprising, including the siege of New Ulm, Minnesota (Danker 1994a; Hughes 1969: 148–154). However, the military commission which passed judgment on the Sioux found "no evidence to support these claims" (Lass 1963: 353). Hysteria about Indian warriors and the prospect of gaining more Indian land prompted some prominent Minnesota men to persuade Congress to pass national legislation to forcibly remove the peaceful Winnebago from their reservation in Blue Earth County. By the end of June 1863, scarcely four months after the Winnebago removal bill became public law, almost 2,000 Winnebago had been relocated to a hastily established reservation at Crow Creek, South Dakota. As the winter of 1863 approached, a severe lack of food, shelter, and clothing forced many Winnebago to leave the new reservation (Hughes 1969: 154; Jackson 1964: 393–394; Lass 1963: 364; Lurie 1978: 700).

4. What remains of the Huichol Indian homeland (some 4,107 square kilometers of rugged mountain and canyon country) is located in northwestern Mexico, about 150 miles north of Guadalajara. The famous Huichol peyote hunt, which until recently required that Huichol temple officers complete a round-trip of some 700 kilometers on foot, is but one of at least ten subsistence-oriented rituals traditionally performed at various aboriginal temples. Peyote *(Lophophora williamsii)* is revered by the Huichol as the heart, mind, or memory *(iyari)* of their Creator and tutelary spirit, *Caoyomari.* Unlocking the wisdom of the Creator's heart-soul, which is incarnate in peyote, is what enables Huichols to heal and sing effectively (Fikes 1985: 255). The immortal wolves are esteemed as "elder brothers" who set precedents in deer, rabbit, and peyote hunting. Huichols are obliged to eat peyote—the Creator's heart—raw, thereby replicating the precedent the wolves set. Huichols neither cook peyote nor use peyote enemas. To take enemas would be sacrilegious as well as unnecessary. Huichols eat peyote raw, or else they dry it out, grind it up, and consume it in water.

The notion that Huichol use peyote enemas is one of numerous bizarre and unverified practices which have been attributed to them since the mid-1960s (Fikes 1993a, 1993b). Other outrageous assertions include defaming *Caoyomari,* their Creator and tutelary spirit, as "one who does not know himself" or "one who makes others crazy" (see Fikes 1993a: 109, 117) and claiming that stunts performed beside a waterfall near Guadalajara are indicative of "shamanic balance" (see Fikes 1993a: 70–78).

5. My observations led me to conclude that Reuben Snake, like other Nebraska Winnebago members of the NAC, felt comfortable participating in either of two major types of peyote meeting. The first type, the Big-Moon peyote meeting, was brought from Oklahoma by John Rave around 1890. The second variety of meeting, the Half-Moon, was introduced to the Nebraska Winnebago in 1912 by Jesse Clay, a Winnebago who had lived among the Arapaho (Stewart 1990: 150–158). Stewart has concluded that the basic beliefs underlying these two most prominent types of peyote ceremony are similar. One obvious way in which the Half-Moon ceremony (popularized by people such as Quanah Parker of the Comanche) differs from the Big-Moon ceremony (disseminated most notably by John Wilson of the Caddo) concerns the shape of the altar. In John Wilson's Big-Moon ceremony the altar was larger

> and in the shape of a horseshoe rather than a crescent. The ceremonial arrangement was also more complex. A mound representing the sun was constructed immediately opposite the door to the east of a heart and a cross. From the center of the doorway and through 'the sun' a line was either imagined or drawn to the center of the altar where the Chief Peyote was placed, sometimes surmounted by a crucifix. This line was called the Peyote Road. (Stewart 1990: 91)

Wilson's version of the peyote meeting brought Jesus, the crucifix, the Bible, and other Christian elements into the ceremony more often than did the Half-Moon way of worship. Wilson's Big-Moon ceremony eventually evolved into the Cross-Fire style of peyote meeting in which the use of sacred tobacco was prohibited (Steinmetz 1990, Stewart 1990: 93).

In 1931 Frances Densmore observed first-hand that differences in peyote ceremonies were obvious but that Winnebago worshipers in both branches of peyote meeting thrived without any antagonism. Densmore also noted that John Rave's ceremony featured fewer aboriginal American elements than did the Half-Moon ceremony popularized by Jesse Clay. "The followers of Rave were said to use songs and customs derived from the Quapaw and Oto tribes while Jesse Clay followed the Arapaho customs" (Densmore quoted in Stewart 1990: 158).

Participants in John Rave's Cross-Fire ceremony were required to give up alcohol as well as tobacco. They were also expected to stop sponsoring traditional feasts, and to destroy their warbundles and sacred medicine bags (Radin 1963: 48–49). In their zeal to abandon traditional Winnebago ways, the Cross-Fire peyotists acquired enemies, especially among members of the Medicine Lodge Society (Lurie 1966: 46–51, 129–130; Radin 1963: 48–49, Radin 1970: 376–378). Radin's research indicated that the greatest opposition to peyote meetings came from elderly Winnebago shamans who felt peyotists denied "the doctrine of reincarnation" and feared that "the Christian doctrine of the immortality of the soul" was not a viable substitute (Radin 1970: 378).

Lurie (1978: 701) suggests that factionalization among the Winnebago was further exacerbated as more and more Winnebagos were converted to divergent denominations of Christianity by non-Indians. By 1959 Winnebago Half-Moon meetings had become quite popular, perhaps partly because they had incorporated prayers and testimonials. During this time the congregation for Rave's Cross-Fire ceremony decreased greatly, at least in Nebraska (Lurie 1966: 51, 130). By 1959 ancient Winnebago ceremonies were performed almost exclusively by a minority of traditionalists centered in Wisconsin (Lurie 1978: 701).

CHAPTER 1

1. The Quapaw, a Siouan-speaking tribe, were evidently living in wretched conditions among the Osage tribe in Oklahoma when they first learned how to conduct peyote ceremonies from John Wilson around 1890 (Stewart 1990: 113). Wilson, one of the most energetic and charismatic Roadmen of his day, and his Quapaw proteges had all been trained by Roman Catholics. The "Quapaw fireplace" which John Painter Sr. inherited had evolved into the Cross-Fire form of peyote ceremony by the time Reuben Snake was baptized.

By 1937 almost all Winnebago peyotists were favorably predisposed toward the Bible. Albert Hensley, a Winnebago who attended Carlisle Indian School, had, perhaps by 1908, persuaded Winnebago peyotists to set Bibles on their altars and to perform Christian baptisms (LaBarre 1989: 73–74; Radin 1970: 372–374; Stewart 1990: 152–153). Biblical references were, and still are, frequently quoted in Winnebago peyote songs, in pre-dawn testimonials and sermons. The three leaders of the meeting—the Roadman, his drummer, and the cedar (prayer) chief—were (and still are) said to represent the Father, the Son, and the Holy Ghost. Hensley called peyote a "Holy medicine" and eloquently conveyed the kind of reverence Reuben Snake always demonstrated for this supreme sacrament of the NAC. Speaking for Winnebago peyotists, Hensley declared:

> . . .to us it is a portion of the body of Christ, even as the communion bread is believed to be a portion of Christ's body by other Christian denominations. . . . Christ spoke of a Comforter who was to come. . . . it never came to Indians until it was sent by God in the form of this Holy Medicine.
> (quoted in Stewart 1990: 157)

2. The Thunder or Thunderbird Clan was "unquestionably the most important of all the Winnebago clans" (Radin 1970: 159). Members of the clan trace their ancestry to a location on Green Bay (Radin 1970: 159) Reviewing his research, Radin concluded that Winnebago society had originally been stratified (1948: 45) and that the peace chief of the Winnebago tribe had been selected from among certain families of the Thunderbird Clan (Radin 1970: 159–161). Lurie states (1978: 693) that there is disagreement about whether the Winnebago peace chief "was necessarily from a particular lineage of the Thunder clan." Fire was regarded as a sacred possession of the Thunderbird Clan, and clan members called themselves "thunderbirds because they, like the true thunderbirds, caused a drizzling rain and fog when they went about" (Radin 1970: 160–162).

The tobacco that Reuben's grandmother offered to the Thunderbirds is the most treasured possession of traditional Winnebago. Earthmaker, the Creator, took pity on humans and gave them tobacco, to be used as their foremost offering to the spirits of nature. After giving each of those nature spirits a puff of sacred tobacco, Earthmaker told them that they would have to obtain tobacco from human beings, "the only ones of my creation who are poor. If a human being gives a pipeful and makes a request we will always grant it" (Radin 1970: 18). Kathleen Danker, citing Paul Radin and Felix White, Sr., has explained how the Winnebago belief, that human beings were created last and considered the least important of all of Earthmaker's creations, does more than underscore the sacredness of tobacco. As Danker notes, this cornerstone of the Winnebago worldview contrasts dramatically with the orthodox Judeo-

256

Christian image of our species being the greatest of all God's creatures, the one given dominion over other plants and animals. "The Winnebagos' belief that human beings were created so lowly accords with their general emphasis on humility" (Danker 1994b). This Winnebago view contributed significantly to Reuben Snake's commitment to being a humble serpent.

CHAPTER 2

1. By 1908, when Radin began studying this ancient religious society, initiation was potentially open to any Winnebago from any clan. Membership could be obtained by applying for admission and, upon acceptance, making the required payments (Radin 1970: 312). To initiate a Winnebago man or woman into the Medicine Lodge Society involves numerous activities, including symbolically killing candidates (by shooting a sacred shell into the body) and then symbolically resurrecting them, by giving away their clothes and redressing them in other clothes (Radin 1970: 320, 330). Instructions for living a new life during the remainder of one's lifetime on earth as well as in one's existence after death were also revealed to the initiates. The Winnebago Creator, Earthmaker, taught Hare (their "culture hero" or ruler of this terrestrial world) how to perform this ceremony, advising him that whenever a man or woman performs

> everything properly he will have more than one life. I will always keep the door (through which he may return to earth) open to him. When he becomes reincarnated he can live wherever he wishes. He can return (to the earth) as a human being or he can join the different bands of spirits, or finally he can become (a being) below the earth (Radin 1970: 307).

When Hare first explained how to perform this ceremony he also promised Winnebago men and women that they would be able to complete their journey through the four hills of life, i.e., live to a ripe old age, if they performed this ceremony properly (Radin 1970: 310–311, 330).

According to Hultkrantz (1979: 122–124), the beliefs animating the complex and esoteric initiation ceremony of the Winnebago Medicine Lodge closely resemble those of medicine lodges existing among central Algonquian Indian tribes inhabiting the Great Lakes region (e.g., Menominee and Chippewa). Lurie, citing Radin (1945, 1950), insists that the Winnebago Medicine Lodge differs dramatically from Algonquian versions and recognizes that the Winnebago sacred shell "shooting rite symbolizes reincarnation rather than magical resuscitation of the dead" (Lurie 1978: 696).

CHAPTER 6

1. During the 1950s the BIA implemented a relocation policy to move American Indians permanently from their reservations to urban areas such as Los Angeles and Chicago. Many Indians received financial assistance "to cover all or part of the costs of transportation to the place of relocation and short-term temporary subsistence." Others were provided relocation services only, including "counseling and guidance prior to relocation, and assistance in establishing residence and securing permanent employment in the new community" (Prucha 1990: 237). The goal of relocation, to facilitate assimilation of Indians into urban America, was resoundingly rejected later by activists such as Reuben Snake.

CHAPTER 9

1. The Johnson-O'Malley Act became federal law (U.S. Statute 48: 596) on April 16, 1934. It authorized the Secretary of the Interior (and thus the BIA) to enter into contracts with individual states to improve the "education, medical attention, agricultural assistance, and social welfare" of American Indians (Prucha 1990: 221–222).

2. The U.S. Supreme Court ruled in *United States v. Sioux Nations,* 448 U.S. 371 (1980) that eight Sioux tribes were entitled to money in compensation for land in the Black Hills region of South Dakota seized by non-Indians. The eight beneficiary tribes have refused to accept the money, which by early 1994 totalled more than $350 million, as it sits in the U.S. Treasury accruing interest (Lazarus 1991). The prominent lawyer and scholar Vine Deloria has concluded that this Supreme Court case is based upon "a history of duplicitous dealings with an Indian nation" and announces a ruling which transforms the presumption that Congress must act in "good faith" when taking Indian property into "a fictional hurdle placed before Indian litigants to narrow the application of the Fifth Amendment to so few occasions as to be meaningless as a protection for the Indian nations" (Deloria 1992: 309).

CHAPTER 10

1. Today over 14,000 Oglala Sioux (Lakota) live on the Pine Ridge Reservation in South Dakota. The Oglala are the westernmost of seven tribes classified as Teton or Western Sioux. The Western Sioux are one of three major linguistic/geographical groups of Sioux (Matthiessen 1992: xxv; Steltenkamp 1993: 5). The Pine Ridge Reservation includes Wounded Knee, the place where over 150 defenseless Lakota were murdered by the U.S. 7th Cavalry in 1890. Wounded Knee epitomizes the end of Indian independence.

Reuben Snake accurately identified the underlying cause of the 1973 conflict at Wounded Knee between AIM supporters and followers of Richard Wilson, the Oglala Tribal Chairman. There was a deep schism between AIM members (and their allies, primarily more traditional Oglala Sioux Indians) and proponents of the Oglala tribal government established under the auspices of the Indian Reorganization Act of 1934 (Deloria 1985: 19–20, 40–41, 63–83, 187–206; Matthiessen 1992: 27–30). Moreover, Richard Wilson was evidently resentful of Russell Means, an AIM leader who returned to the Oglala Reservation in 1972 and announced that he would eventually run against Wilson for the office of Oglala Tribal Chairman (Deloria 1985: 70–71; Matthiessen 1992: 61). Matthiessen also suggests (1992: 61–62) that Russell Means and the Oglala traditionalists were viewed as a threat by hundreds of Oglala tribal government employees whose jobs might be eliminated if Means were to be elected. Fear that an alliance of traditional Oglalas and AIM activists might lead to termination of uranium mining has also been invoked to explain "the government's remorseless attitude toward militant Indians" (Matthiessen 1992: 106). Deloria declares (1985: 48–62, 207) that AIM leaders felt betrayed by the Nixon Administration's indifference toward the Twenty Points they had presented to the U.S. government a few months earlier during the Trail of Broken Treaties. Their disappointment at Nixon's rejection of the treaty rights issues in the Twenty Points surely contributed to the indomitable attitude AIM leaders displayed at Wounded Knee.

Several minor incidents also contributed to the collision between AIM and the Oglala Tribal Council. The siege finally erupted after AIM demanded Congressional hearings on the Twenty Points treaty rights issues and an investigation of alleged misconduct in the BIA. This "Oglala Sioux declaration of independence" triggered a massive U.S. paramilitary operation in which numerous U.S. Marshals, FBI agents, and BIA police surrounded AIM supporters for 71 or 72 days (Deloria 1985; Matthiessen 1992; Redford 1992). The occupation of Wounded Knee ended with neither side victorious. A few weeks later, the letter sent by the same Nixon aide who had discarded the Twenty Points stated that the days of treaty-making had ended in 1871. "Only Congress can rescind or change in any way statutes enacted since 1871, such as the Indian Reorganization Act of 1934" (Matthiessen 1992: 81–82).

Once the siege ended, more than 500 arrests of Indians were made. Subsequently 185 federal indictments were brought but over 90 percent were dismissed or resulted in acquittals (Matthiessen 1992: 82; Redford 1992). Tension between the pro-Wilson faction and AIM sympathizers increased dramatically from mid-May of 1973 until June 26, 1975. In an atmosphere of intimidation and distrust, two FBI agents (whose identity as agents was unknown at that time) were killed in a shoot-out on June 26, 1975, at the Jumping Bull property about twenty miles east of Wounded Knee (near Oglala, South Dakota). Immediately thereafter some 350 FBI agents conducted what was probably "the largest manhunt in FBI history" (Matthiessen 1992; Redford 1992). Of three AIM members who stood trial for the murder of the two FBI agents, only Leonard Peltier was convicted. Critics continue to insist that Peltier's conviction for murder was based on evidence which was flimsy, if not fabricated (Matthiessen 1992; Redford 1992). Before, during, and after the occupation of Wounded Knee and the shoot-out of June 26, 1975, there was intense FBI scrutiny of suspected activists and AIM sympathizers (Churchill and Vander Wall 1990).

AIM sympathizers have attributed some sixty violent deaths at Pine Ridge to supporters of the Wilson administration. Tim Giago, a prominent Lakota journalist, states that the investigation conducted by his newspaper, the *Lakota Times,* discovered that during the years 1973 to 1976, "There were not more than ten deaths directly attributable to the clashes between members of the American Indian Movements and supporters of the duly elected government of the Oglala Sioux Tribe," (Giago 1993). Although the actual number of activists murdered may be debatable, animosity remains strong because nobody has ever been charged for the murders of Joe Killsright Stuntz, Anna Mae Aquash, and other Indian activists.

The greatest tragedy of the 1973 Wounded Knee confrontation is that the media's preoccupation with the more sensational aspects of the siege helped hide the bold call for Indian sovereignty embodied in the Twenty Points. As Reuben Snake remarked twenty years later, "The injustices of the system that we were living in then still exist today. The media . . . never picked up on the message that we were trying to deliver."

CHAPTER 13

1. Karl May (1842–1912) did actually visit America once, in 1908. Four generations later, his fictional Mescalero Apache chief, Winnetou, continues to fascinate German readers and people attending the pageant at Bad Segeberg.

CHAPTER 16

1. Lurie recognizes that Winnebago religion extols warfare and that war bundles were among the tribe's most sacred objects (1978: 695). Radin reported that the war-bundle feast was one of the principal Winnebago ceremonies (1970: 379) and observed that the Winnebago *Herucka* ceremony was a celebration in which victory songs and dances were synchronized to the beating of a large drum (Radin 1970: 336). Visitors from other tribes were

invited and warriors were especially honored. According to Kathleen Danker (1994a), the *herooshga* was a "dance in which warriors unbind tokens of their raids from their hair to give to their female relatives."

The social gathering known today as the "powwow" has its roots deep in such warrior-respecting traditions. At powwows American Indian war veterans, both living and deceased, are always honored. Reuben Snake was proud of having served his country as a Green Beret not only because he considered himself a patriotic American, but also because powwows, *Herucka* ceremonies, and ancient Winnebago religious beliefs reinforced an aboriginal American warrior tradition. Reuben's pride at being a warrior was inherited by his son, Darren, who once explained to me that members of the Winnebago Snake Clan are expected to be among the first to form the front line in combat. It should be understood, however, that Reuben was never an angry militant. Two days before he passed away he received the World Peace Award from the Sikhs, a religious group with an international membership of more than 18 million.

CHAPTER 17

1. Reuben Snake mentioned that the traditional Winnebago system of patrilineal clans was badly eroded in Nebraska by the time he was born. According to traditional clan protocol, the father's family would have chosen his name from the inventory of Snake Clan names. A lavish feast to publicly proclaim a Winnebago child's name would then have been given (Radin 1963: 90–91). Reuben's name, *Kikawa Unga,* is a bona fide Snake Clan name, but it was given a Christian emphasis because Reuben's grandmother's family belonged to the Native American Church. Their actions indicated their intent to embrace Christ's teachings, even if it meant eliminating or altering orthodox Winnebago customs.

EPILOGUE

1. Darren Snake's statement to me, that traditional Winnebago doctrine affirms that the spirit of the deceased journeys toward the west, is confirmed by the Winnebago "origin myth," as recited by members of the Thunderbird Clan. Radin's "informants" reported that the Creator, Earthmaker, placed a part of himself inside the human body and established that this spirit will return to him if the person has behaved properly throughout life. When the first human being died, "his spirit traveled west toward the setting of the sun, making a road for all who were to come after him. He was the chief of the village of the spirits" (Radin 1970: 167–169). My experiences, and similar reports conveyed by several Winnebago confidantes, make clear that the Winnebago

belief that human life continues after death does not require any great leap of faith. "The deceased may appear to a living individual in dreams and visions" and by talking or making his/her "presence felt in a multitude of ways" (Radin 1970: 266). The conclusion reached by Radin some eighty years ago, that faith in reincarnation is a central feature of the Medicine Lodge Society (Radin 1911), and a fundamental tenet of Winnebago society (Radin 1970: 266), still seems valid today. Kathleen Danker (1994b) suggests that today only members of the Medicine Lodge still profess faith in reincarnation, which traditionally meant "that one will be born again into the Winnebago tribe within a relatively short period of time (typically four years)." Similarly, Paul Radin (1970: 378) mentions that the older shamans were fiercely opposed to Winnebago peyotists because those peyotists had abandoned Winnebago faith in reincarnation after accepting Christian doctrine regarding the immortality of the soul. However, it must be remembered that the peyotists Radin described were participants in John Rave's Cross-Fire ceremony. Further research may be needed to determine whether today's Winnebago Half-Moon peyotists, which included Reuben Snake, endorse an orthodox Christian belief in the soul's immortality, or prefer the traditional Winnebago faith in reincarnation.

2. I considered Reuben Snake my friend, mentor, and brother. It should be obvious that this book is not intended to be an impartial anthropological account of the life of an "informant" or a member of Winnebago culture. Two well-known anthropologists have already published that type of orthodox work. Paul Radin's book, *The Autobiography of a Winnebago Indian,* is about Sam Blowsnake, a member of the Winnebago Snake Clan whom Reuben considered his relative. Reuben had read Sam Blowsnake's autobiography as well as Nancy Lurie's autobiography of Sam Blowsnake's sister, *Mountain Wolf Woman.* We wanted this book to be his autobiography. We agreed that anthropological references would be cited sparingly, only as needed to clarify aspects of his life or culture.

Once Reuben agreed to collaborate with me on writing his autobiography we devoted almost two weeks to tape-recording conversations about his life. Virtually all our interviews were recorded in a building owned by St. Augustine's Indian Mission in Winnebago, Nebraska. This location was quiet, free from interruptions, and close to Reuben Snake's home. Reuben Snake passed on three weeks after we finished our conversations.

It would have been wonderful if he had been able to read and correct the unedited transcripts of our interviews. I feel it is futile to speculate about possible changes and additions he might have made to these transcripts. Readers are asked to trust that the emphasis and meaning Reuben conveyed in our interviews are faithfully preserved in this book.

The edited version of our interviews which readers have in this book differs relatively little from the written transcript of our interviews. The greatest change came when I deleted my questions from the transcript of our interviews. This was done after considerable deliberation, and with great caution. Of course I also had to create paragraphs and define sentences. Some minor editing of many of Reuben's statements was also required. Reuben occasionally repeated particular phrases to emphasize the importance of some of his statements. I usually deleted such repetitions if it seemed that Reuben's intent would be clearly conveyed without them. Certain words which could be considered colloquial, or phrases which contained obscure slang, were periodically converted into more standard forms of English. I also corrected inadequate grammar. The pronoun "you" was almost always changed to "one"; e.g., the phrase, "when you get ill" was edited to the third person pronoun, "when one gets ill." In those extremely rare cases when words were added to what Reuben actually said, those words are included inside parenthesis.

The material which supplements our interviews is obvious and clearly separable from the chronicle Reuben told about his life. I alone am responsible for the introduction, the chapter titles, the Epilogue, the explanatory notes, and the bibliography. I feel confident Reuben would have approved these additions.

AFTERWORD

1. See e.g., *Quick Bear v. Leupp*, 210 U.S. 50 (1908), which upheld the use of federal funds to support a religious mission on an Indian reservation, despite a claim that such governmental action violated prohibition of the Establishment Clause of the First Amendment against government support or entanglement with religion.

2. A. Debo, *A History of the Indians of the United States,* (Norman: University of Oklahoma Press, 1970), 349.

3. This test, which had been routinely applied by the Supreme Court in numerous religious freedom cases for decades, states that government may not lawfully infringe upon worship by citizens under the First Amendment unless there is a "compelling government interest" at stake that cannot be protected by any means less restrictive than curtailing worship.

4. Indeed, in the cases following this 1990 decision, courts were forced to deny the right of worship to religious practitioners of many "mainstream" faiths in various contexts—ironically, treating these citizens like Indians in the context of religious liberty under the rule of *Smith.* When the moccasin was on the other foot, it is little wonder that non-Indian citizens would not tolerate government infringement upon their human right of worship—hence,

a firestorm of outrage led Congress to enact the Religious Freedom Restoration Act of 1993 (107 Stat. 1488, 42 U.S.C. 2000bb, et. seq.)("RFRA"). Ironically, the powerful church coalition which worked tirelessly for the passage of RFRA (working nights and overtime beating down the doors of Congress to protect their own religious practices) refused to include specific relief in this legislation for the Native American Church—and asked Reuben Snake and the Native American Church to seek "separate legislation." Thus, RFRA did not protect the religious use of peyote by Indians—the very issue that prompted the need for the law!

5. That "loophole" was first opened by the 1988 decision in *Lyng v. Northwest Indian Cemetery Association,* 485 U.S. 439 (1988), which denied First Amendment protection for native worship at traditional holy sites located on public lands. Although little noticed by the larger society, which has no sacred sites in America, that decision, which remains in effect today, placed the Supreme Court on the doctrinal slippery slope leading to the infamous *Smith* decision in 1990. While Congress overturned the *Smith* decision in the 1993 RFRA legislation, it has yet to overturn *Lyng,* which remains a pressing human rights need by native peoples to this very day. Tribes continue to witness their irreplaceable tribal sacred sites being destroyed by government actions due to a lack of American legal protection.

Bibliography

Atwater, Caleb. 1831. *Remarks made on a tour to Prairie du Chien.* Columbus: Jenkins and Grover.

Babcock, W.M. 1962. "Minnesota's Indian War." *Minnesota History,* Volume 38, No. 3, 93–98.

Blackhawk, John. 1994. Personal communication, August 24, 1994.

Burnette, Robert and John Koster. 1974. *The Road to Wounded Knee.* New York: Bantam Books.

Churchill, Ward and Jim Vander Wall. 1990. *Agents of Repression: The FBI's Secret Wars against the Black Panther Party and the American Indian Movement.* Boston: South End Press.

Collier, John. 1947. *Indians of the Americas.* New York: New American Library (Mentor Books paperback ed.).

Danker, Kathleen. 1994a. Letter to Jay Fikes, August 16, 1994.

_____. 1994b. Letter to Jay Fikes, November 6, 1994.

Deloria, Vine Jr. 1985 (1974). *Behind the Trail of Broken Treaties: An Indian Declaration of Independence.* Austin: University of Texas Press.

_____. 1992. In Lyons, O.R. and J.C. Mohawk, eds. *Exiled in the Land of the Free.* Santa Fe: Clear Light Publishers.

Deloria, Vine Jr. and Clifford Lytle. 1984. *The Nations Within: The Past and Future of American Indian Sovereignty.* New York: Pantheon Books.

Dorsey, J.O. and P. Radin. 1910. "Winnebago." In Frederick W. Hodge, ed. *Handbook of American Indians North of Mexico.* Washington: U.S. Bureau of American Ethnology, Bulletin 30, Volume 2: 958–961.

Fay, G.E. 1966. *Treaties between the Winnebago Indians and the United States of America, 1816–1865.* Wisconsin Indians Research Institute, Volume 2, No. 1: 7–49.

Fikes, Jay Courtney. 1985. *Huichol Indian Identity and Adaptation.* Doctoral dissertation, University Microfilms International, Ann Arbor, Michigan.

_____. 1993a. *Carlos Castaneda, Academic Opportunism and the Psychedelic Sixties,* Victoria, B.C.: Millenia Press.

_____. 1993b. "Anthropological Visualization of the Huichol in Ethnographic Film: A Discussion of the Problem of Contextualization." In *Anthropological Film and Video in the 1990s.* Edited by Jack R. Rollwagen. Brockport, N.Y.: The Institute, Inc.: 221–240.

Fletcher, J.E. 1854. "Origin and History of the Winnebagos." In H.R. Schoolcraft, ed. *Information Respecting the History, Condition, and Prospects of the Indian Tribes of the United States.* Volume 4. Philadelphia: 227–243.

Giago, Tim. 1993. "Movie Promotes Fiction About Occupation of Wounded Knee." *Albuquerque Journal,* Nov. 12, 1993, A–11.

Griffin, James B. 1960. "A Hypothesis for the Prehistory of the Winnebago." In Stanley Diamond, ed. *Culture in History.* New York: Columbia University Press, 809–865.

Grossman, George S. 1979. *The Sovereignty of American Indian Tribes: A Matter of Legal History.* Minneapolis: Minnesota Civil Liberties Union Foundation.

Hughes, Thomas. 1969 (1927). *Indian Chiefs of southern Minnesota.* Minneapolis: Ross and Haines, Inc.

Hultkrantz, Ake. 1979. *The Religions of the American Indians.* Translated by Monica Setterwall. Berkeley: University of California Press.

Jackson, Helen Hunt. 1964 (1881). *A Century of Dishonor.* Minneapolis: Ross and Haines, Inc.

Kneale, Albert H. 1950. *Indian Agent.* Caldwell, Idaho: Caxton Printers.

Krupat, Arnold. 1985. *For Those Who Come After: A Study of Native American Autobiography.* Berkeley: University of California Press.

LaBarre, Weston. 1989. *The Peyote Cult.* Norman: University of Oklahoma Press.

Lamere, O. and P. Radin. 1913. "Description of a Winnebago funeral." *American Anthropologist,* n.s., 13: 437–444.

Lass, William E. 1963. "The Removal from Minnesota of the Sioux and Winnebago Indians." *Minnesota History,* Volume 38, No. 8: 353–364.

Lazarus, Edward. 1991. *Black Hills/White Justice: The Sioux Nation versus the United States; 1775 to the Present.* New York: Harper Collins.

Lurie, Nancy O. 1953. "Winnebago Berdache." *American Anthropologist,* 55: 708–712.

———. 1960. "Winnebago Protohistory." In Stanley Diamond, ed. *Culture in History.* New York: Columbia University Press: 790–808.

———. 1966. paperback ed. (1961). *Mountain Wolf Woman, Sister of Crashing Thunder: The Autobiography of a Winnebago Indian.* Ann Arbor: University of Michigan Press.

———. 1978. "Winnebago." In William Sturtevant, ed. *Handbook of North American Indians,* Volume 15 (Northeast), 690–707. Washington: Smithsonian Institution.

Matthiessen, Peter. 1992 (1983). *In the Spirit of Crazy Horse.* New York: Viking Press (Penguin Books ed.).

McKenney, Thomas L. and James Hall. 1933–34. *The Indian Tribes of North America, with Biographical Sketches and Anecdotes of the Principal Chiefs.* 1970 edition, Frederick Hodge, ed. 3 volumes. St. Clair Shores, Mich.: Scholarly Press.

Michelson, Truman. 1935. "Some notes on Winnebago social and political organization." *American Anthropologist,* n.s., 37: 446–449.

Mount, Guy. 1993 (3d ed.). *The Peyote Book: A Study of Native Medicine.* Cottonwood, Calif.: Sweetlight Books.

Prucha, Francis P. 1990. *Documents of United States Indian Policy.* Lincoln: University of Nebraska Press.

Radin, Paul. 1911. "The Ritual and Significance of the Winnebago Medicine Dance." *Journal of American Folklore,* Volume 24, No. 62: 149–208.

———. 1915. *The Social Organization of the Winnebago Indians, an interpretation.* Ottawa, Canada: Government Printing Bureau, Department of Mines.

———. 1948. *Winnebago Hero Cycles: A Study in Aboriginal Literature.* Bloomington: Indiana University Publications in Anthropology and Linguistics, Memoir 1.

———. 1949. *The Culture of the Winnebago: As Described by Themselves.* Bloomington: Indiana University Publications in Anthropology and Linguistics, Memoir 2.

———. 1950. *The Origin Myth of the Medicine Rite: Three Versions.*

267

Bloomington: Indiana University Publications in Anthropology and Linguistics, Memoir 3.

_____. 1963 (1920). *The Autobiography of a Winnebago Indian*. New York: Dover Publications.

_____. 1970 (1923). *The Winnebago Tribe*. Lincoln: University of Nebraska Press.

_____. 1972 (1956). *The Trickster: A Study in American Indian Mythology*. New York: Schocken Books.

_____. 1983 (1926). *Crashing Thunder: The Autobiography of a Winnebago Indian*. Lincoln: University of Nebraska Press.

_____. 1991 (1945). *The Road of Life and Death: A Ritual Drama of the American Indians*. Princeton: Princeton University Press.

Redford, Robert. 1992. *Incident at Oglala: The Leonard Peltier Story*. Documentary film directed by Michael Apted. Order from Live Home Video at 15400 Sherman Way, Van Nuys, CA 91406.

Slotkin, J.S. 1975 (1956). *The Peyote Religion: A Study in Indian-White Relations*. New York: Octagon Books.

Snake, Reuben A. 1972. *Being Indian Is*. Nebraska Indian Press.

_____. 1992. Executive Producer, *The Peyote Road,* documentary film directed by Fidel Moreno, Gary Rhine, and Phil Cousineau. To order this VHS documentary film send $33.95 (includes handling) to Kifaru Productions, 1550 California Street, Suite 275, San Francisco, CA 94109 or call 800-400-8433.

Steltenkamp, Michael F. 1993. *Black Elk: Holy Man of the Oglala*. Norman: University of Oklahoma Press.

Steinmetz, Paul B. 1990. *Pipe, Bible, and Peyote Among the Oglala Lakota*. Knoxville: University of Tennessee Press.

Stewart, Omer C. 1990 (1987). *Peyote Religion: A History*. Norman: University of Oklahoma Press.

Turner, Katharine C. 1951. *Red Men Calling on the Great White Father*. Norman: University of Oklahoma Press.

Ho Chunk Vocabulary and Pronunciation

by Kathleen Danker and Felix White, Sr.

chiporoke (chi po ro ke)—A round lodge constructed of a framework of bent poles. Traditionally, it was covered with bark in the winter and reed matting in the summer. In more recent times, canvas has been used as the covering.

Choka (Cho ka)—Paternal and maternal grandfathers and fathers-in-law. Direct address. (When speaking *about* one of these individuals, the correct term is **hichoke**.)

Dega (De ga)—Mother's brother or mother's sister's husband. Direct address. (When speaking *about* one of these individuals, the correct term is **hidek**.)

herooshga (he roo shga)—A dance in which warriors unbind tokens of their raids from their hair to give to their female relatives.

Ho Chunk (Ho chunk)—Voice of praise. The Winnebago term for themselves and their language. (There is no consensus on the meaning of this term. Others have defined it as Big Voice, Big Fish, and other meanings.)

Kikawa'oonga (Ki ka wa 'oon ga)—One who rises up.

Ma'oonna (Ma 'oon na)—The Earthmaker, the Ho Chunk creator deity.

Wakan Tanka (Wa kan Tan ka) **(Lakota)**—The Great Mystery.

warooj (wa rooj)—v. To eat. n. Food. n. A dish made of sweetened ground parched corn served in the morning after the night rituals of the Native American Church.

wankwashoshera (wank wa sho she ra)—A group of brave men. The term could be used to indicate a veterans' society.

PRONUNCIATION

a	as in <u>ah</u>	oon	as in m<u>oo</u>n
an	as in c<u>on</u>ked	un	as in s<u>un</u>k
e	as in <u>ate</u>	r	A flapped lateralized "r"
i	as in b<u>e</u>		that often sounds to English
o	as in v<u>o</u>te		speakers like "d" or "l."
oo	as in z<u>oo</u>		

Index

drum society, 86
drummer, 256
drums, 106–7, 225, 231–32, 238, 242; *see also* music
  as sacred instruments, 136
  tying up, 138
  water, 226–27
Dutch immigrants, 83–84

eagle dancing, 201
eagle feathers, 228, 231, 238, 241
eagle-bone whistle, 204, 238, 241
eagles, 8, 181, 228, 241
eagle-tail fans, 227–28, 238
Earth Day activities, 183, 184
Earth, John, 14
Earth Repair Action, 168
Earth, Thomas, 238
Earth Walk, 168, 169, 183
Earthmaker, 256, 257, 261; *see also* Creator; God
East Germans, 76, 80
Echo-Hawk, Walter, 9, 15, 185, 243–50
economic boycotts, 22, 110–12, 125
economic development, 120, 124, 141–53, 144, 149, 167, 173, 247
Economic Development Administration, 143
Egyptians, 229
"El Grande Anaconda," 165
elders, 193, 194, 197, 201, 224
emergency medical service, 148
Employment Division of Oregon v. Smith, 10, 28–29, 183–86, 247–49, 263–64
employment log, 82
enemas, peyote, 27
engineering degree, 99

England, 161
English language, 58, 61
enslavement, 159
environmental issues, 161, 168–69, 183
Escuinapa, Sinaloa, Mexico, 211, 212
Eskimo people, 204
eternal life, 198
ethnic minorities, 126
Euro-Americans, 18, 24, 110, 213
European immigrants, 18, 41
Evangelical Reform Church, 42, 56
excess property, 121
extended families, 30, 32

family, 26, 27, 30, 138, 197–200, 206
  and kinship, 197–200, 206
family portrait, 45
farm, tribal, 149, 173
farm work, 98
Farmer's Home Administration, 144
fasting, 201, 206–7
father-in-law, 123, 124
FBI; *see* Federal Bureau of Investigation
feathers; *see* eagle feathers
Federal Bureau of Investigation (FBI), 125, 126, 128–29, 133, 162, 166–67, 259–60
federal grants, 141, 142, 143, 144
federal guidelines, 142–43
fee simple title, 253
fence post cutting, 38
Fifth Amendment, 258
fighting, 67, 69, 100–101
  at Haskell Institute, 72
  in military life, 77

and Santee Sioux, 18–19, 253
self-sufficiency of, 141–53,
161, 182
and Thunderbird Clan, 256
as warrior society, 260–61
women in, 230
world view of, 256–57
Wisconsin, 42, 59–61, 251, 252
women in tribes, 230
Women's Army Corps (WACs),
75
wood cutting, 86
work programs, 107
Works Project Administration,
33, 37, 38
World Assembly of First
Nations, 161

World Peace Award, 244, 261
World War II, 41, 62, 67
Wounded Knee, South Dakota,
126–27, 128–33, 244, 246,
258–60

Yankton Sioux tribe, 13, 14, 18,
19, 135, 223, 224, 228
Yellowthunder, Raymond, 122,
133
YMCA, 102, 103
youth programs, 102, 105, 153
Yuwipi ceremonies, 135, 223

Zah, Peterson, 185
Zingg, Robert, 288

Jay C. Fikes

Jay Courtney Fikes is the author of *Carlos Castaneda, Academic Opportunism and the Psychedelic Sixties*. He has published numerous scholarly, popular, and technical articles on American Indians. He is finishing a documentary film, *Huichol Indian Ceremonial Cycle*, which interprets both Christian and aboriginal Huichol Indian rituals filmed in 1934 by anthropologist Robert Zingg.

Dr. Fikes obtained his doctorate in anthropology from the University of Michigan in 1984. Since completing his dissertation, *Huichol Indian Identity and Adaptation,* he has taught courses in cultural anthropology, policy research, and social science research methods at the United States International University, Marmara University in Istanbul, and New Mexico Highlands University. He was a post-doctoral fellow in anthropology at the Smithsonian Institution but has been a "recovering anthropologist" for the past several years.

In 1990 Jay began advocating beneficial legislation for American Indians as the Legislative Secretary of the Friends Committee on National Legislation (FCNL). After leaving the FCNL he worked to pass national legislation protecting religious freedom for members of the Native American Church (NAC). He became Reuben Snake's "younger brother" during their crusade to overturn the Supreme Court's infamous 1990 decision against the NAC. He established the Institute of Inter-Cultural Issues to celebrate the lives of successful bicultural leaders such as Reuben Snake. He lives in southern California with his wife and daughter.